THE IMPERIALIST
REVOLUTIONARIES

HOOVER INTERNATIONAL STUDIES
Richard F. Staar, general editor

THE PANAMA CANAL CONTROVERSY
Paul B. Ryan

THE IMPERIALIST REVOLUTIONARIES
Hugh Seton-Watson

THE IMPERIALIST REVOLUTIONARIES

Trends in World Communism in the 1960s and 1970s

Hugh Seton-Watson

Hoover Institution Press
Stanford University, Stanford, California

*

Hoover Institution Publication 193

© 1978 by the Board of Trustees of the
  Leland Stanford Junior University
All rights reserved
International Standard Book Number: 0-8179-6932-2
Library of Congress Catalog Card Number: 77-92342
Printed in the United States of America

Contents

Foreword

In its eleven consecutive volumes that have appeared to date, each comprising between 600 and 1,000 pages, the *Yearbook on International Communist Affairs* has offered to interested readers a wealth of data concerning communist party activities around the world. All of the facts reported in individual *Yearbooks* had their temporary relevance, but some remain historically more important than others.

To distinguish between the ephemeral and the lasting, and to determine which events in the fragmented yet invariably dynamic communist world were shaping history during the period 1966–1977, the Hoover Institution embarked upon a search for a particularly keen observer to prepare an analytical and highly readable survey. We believe, and trust readers will agree, that one could hardly find a more competent scholar in the Western world than Hugh Seton-Watson to handle the difficult task of writing such a book. Professor of Russian History at the School of Slavonic and East European Studies, University of London, a prolific writer and prodigious linguist, the author has gone well beyond the initial assignment. Not only has he surveyed the myriad of facts in trying to establish their hierarchical significance but has applied historical erudition to place the contemporary phenomenon of communism within a wider sociopolitical and cultural framework in given countries, regions, and continents. While discussing the behavior of parties in power or those fighting for power in many tactically differing ways, analyzing the relationship between communism and nationalism, probing reactions of social classes to ideological challenges and political battles, and finally assessing policies of the Great Powers during these turbulent years, the author has been both rigorously objective with facts and engagingly idiosyncratic in their interpretation. He has indeed been both scholarly and humanistic in the best meaning of these terms. He has tried to understand and dispassionately describe the "whys" of undulatory communist moves, and to project these against the background of his deep concern for the survival of Western civilization.

One could say of the present volume that it represents an attempt to transform the quantitative contents of eleven *Yearbooks* into one qualitatively distilled essay. The propositions and conclusions made by Professor Seton-Watson concerning the efforts and failures of the ''imperialist revolutionaries'' in our time may be disputed, but they cannot be neglected. He has attempted to discern carefully the main trends in world communism during the 1960s and 1970s, and these trends will certainly and necessarily affect the course of world events in the future.

The present monograph is the second in a new Hoover Institution Press series on international affairs. The objective of the series is to illuminate the difficult controversial problems and phenomena of our time. Professor Seton-Watson has admirably succeeded in this one particular endeavor.

Stanford, California   RICHARD F. STAAR
                                        Coordinator of International Studies
                                        Hoover Institution

Preface

Since 1966 the *Yearbook on International Communist Affairs*, published by the Hoover Institution, has been an invaluable source of information for all students —both in the strict sense and in a wider meaning—of international politics. It has provided a detailed, systematic, and factually reliable survey of the activities of communist parties—of those struggling for power and of those already wielding it. The *Yearbooks* have concentrated on the political struggle: their contributors have not set out to comment on old or new expositions of Marxist-Leninist theory, or to offer new analyses of their own, though theoretical arguments between communists have been discussed. They have also not set themselves the task of exploring in depth the many and varied social and economic frameworks within which communists have operated, though from time to time they have, of course, been obliged to discuss social and economic forces.

In the summer of 1976 I was invited by Dr. Richard F. Staar, the editor of the *Yearbook,* to write a short book in which I would try to identify certain main trends in communist affairs during the decade of the *Yearbook*'s publication, and to put these in some sort of historical perspective, at least in the limited sense in which practitioners of "contemporary history" can aspire to such an aim. This I undertook to do. I had a completely free hand in my choice of topics for closer study; enjoyed ideal working conditions during six weeks in California; and had the benefit of much expert advice both orally at that time and by correspondence in the subsequent year. Many were generous with their time and advice, but no one attempted to influence my interpretation. I made my own decision as to what were the main trends of the period, and this decision is explained in the first chapter of the book. My themes largely but not entirely overlap with the themes of ten years of the *Yearbook*. Some of the subjects covered in the *Yearbook* are missing from my work; and I have devoted a good deal of space to problems of class structure, historical tradition, political institutions, and national consciousness that are not usually explored in the *Yearbook,* because in the case of certain communist movements this was necessary in order to bring out my main themes. My time range has been somewhat longer, since I have frequently traced problems or trends back to the beginning of the 1960s, and in some cases a good deal further than this.

I have tried to expound the facts and the trends objectively, and to avoid moralizing rhetoric. Yet I have my own views, of which I am not ashamed, and they doubtless intrude themselves from time to time. Apart from this, as a large part of the material consists of polemical literature, I have been obliged to point out the fallacies, and it is virtually impossible to avoid being sometimes forced into counterpolemics.

It gives me great pleasure, in conclusion, to express my gratitude to Dr. W. Glenn Campbell, Director of the Hoover Institution, for his encouragement of my work, and to Mr. Richard T. Burress, Associate Director, who took so much trouble to ensure such excellent working conditions. I have to thank most especially Dr. Milorad M. Drachkovitch for his generous, imaginative, and understanding cooperation. Warm thanks are also due to Dr. Myron Hedlin, whose efficient and resourceful activities as a research assistant in the summer of 1976 enormously facilitated my task. I am also extremely grateful to Dr. Lewis Gann and Dr. William Ratliff for their expert advice, and to Brian Crozier, who read my typescript here in London and made many useful comments.

– 1 –

Communists in World Politics

Is There a World Communist Movement?

It may be useful to begin a general examination of the role of communists in world politics in 1977 by putting the same question that was put in the Introduction to the first of the *Yearbooks*: Is there a world communist movement?

There certainly was once such a thing. It was an international organization, with followers scattered all over the globe, strong in some countries and weak in others, and acknowledging one central leadership: the Central Committee of the Communist Party of the Soviet Union (CPSU), which meant in practice the leader of that party—Stalin until 1953, and Khrushchev until the end of his period in office, by which time the unity began to be in doubt.

In these earlier decades there could be no doubt of the absolute supremacy of the Soviet leaders. The aims of the Soviet government then had to be the aims of the international movement, and the cause of international communism could best be furthered by the promotion of the state interests of the Soviet Union. In order to guarantee those interests, and to achieve those aims, tactics had to be varied from time to time, sometimes drastically. When a change in tactics came, it was normally binding on all parties belonging to the movement, regardless of the fact that the new tactic might be highly advantageous to some parties and most damaging to others. There could be no question of flexibility within the movement. The most striking example was the imposition on all communist parties of the duty to defend the Ribbentrop-Molotov pact of August 1939.

The unity of the movement was broken for the first time in a serious manner in June 1948, when the Communist Party of Yugoslavia was condemned by the Cominform and expelled from the community of the faithful. This decision was taken by Stalin, not by Tito. It was a decision of the Soviet leadership to excommunicate, not a decision by the Yugoslav party to secede. It had repercussions in Eastern Europe in the following years, but looking back after nearly three decades one may say that the schism with Yugoslavia did not substantially disrupt the unity of the movement.

Much more serious was the schism with China, which became clearly visible at the beginning of the 1960s. From that time onward there appeared a series of splits and repeated threats to unity, and there was a great deal of argument about how much variety could be tolerated in "national roads to socialism." Despite tremendous efforts by learned Marxist-Leninist ideologists to formulate and reformulate satisfactory definitions, this question remained unanswered. Apart from these uncertainties within the Soviet-led camp, there were direct challenges to the old principle of subservience to Soviet policy by groups that preferred to look to China for their inspiration. The parties that split off from the traditional communist parties and called themselves or were called Maoist remained small, and did not attract a large organized following anywhere. Nevertheless they were a source of great embarrassment to orthodox communists. Further groups of communists, disillusioned with the Soviet model, looked for inspiration to Cuba, whose policies in the early 1960s were attractively unorthodox. Finally, the late 1960s saw the emergence of numerous extreme-left groups, some Trotskyist, some anarchist, some indeterminate, but all aiming at violent and complete social revolution, and all manifestly dissatisfied with the leadership of the existing communist parties. This proliferation of revolutionaries, usually rather small groups of intellectuals, was another source of embarrassment to the communist leaders of the old school—though it is arguable that on balance the activities of these *groupuscules* did more harm to the enemies of the communists than to the communists themselves.

Thus in the mid-1970s there were three models of communism, and in addition to these a wide variety of dissident revolutionaries.

The Soviet Union remained by far the most important and powerful communist state. Its very strength, however, significantly reduced its revolutionary appeal. Its imposing array of generals, bureaucrats, and managers of vast factory complexes made it unattractive to many of those whose predecessors thirty years earlier had looked to revolutionary Russia as the model for the future society. The Soviet Union of 1977 looked suspiciously like an old-style despotic empire.

In China, by contrast, were visible a revolutionary fervor and an enthusiasm that were much stronger and more genuine than anything to be seen in Soviet Russia in the 1970s. It recalled perhaps the enthusiasm that had been present in the early years of the Soviet regime. However, China also had its paradoxical features. In the first place it seemed that the effective strength of this great nation, from which the left had hoped for great things, was being seriously damaged by the ravages of the Great Proletarian Cultural Revolution, which had disrupted the apparatus of the communist party and the bureaucracy in the late 1960s, and had involved a massive denunciation and repudiation of the old Chinese culture. Campaigns against Confucius or Beethoven were peculiar phenomena that did not fit the pattern of orthodox left-wing thinking. The other paradoxical feature of the Chinese policy was that in the mid-1970s, Chinese spokesmen were strongly defending NATO and urging both the United States and its European allies to increase their military power and to stand up to the Soviet military threat. Chinese arguments to this effect were closer to the exhortations of the "cold warriors" of the 1950s than to the style affected by Western policy-makers of the mid-1970s. The whole Chinese scene was then changed by the deaths of Chou En-lai and Mao Tse-tung, the succession of Hua Kuo-feng, and the disgrace of the "Gang of Four" of extreme radicals, whose consequences were likely to be far-reaching but could not be predicted.

For a time Cuba seemed to be a third distinct center. The Cuban communists emphasized individual acts of heroism, extolled guerrilla warfare among peasants, insisted that victory must be won by armed struggle and not merely by sordid political maneuvers within a bourgeois constitutional framework, and attributed the leading role to an alliance of working-class cadres with revolutionary intelligentsia. For some years this doctrine made a powerful appeal to would-be revolutionaries, especially to the young and to elder persons who longed to recapture their youth. The charms of the Caribbean setting—so unlike snowy Russia or unknown China—had something to do with it. The romantic figure of Ché Guevara, who believed in an intercontinental struggle of all the peoples of Latin America,[1] symbolized the idea of the Caribbean, the Andes, and the Brazilian jungles as the future world center of revolution, and this concept made at least an abstract appeal to many whose lives were spent in safety and comfort by the Hudson and the Seine. Yet Cuban communism as an independent model proved short-lived. Already in the early 1960s dependence on Soviet economic aid limited Castro's freedom of maneuver. The disillusionment caused by Khrushchev's retreat in the missile crisis of 1962 proved less important than the need to market Cuba's surplus sugar. Already in 1964 Castro showed himself complaisant to Moscow's wishes by not inviting the Chinese to his Havana conference of Latin American communist parties; and at the Tricontinental Conference in Havana in January 1966, which the Chinese did attend, Cubans and Chinese exchanged public insults. In 1967 and 1968 Cuban-Soviet relations again deteriorated, first because Castro was angry that the Soviet government maintained relations with Latin American governments, which he regarded as reactionary and oligarchical, and then because the Soviet leaders were angry that Castro had purged his communist party of its former orthodox leader, Anibal Escalante. However, Castro's loud approval of the Soviet invasion of Czechoslovakia in 1968 brought a reconciliation and ever closer cooperation, culminating in the Soviet-assisted Cuban invasion of Angola in 1976. Nevertheless, Cuba as a third center was but an illusion.

---

1. Guevara, an Argentine who fought with Castro in Cuba and then made vain efforts to start a revolution in Bolivia, put his principles into practice, and paid with his life.

A possibility of a fourth model, capable of attraction at least in southern Asia, emerged with the unification of Vietnam under communist leadership. The Vietnamese communists appeared genuinely independent of both Moscow and Peking. Another communist government that succeeded in keeping a balance between the two communist giants, and also had special features of its own, was the North Korean.

Disillusionment with the successive models of communist power did not prevent left-wing groups from pursuing their several utopias. The rhetorical exaltation of violence began to produce results. Murder, piracy, and the taking of hostages were glamorous activities, and attracted devoted bands. It is not surprising that these activities should have been most successful in places where the revolutionary struggle had a national character, and where there was a clear foreign or religious enemy, easily distinguishable and easy to hit. Obvious examples are the Irish Republican Army (IRA) and the Palestinian "Black September." In South America, not so much in the regions of peasant poverty on which the Maoists had put their hopes as in the industrialized and materially civilized states of the south and southeast—Argentina, Uruguay, and Brazil— the national enemies, held up as targets for kidnapping or assassination, were the alleged foreign exploiters of the nation's resources—citizens of the United States or other Western "capitalist" countries, and their "domestic running dogs." In the doctrines that were advanced to justify these actions the nationalist element could no more be separated from the social revolutionary than priority of cause could be assigned to the hen or the egg.

Thus in 1977 the words "world communist movement" were bound to cover at least three political phenomena: the Soviet state and the communist parties outside Russia that proclaimed their devotion to Soviet policy; the Chinese state and the communist parties outside China that looked to the theory and practice of Mao Tse-tung as their model; and a miscellaneous collection of Trotskyist and other heretical groups professing themselves to be Marxist-Leninists. To these might possibly be added the Vietnamese state and groups outside Vietnam that took it as their model; and conceivably the same might be said of North Korea.

However, reality was more complex. In the first place, the heretical Marxist-Leninists were in no sense a single category, but consisted of numerous warring sects. Second and more important, the unity of the first category was in doubt. The last Soviet-sponsored worldwide conference of communist parties had been held in Moscow in June 1969. Thereafter the Soviet leaders and their East European partners had concentrated on assembling a more modest gathering, a conference of European parties, a sequel to the Karlovy Vary conference of April 1967. After much time and effort, it met in East Berlin in June 1976. At this meeting the differences, which had been growing since the invasion of Czechoslovakia, between the "Eurocommunists" of some Western European party leaderships and the Soviet rulers were very openly expressed.[2] There was a widespread belief that the era of such pageants in Moscow was over. The French leader Georges Marchais said that "as far as we are concerned, conferences such as this no longer meet the requirements of our time." The statement issued at the end of the conference omitted the phrase "proletarian internationalism"— the conventional euphemism for subservience to Soviet policy—although Brezhnev himself had used it in his own speech. The decisive sentences in the statement regarding relations between communist parties were:

> [Communist parties] will develop their internationalist, comradely and voluntary cooperation and solidarity on the basis of the great ideas of Marx, Engels and Lenin, strictly adhering to the principles of equality and sovereign independence for each party, non-interference in internal affairs, and respect for their free choice of different roads in the struggle for social change of a progressive nature and for socialism.

If we now ask ourselves whether there still existed in 1977 a single organized and disciplined world communist movement, then the answer must be "no." There were a Soviet-led movement, a Chinese-led movement, and several other small movements with followers in many countries. The Soviet-led movement was no longer a hierarchically ordered organization: at most it was a rather loose association of like-minded parties.

At the same time, the passage quoted above from the Berlin statement should not be dismissed as simply a face-saving formula. The Marxist-Leninist doctrinal foundation, which all the signatory parties shared, was more than rhetoric. All the party leaders had often denounced their common enemies of "imperialism" and "capitalism"; had identified the first of these exclusively with the United States and its European and Japanese allies; and had refused to apply the epithet "imperialist" to the Soviet Union.

In a wider sense, it could be argued that not only all the European communist parties that accepted the Berlin statement, and all the orthodox communist parties outside Europe (including the Cuban), but also the Chinese, Vietnamese, and North Korean parties and all the heretical *groupuscules* all over the world, shared a common residue of Marxism-Leninism, and regarded "U.S. imperialism" as their permanent long-term enemy. This argument has some force, but it does not take into account the fact that intracommunist feuds do affect relationships between individual communist countries and the West. "Eurocommunism" has been described by some as a "communist Reformation." The historical analogy is not unattractive. In the mid-sixteenth century it was certainly true that Catholics, Lutherans, and Calvinists shared a great residue of Christian belief, which

---

2. These differences are discussed at greater length in chapter 2 and again in chapter 7.

united them all in doctrine in contrast with the Muslim Ottoman Turks who then threatened Central Europe. This did not prevent His Most Christian Majesty François I, king of France, from making a treaty with the sultan: he preferred the infidel tyrant to the Habsburg ruler of Spain and the Empire. In 1977 the Chinese rulers did *not* consider the United States their most dangerous enemy: that role they assigned to the "new tsars" and "modern revisionists" of the Soviet Union.

Thus, the common residue of ideology makes it possible to attempt a meaningful discussion of the activities of "communists" in world politics in the 1960s and 1970s; yet the notion that there was still a single world communist movement in this period must be abandoned.

Communist Successes and Failures: A Preliminary Balance

At this stage it may be useful to make a brief list of what appear to be the successes and failures of communists during the 1960s and 1970s-to-date.

The most outstanding success was certainly the victory of the Vietnamese communists. It was a success in the most obvious sense—that a communist form of government was extended from North Vietnam to cover all Vietnam; and that this was followed by the access to power of communist parties in the two neighboring states of Indochina: Laos and Cambodia. But the success was far greater than this. It was the culmination of a struggle of thirty years by the Vietnamese communists—surely one of the most costly, painful, and protracted efforts ever made by any group of revolutionaries, revealing the Vietnamese communists as even more single-minded and implacable than the original Russian Bolsheviks. But even more important than this, it was a tremendous defeat for the United States, which had been slowly dragged into a war it could not win, in which it had fought by the wrong means, thereby enabling its enemies to maximize the odium attached to the United States in a very large part of the world. Not least was the harm done by the years of war in Vietnam to the internal strength and cohesion of American society and political life. Some would say that the withdrawal from Vietnam was a glorious victory by the American left, and by the young people of America, who had obliged their government to yield to their wishes. Others would say that it revealed above all a failure of nerve on the part of the American political class, an inability of elected politicians to stand up to a public mood largely created by the mass media. Another argument sometimes heard was that it was above all a revelation of the impact of television on the citizen of the modern state; and that it would never again be possible for any society, in which there was genuine freedom to show contemporary events on the television screen and to offer any comment on them, to fight a war at all. (This consideration would not, of course, apply to any government that could ensure by censorship of television the showing only of incidents of war that glorified its own troops and cast discredit on enemy forces.) However these things may be, it was clear that the events in Vietnam not only were a military victory for communists, but made a tremendous psychological impact on the people of the United States, and transformed the image of the United States in the minds of millions of persons all over the world—for the worse. With regard to the consequences of these events in Indochina itself, it seemed that the emergent regime in Vietnam was likely to be relatively independent both of Soviet Russia and of China, while the affiliation of the regime in Cambodia was for the time being unpredictable.

The advent to power in Chile in 1970 of the Popular Union led by President Allende, in which the communists participated, aroused great hopes among communists, especially in Western European parties. These were disappointed when Allende was overthrown by a military counterrevolution in September 1973.

A new hope appeared in April 1974 when a military revolution overthrew the dictatorship in Portugal, and political parties reemerged, among which the communist party appeared at first to be the strongest. The communists met with resistance, however, and after their reverse in November 1975 their fortunes ebbed rapidly. Even so, it was too soon to say whether Portugal was or was not on balance a success for communism. The regime within Portugal itself was in process of evolution during 1977, and was subject to severe economic pressures. Meanwhile, in the Portuguese colonies, the establishment of independent governments appeared strongly to favor the communist cause. The new government of Mozambique was greatly indebted to both the Soviet Union and China for supplies of arms and for training, but soon after, victory appeared to be leaning strongly to the Soviet side. The victory of the MPLA (the Popular Movement for the Liberation of Angola) in Angola was brought about by indirect Soviet intervention in the form of Cuban troops equipped with Soviet materiel.

In mid-1977 the outlook for communist parties appeared rather promising along the whole northern coast of the Mediterranean. The greatest international attention was attracted by Italy, in which the communist party made substantial progress at the election of June 1976. In Spain the beginnings of a freer political system after the death of General Franco in November 1975 offered new opportunities for communists. In France the alliance of communists and socialists was gaining ground at the expense of the followers of President Giscard d'Estaing. In Greece the overthrow of the military dictatorship in the summer of 1974 enabled the communists to reappear legally (as two rival parties), but they had little success at the election of the following autumn.

Against these successes, or promises of success, may be set a reverse for communism in the events in Czechoslovakia in 1968. In the view of the Soviet leaders the policies of the Dubček leadership were disastrous. They did not publicly admit that these events showed a desire by the Czech working class for "socialism with a human face": they preferred to attribute the events to imperialist intrigues. However, they knew the facts, and they could take little comfort from them, though consoling themselves with the reflection that they had acted in time, that the military operations of the Soviet army had been efficiently conducted, and that the Western governments had accepted the facts.

Three groups of problems, which belong to the environment of Soviet foreign policy rather than to communist-party activity, must be briefly mentioned.

First was the India-Pakistan war of 1971 and the establishment of Bangladesh. This was, in the short term, a blow to Chinese interests, and it strengthened the links between India and the Soviet Union. It also strengthened the position in India of Indira Gandhi, who had for some time inclined toward the Soviet Union, and of the pro-Soviet Communist Party of India, which supported her, while weakening that of the rival CPI (Marxist) in Bengal. Indira Gandhi's decision to introduce a dictatorship probably increased her dependence on the Soviet Union and on the support of the CPI. However, the disastrous defeat of her Congress party in the election of March 1977 transformed the whole Indian situation and placed the political influence of the Soviet Union in India in doubt.

The second set of problems was in the Middle East, where Soviet support of the Arab states against Israel increased Soviet popularity in the "Third World," but it was arguable that Soviet political success was more verbal than real. Israel defeated her enemies in 1967, and recovered quickly from the initial surprise in the Yom Kippur war of 1973. Tensions existed between Egypt and the Soviet Union from 1972 onward, and Soviet influence seemed to be diminishing in Syria in 1976. Iraq was the Soviet Union's best remaining client, but the significance of the reconciliation between Iraq and Iran for Soviet interests was uncertain. In none of these countries were communist activities important. The terrorism of various Palestinian groups, when directed against Western subjects, could give Soviet observers a certain *Schadenfreude,* but in reality it was a dubious asset. On the borders of the Middle East, in the Horn of Africa, Soviet influence was considerable, but it could hardly accommodate the conflicting interests of the two prospective Soviet clients, the Somalis and the Ethiopians.

The third set of problems arose from the economic difficulties of the Western nations beginning with the fuel crisis of 1973. It was pleasant to talk of the "crisis of capitalism," but the Soviet leaders were well aware of their own economic difficulties, and were not sure whether they were more eager to see the collapse of capitalism or to receive an injection of Western technological expertise.

Revolutionaries and Imperialists

Anyone who thinks seriously about contemporary communist politics must be aware of the dual nature of the subject, and is bound to be frustrated by it.

Communism is an extreme revolutionary ideology, proclaiming an earthly paradise; it is pursued in some countries openly and in freedom, and in others clandestinely by brave men and women who suffer all manner of cruel persecution. Communism is also a form of government whose foremost exponent is a vast empire ruled by men who are extremely conservative and extremely resistant to change within their own frontiers while pursuing abroad ambitious enterprises that strikingly resemble the imperialist ventures of earlier empires with different ideologies, or none at all. A complete survey of contemporary communism would require a discussion of almost the whole fields of international relations and political science, not to mention economics and sociology. This would exceed not only the limits of a short book, but the powers of this author, and perhaps of any writer at all. I have therefore decided to confine myself to four main topics, affecting both aspects of communism, which seem to me to have been especially important during the last decade.

First are the attempts of communist parties to obtain power by peaceful means —by what has sometimes been called the "parliamentary road to socialism." My survey of this subject begins with Chile and Portugal and proceeds to Italy, France, Spain, and Japan, with some mention of some less important parties elsewhere. A term often used in recent years to denote this set of problems is "Eurocommunism." However, the strategy of peaceful pursuit of power was not confined to Europe: the subject cannot be adequately examined without reference to Chile and Japan. It is also not strictly true to say that this is a strategy for industrially advanced countries, because those words could not fit either Portugal or Chile. Therefore, if my treatment of the efforts of communists to attain power by peaceful means lacks geographical tidiness and precise political definition, this is because the phenomenon itself defies definition and is incurably untidy.

The second theme, which is discussed in the third chapter, consists of the opportunities available either to indigenous communists or to communist-ruled foreign governments in connection with "national-liberation" movements in the developing countries, especially in the Muslim world, Africa, and Latin America, and the use made of these opportunities for the communist cause. Here it is necessary to consider at some length the social forces that favor revolution, and the natures and actions of the indigenous revolutionary movements, in which the elements of "nationalism" and of "socialism" are barely distinguishable.

The fourth and fifth chapters are concerned with communism in power, and especially with the complex of problems arising from the fact that the Soviet leaders, who consider themselves the world's chief defenders of "national liberation" from "imperialism," are the rulers of the only remaining great empire in the world, and also have a chain of semisovereign states that are in a "neocolonialist" relationship to them. Something also has to be said of the communist-ruled states that escaped from this semicolonial status—Yugoslavia and Albania.

The theme of the sixth chapter is the situation of the communists in the Far East and southern Asia. Here the emphasis must inevitably be placed on relations between states—between the two major communist governments and between them and the two major noncommunist powers—the United States and Japan. These relationships also affect, and are affected by, the situations in India, Bangladesh, Pakistan and the Southeast Asian lands, and the efforts of communists in those countries.

This is, then, a book about communists, but it does not claim to cover the whole reality. It is a summary and a discussion of those communist activities in world politics in the 1960s and 1970s that seem to me to be the most important. It is concerned above all with the great underlying paradox: communists and their associates fight in the name of scientific socialism against economic exploitation and foreign domination, while the great Soviet empire exploits its own citizens and the citizens of lands in which its neocolonialism goes unchallenged, and prepares its vast armies, fleets, and stocks of missiles so that it can impose its foreign domination over more and more foreign lands, whether by the use of force or merely by its threat.

$-2-$

The Peaceful Road to Socialism

Communist Revolution: The Historical Paradox

The paradox that communists, who form parties claiming to embody the interests of the industrial working class and seeking to establish a form of society more advanced and more sophisticated than bourgeois democracy, won their victories in countries in which, at the time of the revolution, the economy was predominantly agrarian, the system of education extremely inadequate, and the political system a crude form of indigenous autocracy or imposed foreign rule, has been well known for many years, not least to the communists themselves. It was first revealed in Russia, then in China from the late 1920s onward, then in Yugoslavia and Albania in the Second World War, and after the war in China and Vietnam. The establishment of communist rule in East Germany and in Czechoslovakia, both of which had industrialized economies, educated peoples, and substantial experience of forms of government that might be called "bourgeois democratic," was a result of Soviet military domination—though in the case of Czechoslovakia things were complex, as will be argued later. Cuba is a difficult case to classify. The economy was lopsided, and dependent on foreign capital; the level of education was rather high (at least by Latin American standards); there had been substantial periods of democratic government in the past; and North American political domination, imposed by brutal force at the end of the nineteenth century, had been virtually removed by Roosevelt's "good-neighbor policy" in the 1930s. However, the sporadic repression of Batista's regime, the existence of great poverty (especially among the blackest portions of this racially mixed people), the ubiquity of foreign capitalists and foreign tourists, and the romantic aspects of Castro's guerrilla warfare gave the Cuban revolution something of the glamor of the Yugoslav or Chinese. Thus none of the cases mentioned above radically modifies the generalization that until the 1970s, communist successes had occurred in underdeveloped societies ruled by dictatorial methods.

However, this fact was never accepted as some immutable law of history by communists, least of all by commmunist intellectuals in Western countries or by the planners of strategy in Moscow. From the very beginning, hopes were set on the proletariat of the advanced industrial countries. The old belief that the workers themselves could seize power if only they were properly led by persons possessing a full understanding of Marxist theory survived for the first decade and a half after 1917. If there was no socialist revolution in Germany, this was simply because the social democratic leaders were renegades, and the workers themselves still had too little political consciousness. However, although the victory of Hitler in Germany was at first greeted in Moscow as a preliminary stage during which the workers, finally disillusioned about social-democratic fatuity, would reorganize their ranks and fight the last great fight to victory, it proved to be rather more serious, not least because the Third Reich directly threatened the Soviet Union. Rethinking by communist leaders produced the first successful attempt in an advanced industrial society at an alliance not only with noncommunist parties but also with social classes other than industrial workers. This was the Popular Front, which was prepared in France in 1934, accepted by the Seventh Congress of the Comintern in 1935, and victorious at the French and Spanish elections in 1936.

The Popular Front of the 1930s: Promise and Failure

The Popular Front, which undoubtedly won widespread and enthusiastic support from workers and from members of the intellectual professions throughout the lands of Western democracy in the late 1930s, was defeated as a result of the Spanish civil war. The most obvious explanation is that the fascist powers, Germany and Italy, had not only the arms and the men, but also the political will to back their candidate Franco to victory; the governments of France and Britain, on the other hand, which were subject to conflicting pressures and fears and lacking in political will, did not help the Republic. This is true, but it is not the whole truth. The Soviet Union, whose leaders loudly proclaimed their devotion to the Spanish people's cause, was devastated during the years of the Spanish civil war by Stalin's mass purge, which removed probably more than half the senior officers of the Soviet Red Army (including some who saw service as "volunteers" in Spain) and turned the political and economic structure upside down. This cataclysm not only limited the capacity of the Soviet leaders to help the Spanish Republic, but also affected the position of the Spanish communists. Nevertheless, the International Brigades, organized by the Comintern and manned largely by communist volunteers from Europe and America, undoubtedly made a major military contribution.

 The Soviet leaders wished the Republic to resist Franco and keep German and Italian military forces engaged far from the Soviet borders. The communists were therefore urged to avoid all revolutionary excesses and to give absolute priority to military needs. This they did, to the best of their ability. However, there were powerful revolutionary forces in Spain, the anarchists and anarcho-syndicalists, who were entirely unimpressed by arguments from military expediency, and who insisted on fighting the bourgeoisie and the church, thereby terrifying many Spaniards who might otherwise have served the Republic and driving them into support of Franco. This was the first occasion when "ultraleft" enthusiasm seriously damaged the revolutionary cause, as it was understood by communists; it was not to be the last.[1] The Spanish communists' efforts to become the main "party of order" on the Republican side, and thus to win the respect of professional soldiers, were rather effective. They were well set to take over the Republic from within. They were, however, limited by the fact that Stalin, who was determined to root out and destroy any groups of revolutionaries owing allegiance to his enemy Trotsky, insisted that the Spanish communists should destroy the small Trotskyist party, the POUM, which existed in Barcelona (and was quite distinct from the anarchists). Their vindictive persecution of POUM won the communists a good deal of hostility, and further contributed to the weakening of the Republic and to Franco's victory. Final military defeat destroyed communist hopes, as well as Spanish liberties.

In France the Popular Front broke up partly as a result of the war in Spain and partly because of internal contradictions. The inability of Léon Blum's government to get British consent either to joint support of the Republic or to French unilateral help brought on the French socialists floods of abuse from the communists, who, though members of the Popular Front, had decided that there should be no communist ministers in the government. The government was also bitterly divided on whether priority should go to social reforms—long overdue but very costly to the state's finances—or to national defense. On the left of the socialist party were pacifists, antimilitarists, and champions of immediate social upheaval equally objectionable to the socialist leaders and to the communists, and comparable to the anarchists in Spain, in their influence on government cohesion and on France's ability to resist the fascist powers.

The Popular Front Revived, 1941–1947

The popular-front strategy was abandoned when Stalin made his alliance with Hitler in August 1939, but was hurriedly revived after Hitler attacked his ally in June 1941. It was most effective in the Resistance in France and in Italy. The main movements kept their independence and did not entirely trust each other, but they did cooperate—in contrast to the civil wars that developed in Yugoslavia, Greece, and Albania. In France the growing authority of General de Gaulle was something that the communists, despite the large number of their

---

1. It is perhaps worth recalling that extremist groups played a similar part in the Russian civil war in 1918 and 1919, but this was so different a situation that comparison is difficult.

own organized resisters, had to recognize. Antifascist solidarity was more powerful in Italy than in France. For more than a decade before 1940, both intellectuals and workers, both in exile and within Italy, had been fighting a bitter
underground struggle; though the distinct factions of socialists, communists, and
Party of Action involved in it remained apart, they felt themselves to some extent
to be comrades. The intellectual tradition of antifascism, consciously modeled
both in rhetoric and in reality on the intellectual tradition of the Risorgimento,
provided a more solid foundation for common action in Italy than was the case
in France. It also marginally affected the left wing of the Catholic *popolari*, the
nucleus from which the Christian Democratic party later developed.

At the end of the Second World War, communists were members of the government in both France and Italy; their cooperation reflected the cooperation
between the governments of the four Allied great powers, and a similar pattern
of popular-front governments emerged in the countries in Central and Eastern
Europe that were occupied by the Soviet army.

This proved to be a very brief phase. Most of the Soviet-sponsored coalitions
quickly came under communist control, and with the assistance of Soviet political advisers and security policemen, copies of the Soviet form of government
were imposed on these peoples; in Czechoslovakia, elements of liberal democracy survived until the summer of 1948, which also saw the excommunication
of the Yugoslav communist-led regime by the Cominform. During these same
years the wartime Alliance broke down. Various causes contributed to the breakdown, and these continue to form the subject of polemics between "revisionist"
and other historians. At least it is certain that one important cause was disagreement between the West and the Soviet Union about Poland, which goes
back at least to 1943, and that another was pressure on Western governments
of public indignation at what was happening in Central Europe between 1945
and 1948.[2] The breakdown, in turn, inevitably led to the departure of the communist ministers from the governments of France and Italy.

The Peaceful Road at the Twentieth Congress
of the CPSU

In the following years the climate of "cold war" meant that communists in
Western European and South American countries were isolated from the democratic left. Stalin accepted the fact with equanimity. It was when the denun-

---

2. Even if it is true (and it is far from certain) that Churchill, Roosevelt, and their expert advisers
had "written off" these countries at Yalta, it is equally true that British and American observers
of international affairs were appalled by the manner in which the Soviet leaders interpreted the
concepts of "democracy" and "friendship to the Soviet Union" in the lands they occupied, and
that this indignation, expressed in Congress, Parliament, and the press, was bound to influence
American and British policy from 1945 onward.

ciation of Stalin began, three years after his death, in the Soviet Union itself, that the first hints of a new communist attitude were made. In his speech to the Twentieth Congress of the CPSU in February 1956, the veteran Politburo member A. I. Mikoyan spoke of the possibility of a "peaceful road to socialism." After quoting massively from both Marx and Lenin, and after repeatedly stressing "the strengthening of the mighty camp of socialism" as "the principal factor in the fundamental changes in the international situation," Mikoyan stated that "peaceful development of a revolution is possible, of course, only as a result of the strength, the high degree of organization and the class consciousness of the working class." As an actual example he cited Czechoslovakia, where "the communists came to power after concluding an alliance not only with the working people's parties that were close to them but also with the bourgeois parties that supported the national front."

At the time, this formula was not very attractive. It was precisely by provoking their partners, the "bourgeois parties," into ineffective protest at disloyal communist behavior, especially in packing the security police with communists in anticipation of the forthcoming parliamentary election, that the communist party leaders were able to seize power in February 1948. It was a peaceful seizure of power in the sense that there was no civil war, no one was killed in the process, and even intimidation by communist factory guards and action committees was on a rather small scale. However, it was followed by executions, tortures, judicial murders, and imprisonment on false charges that added up to a large volume of violence. Thus, Mikoyan was saying little more than that communists could choose from two alternatives, according to expediency—violent suppression of their opponents both before and after their victory, or only after it. Even so, in the excitement of the Western media about the Twentieth Congress (at which the main event had been Khrushchev's "secret speech" denouncing Stalin), more was made of the "peaceful road to socialism" than was justified by the words of the speakers.

The Soviet counterrevolution in Hungary in November 1956 reinforced the earlier antagonism of the democratic left in Western Europe toward communists.[3] During the next decade overtures by communists in Western countries were not very successful, though the resistance to them certainly diminished.

---

3. It is curious that Hungary should have been the scene of three of the clearest cases of counterrevolution in modern history (using the word not as a term of abuse but as a precise description of a political phenomenon: the forcible destruction of a revolutionary regime with the purpose of restoring the previous regime). The first was in 1849, when Russian troops crushed the Hungarian revolution led by Louis Kossuth and the authority of the Austrian emperor in Vienna was reasserted. The second was in 1919, when the revolutionary regime of the communist Bela Kun was overthrown by Romanian troops and in its place came the restoration of the old oligarchy embodied by Admiral Horthy. The third time was in November 1956, when the revolutionary regime created by Hungarian workers and intellectuals was overthrown by invading Soviet Russian troops and the previous regime was restored. It is true that in all three cases restoration proved to be much less complete than its initiators had hoped, but that is another story.

It was not until the end of the 1960s that the first serious attempt since the postwar governments of de Gaulle and de Gasperi was made to set up a parliamentary government that included communists. This occurred not in Europe, but in the South American republic of Chile. The ultimate failure of this attempt set off a series of experiments in communist tactics in Europe—in Portugal, Italy, France, and Spain, as well as in the only country of advanced industrial society in the Far East, Japan. These various policies form the main subject of this chapter.

Chile

Chile was one of the few countries in Latin America in which democratic government had flourished in the twentieth century; it was perhaps surpassed in this respect only by Uruguay and Costa Rica. The great majority of the population were of European stock and lived in towns, and there was a fairly well-developed system of education. The army had a tradition of keeping out of politics. Numerous political parties existed, covering the normal range of European-type parties from conservatives to communists. It is true that there had been periods of dictatorship, and Chilean democracy was potentially fragile owing to the economy's dependence on export prices and to the large share of its resources held by foreign business. Nevertheless, talk of the Chilean people's pride in democracy was more than empty rhetoric.

The Chilean Communist party was formed as a socialist party in 1912, and took the name Communist in 1922. In 1938 it was one of the partners in a Popular Front, which supported President Aguirre Cerda, but there were no communist ministers in his cabinet. In 1946 this Popular Front was renewed, and three communists served in the cabinet of President González Videla (the first communist ministers in Latin America). However, the crisis in relations between the Western powers and the Soviet Union in 1948 inevitably led to conflict between the communists and the other parties; communists were excluded from the cabinet, and from 1949 to 1958 the party was illegal.

At the end of the 1950s the Chilean socialist party moved definitely to the left, and in 1958 it concluded an alliance with the communists—the Popular Action Front (FRAP)—and won nearly 40 percent of the votes at the 1964 election. In the following years efforts were made to extend the alliance of the left. During these years Marxist ideas spread very rapidly among students and younger professional people, and the prestige of Castro strengthened this trend. Anti-North American nationalism also spread. For a time it appeared that the Christian Democrats would canalize the discontents of agricultural laborers and of middle-class radicals. However, the administration of the Christian Democratic president Eduardo Frei failed to satisfy these aspirations. Left-wing groups split off from both the Christian Democrats and the Radicals, and an ultraleft group seceded from the socialists to form in 1965 the Movement of the Revolutionary Left (MIR). In 1969 a new alliance was formed with the name Popular Unity (UP). It consisted of the communist and socialist parties and four other smaller groups, many of whose members were former Christian Democrats or Radicals. After bitter struggles between the left and right wings of the socialist party, a compromise leader was chosen, Salvador Allende. He became the joint candidate of the UP at the presidential election of September 1970.

Allende won 36 percent of the poll, the candidate of the conservative National Party had 35 percent, and the Christian Democrat, 28 percent. It was for the elected congress to decide between the three, which meant that the supporters of one would have to transfer their votes. The Christian Democrats decided to vote for Allende after he had given precise promises to uphold constitutional liberties. The congress voted for him on 24 October, and he became president on 3 November.

The communists' main strength lay in the workers of the nitrate fields in the north and the coal mines around Concepción. Their public-policy statements were studiously moderate. They wished to avoid antagonizing the middle classes, and to concentrate their attacks on the landed oligarchy and foreign capital. The top priority was given to arousing anti-North American nationalism. A statement by the party leader, Luis Corvalán, in *World Marxist Review* in December 1970 made this clear. The left, he stated, was now in power, but "the oligarchy still holds strong positions in the legislature and judicial branches, controls the communications media and, as the partner of U.S. Imperialism, dominates the economy." The UP government planned nationalizations, and intended to pursue an anti-imperialist foreign policy, including "exposure of the OAS as a tool and agent of North American imperialism, opposition to pan-Americanism and the establishment of a new representative continental body" to replace the Organization of American States. Corvalán stressed the UP's intention to "strengthen the national character and professional orientation of the armed forces," to "assure material and technical equipment," and to "create a fair democratic system of pay, promotion and pensions." He noted that the army was recruited from all classes of society. "The military establishment too needs change, but that change should not be imposed on it. It must be initiated by the military and based on their awareness of its imperatives."

In this statement Corvalán showed himself well aware of the menace to the party from the ultraleft—the MIR, which had not joined the UP but had voted for it and hoped to use its victory for its own purposes. During the electoral campaign, he noted, the communist party "had to contend with numerous overt and covert enemies, from double-dyed reactionaries to ultraleft groups with their slogans of rifles instead of ballots." These "phoney lefts" had denounced the communists as "reformist" and "bourgeoisified," and as "sybarites," "conservatives," "traditionalists," "parliamentary time-servers," and "status-quo defenders."

The argument for nationalizing the copper industry had been that in publicly owned plants there would be less wastage; foreign penetration of the economy would be checked; profits would not be exported but retained by the people of Chile; demand for the products of Chilean industry would rise; and the standard of living would be improved. In reality, after nationalization had been carried out wastage increased, because jobs had to be found in the new management for deserving militants of several parties, production declined as less work was done, and wage increases were met by printing more money. For some months there was an appearance of prosperity because there were stocks of goods to be run down and currency reserves to be spent, but toward the end of 1971 shortages became serious. The government decided to postpone repayments of foreign debts, while at the same time asking for further foreign credits. It was not surprising that foreign bankers were unwilling to make loans to a government whose spokesmen loudly denounced foreign investors and refused to pay compensation for expropriated properties, but the leaders of the UP, who were not surprised by the unwillingness, took it as evidence of a conspiracy of the imperialists against them. Help was promised by the Soviet government and by communist-led governments in Eastern Europe; but it tended to be long-term and based on rigid criteria, when the need was for quantities of hard currency for short-term tasks.

The land reform, which had been started by previous administrations, was pursued with much greater speed. The ceiling for landholdings was, in practice, often brought below the legal figure of eighty hectares. The reform was not confined to the great estates (*latifundios*) of the central valley, but was extended to the holdings of small farmers. The Agrarian Reform Corporation (CORA) became an institution exercising dictatorial powers over the peasantry. In large areas, the ultraleft MIR illegally occupied farms both large and small, and set up little local states within the state. The MIR also established strongholds in some working-class districts in, and on the periphery of, Santiago and other industrial centers (the "revolutionary *cordones*"), and in squatter communities on the periphery of the capital (revolutionary *campamentos*). Here it accumulated supplies of arms and created "liberated territories" under its own sovereignty, assisted by foreign volunteers and by military instructors from Cuba and some East European states. Its activities were exceedingly unwelcome to the communists, both because it was building itself up as a military rival, and because it was antagonizing middle-class persons from whose support, or at least passivity, the communists had hoped to benefit. However, the MIR's actions enjoyed sympathy in the left wing of the socialist party, as well as in the smaller factions that belonged to the UP; President Allende himself, who had personal connections with some of the MIR's members, would never formally denounce the movement as such, still less give orders to the armed forces to destroy MIR bases and disarm MIR units.

As economic conditions deteriorated, and armed occupations and incidents multiplied, the Christian Democrats united with the National Party in Congress in opposition to Allende, and demonstrations by housewives and a truckdrivers' strike in October 1972 directly threatened the government. Allende was saved in this crisis by the armed forces, which controlled three cabinet posts under him between November 1972 and March 1973.

The soldiers left the government in March 1973. Allende was able to persuade them to cooperate in a new cabinet, thanks to the support of the chief of the general staff, General Prats, who was his friend. However, the new cabinet only lasted two weeks; General Prats resigned his position and later went abroad, and the armed forces now became clearly hostile to the administration. The congressional election of March 1973 was a success for the UP: its share of the poll went up from the previous 36 percent to nearly 43 percent. It could, however, be argued that this showed a decline in the popularity of the UP, since its candidates had obtained over 49 percent of the votes at municipal elections held in 1971. Whether the municipal and congressional elections were comparable may be a matter of argument. The communist share of the poll remained unchanged at around 17 percent, but the number of communist voters had increased from 383,000 in 1969 to 628,000 in 1973.

In the following months relations between government and opposition grew rapidly worse. Allende was accused of breaking the constitution by his failure to order his ministers to carry out decisions of the courts that were inconvenient to them. When the minister of interior was successfully impeached, Allende merely transferred him to another post. MIR illegalities continued. The government's plan to arm a workers' militia as a rival to the regular armed forces finally destroyed the generals' patience. On 11 September the commanders of the armed forces seized power. Allende committed suicide or was killed; fighting occurred in some of the working-class strongholds, with many casualties; leaders of the UP parties and some of the MIR were hunted down and arrested, and a military dictatorship ensued.

The overthrow of the Allende regime aroused an outcry from communists all over the world, and was also viewed with dismay by socialists and liberals in a broad sense. This protest was increased by the subsequent news of the repression and torture of political prisoners. The Chilean military dictatorship took a place in the rogues' gallery of left opinion second only to that of South Africa.

Much was heard of the argument that a peace-loving left government, which had combined respect for civil liberties with progressive social legislation, had been brutally destroyed: "the bourgeoisie" and "the imperialists," it was argued, had trampled on their own democratic principles. This was not a very convincing argument. Allende himself seems to have been genuinely devoted to freedom of opinion, and at least the leading newspapers of the opposition had been permitted to attack his administration in savage terms. Even so, the persecution of *El Mercurio* by his regime makes it impossible to argue that true freedom of the press prevailed under Allende. Moreover, it could hardly be said that civil liberties had been respected throughout the country: hundreds of thousands had been affected by MIR's illegalities, and also by the despotism of communist bosses in places where they were in command. Hundreds of thousands had suffered heavy economic privations, and saw themselves faced with ruin. To interpret the duty of bourgeois democrats to observe liberty as a duty to submit without resistance to ruin or violence was hardly realistic.

This was in fact understood by communists in other countries. Long, public, and intelligent discussions of the reasons for the Chilean disaster were held, and from a fairly unanimous view of them emerged two different sets of conclusions about future action.

There was general agreement on several points. First, the UP had alienated those elements in the middle classes on whose support they had counted. Second, the violent behavior of the MIR had made even more enemies, and had undermined the effective power of the government. Third, congress, the courts, and the apparatus of government had remained in the hands of persons who were not disposed to sacrifice their institutions to the priorities of the revolution. Fourth, the political neutrality of the armed forces had been overrated, and the UP had not successfully managed its relations with the military commanders. Finally, the hostility of foreign capital and foreign banks had made the economic situation desperate.

Opinions differed as to whether in the future communists should take a much tougher line from the beginning with the armed forces, civil bureaucracy, judiciary, and mass media, or, on the contrary, should make concessions to the middle classes, go much more slowly, and show more genuine respect for constitutional legality and for the rights of other classes and parties. The first view was, of course, taken by the MIR and by the left wing of the socialist party within the UP. It would seem from subsequent events that this conclusion inspired the communist leaders in Portugal, the next country in which an opportunity for action presented itself. The second view, which had on the whole been that of the communist leaders in Chile during the Allende administration, was strongly defended in the following period by the Italian communist leader Enrico Berlinguer, and even more emphatically by the Spanish communist leader Santiago Carrillo.

Portugal

Portugal was the oldest dictatorship of the right in Europe. Its dictator, António de Oliveira Salazar, ruled it from 1928 to 1968. It was also a country with a very backward economy. Salazar believed in free-enterprise capitalism, but he also disliked modern industrial cities and proletariats. At the same time he had a profound belief in the mission of the Portuguese empire and of Portuguese culture; in consequence, the country's wealth tended to be invested more in the African colonies than in industry at home. Since agriculture was poor and overpopulated, Portuguese farmers' children sought employment abroad, and this continued under Salazar's successor Marcelo Caetano; in 1975 about a million and a half Portuguese were resident abroad, of whom seven hundred thousand lived in France. Portugal itself had a population of a little over eight million. In the 1960s the tourist boom brought more prosperity, offering jobs in the building of hotels or of houses bought by foreigners. Foreign capital was also attracted into a rather wider range of business because Portuguese wages were very low by European standards. All this improved material conditions, but also increased discontent, since the disparity between the standard of living of the European holiday-makers and that of the indigenous people was flagrant. Returning workers from abroad told more of this, and their ability to build themselves decent houses with their foreign earnings at a time of housing shortage also aroused envy.

A still more important cause of discontent was the war in Africa. Since the early 1960s guerrilla action had grown in Guinea, Mozambique, and Angola. In 1974 the overseas army numbered about two hundred thousand and about a million and a half Portuguese had at some time seen service overseas. In 1973 a group of captains and lieutenants, discontented about the prospects of promotion as well as about the conduct of the war, formed the conspiratorial Armed Forces' Movement (MFA). At a higher level, the former commander-in-chief in Guinea, General António de Spínola, who had a fine service record, published a book in February 1974 criticizing the whole war policy and advocating a "political solution." It seems likely that Spínola and the MFA were in touch with each other, but it was the MFA that, after an abortive attempt in March, successfully deposed Caetano on 25 April 1974 and seized power. This revolution at once aroused enthusiastic hopes, and was followed by the free expression of all sorts of political opinions and the emergence of political parties.

The best organized of these at the beginning was the Portuguese Communist Party (PCP). Led by the veteran Alvaro Cunhal, and largely organized by workers who had been recruited to communism while working in France (some of whom had been trained in Czechoslovakia), it also had an effective illegal apparatus inside Portugal.

With the example of Chile in mind, Cunhal set himself to apply its lessons, as well as those of Soviet experience. His most important goal was to get on good terms with the army leaders, and to penetrate the officers' corps. Second only to this was his intention to place his men in the civil state machine, in economic management, and in the apparatus of publicity—the press, radio-television, and the Fifth Division of the army (which was responsible for

education of the forces). In all these things the communists, who were first off
the mark, gained quick advantages over their rivals. It was also important to have
an alliance of parties of the left, and to bring them under communist leadership.
Here the communists were less successful. The Portuguese Democratic Movement (MDP) was no more than a communist-front organization, and was soon
recognized as such. It did not bring much added strength to the PCP. The socialist party, led by Mário Soares, was willing to cooperate with the PCP, but
not to be led by it. Maneuvers designed to split it had small effect. On the other
hand, ultraleft groups appeared that, like the MIR in Chile, seriously embar-
rassed the communists. Cunhal's action program was extremely moderate; this
too was designed to avoid the mistakes made in Chile. The PCP urged a "battle
of production," and opposed strikes or large wage increases. However, the Portuguese workers, who had been among the worst paid in Europe, did not show
much enthusiasm for these slogans, and the ultraleft urged them to demand more.
The PCP found itself in much the same awkward middle position as had the
Chilean communists: it tried to limit the workers' pressure, while at the same
time showing its revolutionary prowess by bullying engineers and managers.
The main issue on which the PCP was not moderate even in words was decol-
onization: it insisted on immediate transfer of power to the guerrilla movements
in Guinea, Mozambique, and Angola. In this it had the support of many MFA
officers but not of Spínola, now President, who aimed at the creation by slow
negotiation of a Portuguese commonwealth.

Disagreement about colonial policy, and alarm both at the disorder in the
factories and at the seizure of lands by communist-led agricultural workers in
the south, brought the conflict between Spínola and the left to a head. In September 1974 Spínola summoned a rally of his supporters, of the "silent majority," to be held in Lisbon. Both the PCP and the ultraleftists organized road-
blocks to prevent the entry of demonstrators into the capital, and the armed
forces in Lisbon (under the orders of the Commando for Continental Portugal
—COPCON—headed by a leading MFA officer, Otelo de Carvalho), supported
them. Spínola was forced to call off the rally, and on 30 September he resigned
the Presidency.

In the next months the PCP gained in strength. The premier appointed on 17
July, Colonel Vasco Gonçalves, cooperated closely with Cunhal. In January
1975 the MFA put into force, against socialist and ultraleft protests, a law creating a single trade-union organization, Intersindical, which was under communist control. The press was also dominated by the PCP. Its main strongholds
were the working class of Lisbon and the agricultural laborers of Alentejo Province. Both of these policies were, however, disputed by the ultraleftists, who
urged their followers on to more violent action. Communist spokesmen denounced the "irresponsibility" of these "minor" groups of "students, intellectuals, and petty bourgeoisie" who were playing into the hands of the extreme

right. However, when clashes with the police or military units occurred, PCP speakers could not bring themselves openly to defend "law and order" against "the masses." Inevitably, the PCP got the blame for the disorders. Within the MFA, and among the army commanders in general, there was as much dismay at communist influence as there was sympathy for it. The north of Portugal was overwhelmingly anticommunist: here the land was in the hands of small- and medium-scale farmers, and the Catholic church had strong support.

The next crisis came on 11 March, when a coup d'état by followers of Spínola was easily crushed by COPCON. The whole affair was so ridiculously mismanaged that it even looked as if it might have been a provocation organized by the left MFA or PCP to compromise Spínola, but this could not be proved. The general fled abroad. In the next months the PCP's influence was at its height, yet real power was in the hands of the MFA. Though Gonçalves was on the communist side, this was not true of most MFA radicals; rather, they thought in terms of some "Third World solution" for Portugal, a revolutionary military dictatorship of an African type. Many had been influenced by the ideas of the Guinea nationalist Amilcar Cabral, the leader of the Partido Africano de Independência de Guiné e Cabo Verde (PAIGC), whose analyses stressed the role not of the proletariat (which did not exist in Guinea), but of the exploited lower-middle classes (to whose equivalent in Portugal many MFA officers belonged).

Against the communists' wishes, the MFA decided to proceed with the planned parliamentary election, which duly took place on 25 April 1975, the anniversary of the revolution. Despite a good deal of intimidation by the PCP and the ultraleftists, the results were disappointing for them: the socialist party had 38 percent of a 92 percent poll; the moderate Popular Democrats (PPD), 26 percent; and the PCP and its creature the MDP together, only 16 percent. The communists won more than a third of the votes only in two southern provinces, Evora and Setubal; the PPD were strongest in the medium-sized cities; and the socialists won a high proportion all over the country.

The arguments with which Cunhal reacted to the election results were strikingly similar to Lenin's reaction to the results of the election of the Constituent Assembly in Russia in November 1917. The election results did not really matter, since the aim of the revolution was not a parliamentary regime, but "people's power," which Cunhal equated with the rule of the proletariat, which he equated with the rule by the PCP. If the people had had more than the inadequate period of twelve months between the seizure of power by the MFA and the election, they would have acquired a fuller political consciousness, and thus would have voted for the PCP. The PCP's first priority must be to penetrate the army through its connections with the MFA; parliamentary opponents could then be dealt with in due course.

The election did not appear to affect the MFA-PCP alliance. On May Day the PCP staged a huge workers' rally in Lisbon, and Mário Soares, the socialist leader, was forcibly prevented from attending it. The next day the socialists held a great mass rally in reply. A few days later communist-led printing workers took over *República,* the main Lisbon paper that expressed the socialists' views. Communist radio workers also took over the Catholic radio station *Renascença.* This led to demonstrations by Catholics in Lisbon and in the north, and some revival of support for the church among persons of liberal outlook who had detested it in the Salazar and Caetano periods because of its support for the regime. In the north there were mass attacks on communist-party buildings and on individual communists.

During the summer of 1975 the crisis sharpened. The radicals in the MFA produced in July a project for a new constitution, a form of "people's power" based on "basic assemblies" of inhabitants. This proposal was opposed by the socialists, who resigned from the government. Within the MFA there was a division between Gonçalves, who clung to the PCP, and Carvalho, who was nearer to the ultraleft. In the north anticommunist violence grew, and the loyalty of military commanders was increasingly strained. Carvalho's COPCON was hostile to the Fifth Division of the army, a propaganda force controlled by Cunhal's men. Relations between the communists and the ultraleft continued to be bad. At the end of August COPCON units took over the Fifth Division, and Gonçalves was replaced as premier by Vice-Admiral José Batista Pinheiro Azevedo. His cabinet included five MFA moderates, four socialists, and only one communist. This provoked demonstrations by the left and some mutinous actions in the army, and counterdemonstrations by the socialists. On 22 November Carvalho was relieved of his COPCON command. Three days later an attempt by paratroopers with left sympathies to seize airbases and radio stations was crushed by loyal troops. The PCP was doing its best to develop left insurrectionary groups within the army, but at the last moment Cunhal drew back from committing his party to the abortive coup.

From this time the power of the PCP rapidly declined. Pressure from the small farmers' organizations led to some action against land seizure, and to more orderly procedures in land reform. Carvalho, who was implicated in the November revolt, was removed from his post. The government carried out a second election, under genuinely free conditions, on 25 April 1976. This time the socialist party won 35 percent of the poll; the PPD, 24 percent; the more conservative CDS, 16 percent; and the PCP, 14.5 percent. A new constitution was adopted, which gave large powers to the president of the republic, embodied the nationalization measures that had previously been enacted, and confirmed the agreement of the military leadership to transfer political power to a multiparty democracy. On 27 June the presidential election followed. General António Ramalho Eanes was elected, winning 61.5 percent of the votes cast, while Carvalho won 16.5 percent, and the communists' candidate got 7.5 percent. The new president called upon Soares to form a government, and he decided to rule with a cabinet formed only from his socialist party. Meanwhile the economic situation became more and more difficult.

At the end of 1975 it could be said that the communists' bid for power had failed; but it did not follow from this that there would not be further bids, or that the economic crisis, though largely caused by their actions, could not be turned to their advantage. The prospects before Soares were also uncertain. He had been sustained through the most difficult period by the support of West European socialist movements, especially the West German party, and his government received economic aid from European Economic Community (EEC) countries, but the tasks remained formidable.

The communists' failure in the first two years may be regarded as due to a wrong interpretation of the lessons of Chile, or a failure to apply the lessons learned. Cunhal had, probably rightly, concluded from the Chilean case that it was important to infiltrate the machinery of government, and to place no confidence in the impartiality of ministerial or judicial officials, still less of policemen. He had tried much more systematically than Allende to make these officials harmless. He had also learned the lesson that the army must be won over. It was here that he had had his biggest successes, but they had not been lasting. If Allende had been unwise to trust the army, Cunhal had proved a poor diplomatist in his handling of conflicting army factions. Cunhal had shown even less respect for the freedom of the press than had Allende's regime, presumably because, in the retrospective view of many communists, relative freedom of the press had been a main cause of Allende's fall. Yet it is arguable that the PCP's treatment of the press and radio had strengthened rather than damaged its enemies. Like the Chilean communists, the members of the PCP had suffered much from the outrages committed by the ultraleft; like their Chilean comrades, they had tried to pursue moderate policies and win the middle classes, yet like Allende, they had been unable to take actions against the ultraleft, since their own members in the last resort preferred ultraleft workers to "the bourgeoisie." Perhaps the most important single failure of Cunhal was that he could not cooperate with the socialists. Whereas in Chile the left wing of the socialist party had prevailed —which benefited the communists even if it saddled them with some unpredictable ultraleftists inside the official socialist party—in Portugal the believers in democratic methods, though rather "left" by North European labor-movement standards, were in control; they also had the advantage that Portugal, unlike Chile, was geographically close to countries with strong democratic socialist movements. On the other hand, the Soviet Union was far away, and Soviet naval forces in the Atlantic could not be useful unless the PCP was in power.

A curious feature of Cunhal's record in 1974–1975 is a certain superficial parallel to the events in Russia in 1917. There were "July days" in September 1974, a potential Kornilov rebellion in March 1975, and an abortive "October" in November 1975. One is tempted to wonder whether Cunhal thought of himself as reenacting the Bolsheviks' role, as the Bolsheviks had once thought of them-selves as reenacting the first few acts of the French Revolution.

However this may be, and though the action had failed by the summer of 1976, there were no grounds whatever for disparaging the Portuguese commu-nists. They made a gallant effort, and showed themselves to be a powerful force, ready for another try later. Moreover, by their contribution to a Portuguese gov-ernment policy that made possible the victory of the Liberation Front of Mo-zambique (FRELIMO) in that country and of the MPLA in Angola, they pow-erfully promoted the cause of communism and of the Soviet empire.

Italy

Three well-known special features of modern Italian history must be briefly stated at the beginning of any discussion of Italian communism. The first is the strength of the Catholic church among the people. Not only was Rome the center of the papacy, but devotion to the church was deeply rooted in the country and in towns in forms varying from semi-pagan superstition to robust intellectual conviction, and in regions stretching from Sicily and Apulia to Venetia and Pied-mont. The second feature is the division between north and south, which is so great as almost to justify talk of two nations. Many cities of the south could claim cultural histories equal to those of the north, but under Spanish and Bour-bon rule the kingdom of Naples had remained centuries behind Milan or Turin, which belonged fully to twentieth-century Europe; these differences were not ironed out by the first hundred years of the united Italian state. The third was the Fascist dictatorship, the creation of Mussolini's ambition and vanity, which was welded together by a combination of bombastic rhetoric and police terror; in some ways it was an agency of modernization, and in others a preserver of all that was most backward. In its days of success Fascism had been supported not only by party stalwarts and stolid bureaucrats but also by mass consent; but for independent-minded Italians, above all in the intellectual professions, it had been a hated enemy whose political perversion and moral corruption could not easily or soon be forgotten.

The Italian communist party had begun as a breakaway faction of the out-wardly impressive and large, but sprawling and shapeless Italian socialist move-ment. After Mussolini tightened his dictatorship in 1926, the leading socialists went into exile. The anti-Fascist emigration, based chiefly in France but also in other western countries, included some of the finest minds of Italy; but as the years passed, their links with the people at home wore thin. The main exception was the communist party, whose leaders from the first gave a high priority to the maintenance of an underground organization inside Italy, even if there was not very much that they could do with it. For a time they had an able leader in

Antonio Gramsci, but he was arrested and died in prison in 1937. His successor, Palmiro Togliatti, who spent the years of Fascist dictatorship in exile, was also a brilliant man, who seems to have maintained his own independence of judgment under an exterior of complete compliance with the fluctuating wishes of the Comintern and of Stalin. He was at least able to protect his fellow Italian communist exiles in Soviet Russia from the fate that, during Stalin's purges, befell the members of most persecuted communist parties from countries in which dictatorships of the right held power. Italian casualties of the NKVD seem to have been few; in any case there were more Italian communists in France, and several thousand of these went to fight for the Republic in Spain.

Inside Italy effective mass resistance to Mussolini began in 1943, with large-scale strikes in the north in which both communists and socialists were involved, and developed into partisan warfare when the Germans occupied Italy after Mussolini's overthrow. In the resistance were communists, socialists, independent radical intellectuals of the Party of Action (heirs to the *Giustizia e Libertà* group), and Christian Democrats, but it was the commmunists who contributed the most. When the war ended, their prestige from the resistance and the diplomatic skill of Togliatti in dealing both with "bourgeois" Italian politicians and with the Allied governments enabled the communists to emerge as the strongest party of the left and of the working class. As in France, they took part in the first postwar governments, but were forced out in 1947 as a result of the breakdown of the alliance between the Western powers and the Soviet Union. They were joined in opposition by the socialists, but at the cost of a split in the socialist ranks that further increased the superiority of the communist party over the socialists.

From 1948 onward Italy was ruled by the Christian Democrats. This name covered a number of political trends, and as time passed a number of rival factions were formed, based as much on personalities, on regions, or on power bases within individual ministries as on differences of political principle. The Christian Democrats became the party of the established order, closely linked both with big business and with the bureaucracy, which had maintained considerable continuity, for better or worse, from nineteenth-century Piedmont through the early kingdom of Italy through the Fascist era. Inevitably, nearly thirty years of rule by the same party created boredom in the politically conscious intellectual classes, and spread through the mass media. There were also periodic scandals, showing widespread corruption in high places and wealthy circles, which damaged the party's reputation. To judge by public comment, disillusionment with the Christian Democrats increased steadily from year to year; yet the vote given to them at elections did not fall very far. Their highest peak was reached in 1948, when they won 48.5 percent of all votes cast. By 1963 their share had fallen to 38 percent, and it remained at this level with but slight variations, through the election of June 1976. The Christian Democrats thus remained in control of the center and the moderate right. There were also fascist groups on the extreme right, but over a span of thirty years, their rise and fall and their fluctuating efforts were not impressive.

The left was divided during the same period; a series of splits occurred among the socialists, and the small radical groups, which had once had the support of some of the most intelligent and generous minds in Italy, declined steadily (first the Party of Action and then the Republican party). Throughout the period the communists gained in popularity, with their proportion of the vote rising from 19 percent in 1946 to 35 percent in 1976, while the socialist vote declined during the same time span from 21 percent to 10 percent. The occasions and results of the socialist splits should be briefly recorded. In 1947 those who opposed an electoral alliance between socialists and communists seceded to form the Social Democratic Party (PSDI). In 1963 the socialists (PSI) decided to form a coalition with the Christian Democrats—the so-called "opening to the left." This provoked a secession on the left and the formation of the Socialist Party of Proletarian Unity (PSIUP). In 1972 the PSIUP was dissolved by its members: most joined the communists (PCI), but a remnant joined with a splinter group from the PCI to form an ultraleft extraparliamentary opposition. Meanwhile, in 1966 the PSI and PSDI decided to reunite, but this attempt broke down in 1969. The socialists remained faction-ridden in the late 1970s; although they were far outdistanced by the communists, their support was needed by any combination of parties to form a parliamentary government.

The PCI steadily expanded its numbers and gained support in the south, which before Fascism had been virtually closed to the left. Under Togliatti's leadership, it maintained a moderate posture on the whole. In 1956, in connection with the publication in the West of Khrushchev's "secret speech" to the Twentieth Congress of the CPSU, Togliatti told an interviewer from the review *Nuovi Argomenti* that the horrors revealed by Khrushchev could not simply be attributed to Stalin's personality; thought must also be given to the nature of the Soviet system itself. In the same interview he used the word "polycentrism" as an ideal for communist parties: it could no longer be assumed that Moscow's wishes should be binding on all. In the following years the communists acquired experience in administration at the provincial and municipal levels, especially in Emilia and Tuscany. Communist local government acquired a reputation for honesty and efficiency. The city of Bologna became something of a model. In 1975 the PCI had sweeping successes in local elections, including those in the cities of Milan, Naples, and Turin.

The communists were also rather successful in appealing to the younger generation of intellectuals, as representatives of the great tradition of the Risorgimento. This was an important and specifically Italian phenomenon. The anti-Fascist emigration of the 1930s had laid great stress on this heritage, and it remained alive into the 1970s. There is nothing quite like it in the political mythology (blend of historical truth and fiction) of any other nation. The intellectuals most active in the resistance of 1943–1945 were suspicious of the communists, and preferred to maintain their own political organizations. But a generation later, things were different. *Giustizia e Libertà* and the Party of Action were only names. To many intelligent, highly educated young Italians it now seemed that the only political team capable of creating a new Italy, in which social justice for the people would be combined with the best humane traditions and the disinterested ideals of the Risorgimento, were the communists. This category of potential supporters was not very large, but it was influential, and it was a source of future leadership. Communist attempts to tap this source were rather successful.

The tendencies to independent thought in the leadership of the PCI were strengthened in 1968, both by the Soviet invasion of Czechoslovakia, which the party condemned, and by the student unrest and ultraleft activities, which were visible all over Europe, especially in Paris but also in Italian cities.

In 1971 Enrico Berlinguer became the secretary-general of the PCI. Under his leadership the party's policies appeared increasingly to diverge from those of the Soviet leadership.

One important object of disagreement was the European Economic Community. Whereas this organization was treated with unrelieved hostility in Moscow, Berlinguer and PCI spokesmen favored continued Italian membership in the EEC, hoping, of course, that in time the left would be dominant within it, that a socialist Western Europe would come into being.

Italian writers of the left also began to study seriously the changes in the Italian social structure since 1945. The economist Sylos Labini made a new classification of Italian society[4] that was taken seriously by communists as the work of an independent Marxist. He divided the population into the bourgeoisie (2.6 percent), the middle classes (49.6 percent), and the working class (47.8 percent). In his terminology, the bourgeoisie consisted only of large owners of property and persons at the top of the professions. He divided the middle classes into a "petty bourgeoisie of employees," which comprised 1,750,000 employees of private firms, 980,000 public employees, and 600,000 teachers; and a "relatively autonomous petty bourgeoisie" of 2,380,000 farmers and tenants, 1,250,000 artisans, 1,700,000 tradesmen, and 400,000 workers in transport and services. The working class included 1,230,000 in agriculture, 4,800,000 in industry, 1,670,000 in building, 600,000 in commerce, 800,000 in transport and services, and 300,000 in domestic service. It was clear from his analysis that a party of the left would have to extend its support beyond the working class if it hoped to obtain a substantial majority. This was recognized by the PCI

---

4. Paolo Sylos Labini, *Saggio sulle classi sociali* (Bari, 1974).

leaders, though they did not necessarily accept Labini's categories. They interpreted the phrase "working class" liberally. For example, a member of the party's Politburo, Giorgio Napolitano, told an interviewer that "one must speak of working class in a broader sense than hitherto, referring not only to the manual worker who produces surplus value, but also to other strata of workers, whose objective position in the process of production closely approaches that of the working class and whose level of political and social consciousness makes it easier for it to be welded together with the working class."[5] Such terminology lends itself to very wide interpretation.

It was the Chilean disaster that caused Berlinguer to formulate his political strategy more clearly, in three articles that appeared in the PCI weekly *Rinascita* on 28 September, 5 October, and 12 October 1973. After paying due respect to the doctrine that the events in Chile were the result of American imperialist intervention, he proceeded to look at the prospects in Italy. Here he clearly indicated that greater moderation than had been used in Chile, rather than fiercer revolutionary action, was what was needed. He insisted that the Italian party had always wished "to take into account the whole of Italian history, and thus of all the historical forces (of socialist, Catholic and other democratic inspiration) that were present on the scene and were fighting together with us for democracy." The party's aim was "to rally the great majority of the people round a program of struggle for a democratic healing and renewal of the entire society and state . . . and to marshal the political forces necessary to realize it." The party leadership believed that this could not be done by combining only the parties of the working class and of the left. The main task was "to avoid a stable and organic welding together of the center and right, a broad front of clerical-fascist type, and instead to succeed in shifting the social and political forces situated in the center onto coherently democratic positions." The PCI was therefore speaking not of a "left alternative" but of a "democratic alternative." The Christian Democrats were a "very varied, a very changeable reality." The PCI must deal with them, and it must aim "to isolate and to defeat drastically the tendencies that are wagering, or might be tempted to wager, on a confrontation and on a vertical cleavage in the country," and on the other hand to act so as to give increased weight, and ultimate predominance, to those forces that "with historical and political realism recognize that it is necessary, and that the time has come, to have a constructive dialogue and an agreement between all popular forces." In his last sentence he called for "what can be defined as the new great 'historic agreement' between the forces that assemble and that represent the great majority of the Italian people."[6]

---

5. Giorgio Napolitano, *Intervista sul PCI* (Bari, 1976).

6. The words I have translated as "historic agreement" (in Italian *compromesso storico*) were placed between quotation marks by Berlinguer himself.

Berlinguer was claiming that the PCI was a democratic party, accepting the Italian political heritage as a whole, and asking to share power with the other great political force, which had its following in all social classes, and accepted in one way or another the leadership of the Catholic church. At the same time he also had a second aim. For thirty years the great majority of the center and right had been united, while the left had been divided. In the 1970s the great majority of the left was moving toward unity, and it must be its aim to stimulate disunity in its antagonist. What Berlinguer was seeking was not partnership of the whole communist party with the whole Christian Democratic party, but a split in the Christian Democratic ranks, with those who utterly rejected cooperation with the communists going into opposition, and the rest—preferably a substantial majority of the party—joining a coalition in which the communists would be the strongest partner. Should such a split lead to some sort of alliance of the right-wing secessionist Christian Democrats with the neofascists, it would be possible to argue that there was a dangerous fascist revival, and that exceptional powers must be taken to combat it. The use that could be made of the fascist bogey had been amply demonstrated by communist actions in Hungary and Czechoslovakia in 1947 and 1948. The bogey would be the more effective because many thousands of Italians had very vivid and very bitter personal memories of Fascism.

To suggest that the PCI was capable of maneuvers of this sort is not necessarily to deny that Berlinguer and other leaders might genuinely intend to use strictly constitutional methods to obtain power, and even to wield power after victory. That many thousands of party members, and millions of voters for the PCI, were good democrats was beyond dispute. The question often asked in Anglo-Saxon countries, "Have the Italian communists abjured violent methods, and committed themselves to abide by the rules?" was unanswerable. Neither Berlinguer nor anyone else could know the answer.

Meanwhile the Christian Democrats did fairly well in the 1976 election, and did not accept the *compromesso storico*. A minority Christian Democratic government under Giulio Andreotti ruled with the consent of the communists in the parliament. In July 1977 a further step was taken: the government agreed to discuss its legislative plans in advance with five other parties, one of which was the communist. But economic difficulties, public boredom with the old team, efficient communist local government, and the inevitable surprises in both Italian and international politics that must lie ahead, made the future unpredictable.

France

In 1920, at the time of the split in the French socialist party that gave it birth, the French communist party, in contrast to the Italian, represented a majority of the socialist movement. In the following decades it was able, again unlike

the Italian, to operate freely within a democratic state. It did not stand the test
very well, since it soon fell behind the socialist party; though it made some gains
in the Popular Front period of 1935–1937, it remained a minority group within
the French labor movement. The Soviet-German pact of 1939 further discredited
the French communists, but they made a big recovery during the years of the
Resistance. Partly through their genuine merits in the struggle against the Germans, and partly through their skill and ruthlessness in placing their men in
positions of power in the embryonic trade-union and state apparatus, they
emerged in 1944 definitely stronger than the socialists. As in Italy, they took
part in the first postwar governments, and as in Italy, they were forced out of
power as a result of the breakdown of the great-power Alliance.

In opposition, the French communists, to a greater extent than the Italians,
became isolated from the majority of the people. They continued to enjoy the
loyalty of the majority of the French working class, and their isolation meant
in fact the exclusion of the workers from French political life, a weakness of
the body politic that was largely responsible in the long term for the collapse
of the Fourth Republic. The communist leaders displayed a sullen hostility to
the rest of the French nation that was in contrast with the much milder and more
conciliatory public posture of the Italian communists even under Togliatti. At
the same time they tried to provide for the material and spiritual needs of their
followers within the bosom of the party, to form a state within a state, a society
within society, and a church in competition with the Christian church. This peculiar isolation and self-sufficiency of the French communists have often been
pointed out.[7] Two points that are connected with this contrast between the two
parties, though they do not suffice to explain it, deserve mention.

One is the memory of the Soviet-German pact. In 1939 the French party suddenly had to veer round from militant anti-Nazism to advocacy of peace with
Hitler; Maurice Thorez deserted from the French army; and in the summer of
1940 some communist spokesmen, making a conscious analogy between the
situation of their party after national defeat and the situation of the Bolsheviks
after the Treaty of Brest-Litovsk, went so far as to approach the German authorities with a request to resume their activities legally. These things embittered
many Frenchmen against the communists, but they also hardened the cadres of
the party in unrepentant defiance. A good case could, of course, be made for
the view that the Soviet Union, the glorious model for communists, had saved
France from Hitler. But Thorez went further than this, declaring that the French
workers would not fight if a Soviet army entered France, and that "la France
est mon pays, mais l'Union Soviétique est ma patrie." The Italian communists
found themselves in no such dilemma. They had never been associated with the
nation's enemy: the Italians had never in modern times had a "national enemy"

---

7. Especially by Annie Kriegel, *Les communistes français* (Paris, 1968).

in the same way that Germany had become the national enemy of the French. The long struggle of the Italian communists first against Fascism and then against the German Nazi invaders who had taken over from the Fascists was something of which they could be unreservedly proud.

A second difference is that political liberty was dearer to the Italians than to the French. This is not to deny that in European history as a whole the French, together with the English, have been the leaders in the struggle for political liberty. The point is that in France that struggle had been won long ago: the interlude of Nazi occupation had been painful but had not deeply affected men's thinking. In Italy, however, the victory had been only partially won in 1860, and it had been brutally reversed after 1922. In France the struggle for liberty had been replaced by the struggle of classes in the second half of the nineteenth century. Especially in industrial northern France class hatred was extremely bitter, and both sides were tempted to forget the need to maintain liberty and respect the achievements of past centuries. This was not true in Italy, where the struggles for political liberty and social justice were inextricably linked. This accounts for a significant difference in thinking between the leading figures in the two parties and the left intellectuals from whom they recruited many of their cadres; it is arguable that this difference was also reflected in the attitudes of working people.

The French communists maintained their dominance in the working class during the Gaullist era in France. They were strengthened by the fact that a significant part of the former socialist following transferred its loyalty to General de Gaulle. They suffered, however, from a new difficulty: the general's foreign policy, increasingly hostile to the United States, was very welcome to the Soviet government, which therefore discouraged the communist party (PCF) from active opposition to his regime.

The year 1968 was a fateful time for the PCF. First came the May riots of students in Paris, with their explosion of ultraleft, Trotskyist, or Maoist revolutionary rhetoric and demonstrations. As the movement gained strength, and solidarity between students and workers became more than a slogan, the leaders of the PCF were placed in an awkward situation. They detested the ultraleft intellectuals and still more the Trotskyist working-class groups, yet they clearly could not come out in favor of repression by the police. When the students, the CGT (the communist-led trade unions), and the CFDT (Catholic and miscellaneous left trade unions) decided to call a general strike for 13 May, the PCF had to give its approval. In the following days of mass strike action, the PCF and CGT leaders did their best to make the workers concentrate on economic claims rather than ideological issues, but the CFDT and the ultraleftists began to talk more and more of the overthrow of capitalism. Most reluctantly, the PCF was drawn in this direction. On 29 September it organized a march through Paris from the Place Bastille to Gare Saint-Lazare in which it claimed that eight hundred thousand took part; the next day the Politburo officially called for a popular-front government. A few hours later de Gaulle made his long-awaited speech, and the same evening the PCF withdrew its demand, stating only that it would contest the election called by de Gaulle. This proved to be a massive victory for the Gaullists and a rout for the left.

In August 1968 the PCF was confronted with a second odious dilemma as a result of the Soviet invasion of Czechoslovakia. This was a horrible blow to many French communists, especially to intellectuals, in whose minds the anti-fascist role attributed to Czechoslovakia, and Hitler's invasion of Prague, had a special place. An official statement by the PCF referred to its "surprise and disapproval of the military intervention in Czechoslovakia." However, when the leading communist intellectual Roger Garaudy gave an interview to the Czechoslovak news agency on 28 August, calling the invasion a return to Stalinism, the PCF Central Committee described this as "an inadmissible interference in the internal affairs of fraternal parties," and Garaudy himself publicly accepted this criticism. The PCF was the first nonruling communist party to accept the policy of "normalization" imposed by the Soviet nominees in Czechoslovakia. When the PCF secretary Waldeck Rochet (successor to Thorez in 1964) led a PCF delegation to Moscow on 3 November for talks with Brezhnev, a communiqué was issued that spoke of the traditional friendship and cooperation between the two parties and made only a vague reference to Czechoslovakia.

During the next years there was some discussion in the PCF, as there had been in the Italian party, about changes in the social structure and their implications for the party. At the PCF's Nineteenth Congress, in February 1970, Georges Marchais (who had been secretary since 1972) claimed that the proportion of wage-earners in the labor force had increased from 70 percent in 1962 to 76 percent in 1968. He also asserted that the working class numbered about 9,000,000. These statements were not supported by the official statistics published in 1971, which from a total labor force of 20,680,000 estimated the industrial workers at 7,700,000 (37.4 percent) and the agricultural workers at 388,000 (1.5 percent), as opposed to various middle- and upper-class groups that totaled 10,770,000 or 53 percent.[8] Garaudy argued that potential revolutionary elements should not be excluded from the PCF's concept of the forces of revolution just because they were of bourgeois origin. "New social layers" (*couches nouvelles*) of intellectuals, who do not own the means of production and who are themselves objects of the extraction of surplus value, should be

---

8. These consisted of: farmers (*agriculteurs exploitants*), 1,900,000 or 9.5 percent; businessmen (*industriels et commerçants*), 2,000,000 or 10 percent; liberal professions, 145,000 or 0.7 percent; employees, 3,256,000 or 15.7 percent; *cadres moyens*, 2,471,000 or 11.9 percent; and *cadres supérieurs*, 1,000,000 or 5.2 percent. The further category of *personnel de service*, numbering 1,200,000 or 5.9 percent, might arguably be added to the working class. These figures from official 1971 statistics are quoted in André Laurens and Thierry Pfister, *Lex Nouveaux communistes* (Paris, 1973).

accepted as allies. There should be not just tactical cooperation with them, but a strategic alliance. The party should create a new *bloc historique*. These ideas were rejected by Marchais. Garaudy had already in 1964 polemized with the Soviet ideological official Ilichev about cooperation between communists and Christians. These two groups, he argued, could be allies not only in the class war, but also in the construction of socialism after victory. Marchais denied this. Once the PCF's policies of complete separation of church and state and nationalization of state schools had been carried out, no member of a church would be allowed to be a state official or a teacher. Marchais admitted at the Nineteenth Congress that the number of "intellectuals" had increased between 1954 and 1970 from about one million to three million. Of these he estimated that perhaps 4 to 5 percent could be regarded as working-class; it was possible and desirable to win the support of the others, but there must be no diminution of the leading role of the working class, and talk of a *bloc historique* was unacceptable. Disagreement on these issues eventually led to the removal of Garaudy from the party.

After the departure of General de Gaulle, the main new factor affecting the PCF's fortunes was the recovery and reunification of the socialists. Already surpassed by the PCF in 1945, the old party—the French Section of the Workers International (SFIO)—had split in 1958 on the issues of French policy in Algeria and the attitude to adopt to de Gaulle. The SFIO continued to exist, but a new United Socialist Party (PSU) also came into being, which included former members of SFIO, former communists, followers of the former nonsocialist premier Mendès-France, and other groups. All socialist trends were to be found in it, including syndicalist ideas that were gaining ground in the formerly Catholic trade-union organization CFDT.[9] There were also former members of the Catholic youth movement JOC (Jeunesse Ouvrière Catholique). Other small groups, clubs, and study centers of socialist outlook joined in April 1965 to form the Convention des Institutions Républicaines (CIR). They supported the presidential candidacy of a former politician of old-style radical background, François Mitterrand, who had become converted to socialism. Defeated by de Gaulle, Mitterrand persisted in his efforts to unify the socialist groups and to make himself their leader. During 1969 and 1970 a series of meetings were held, and programs issued, the most important being the "Plan for Socialist Action" of the SFIO and the "Socialist Contract" of the CIR. Discussions were also held with the PCF, and a statement was issued of the points of agreement and disagreement between them. These activities reached a climax at the Congress of Epinay on 11–13 June 1971, at which it was decided to fuse the different parties

---

9. Originally named the French Confederation of Christian Workers (CFTC), it decided, at an extraordinary congress held in November 1964, to "deconfessionalize" itself, and took the name French Democratic Confederation of Labor (CFDT).

into a single socialist party (PS) which included both the SFIO and the CIR. The maneuvering at the congress led to the election as first secretary of the new party of the recent convert Mitterrand, with the support of groups of the left. The new party leadership was determined to make an alliance with the PCF. On 27 June 1972 a "Joint Program" was published, which both parties ratified in the following month.

At the parliamentary election of March 1973, this new Popular Front won over 46 percent of the poll. In the presidential election of 1974, Mitterrand stood as the candidate of the left, and in the second ballot on 19 May he was defeated by Giscard d'Estaing by less than 2 percent. At the municipal elections of March 1977, the left achieved a vote of more than 50 percent.

Thus the 1970s had seen a remarkable recovery of the French communists, which in mid-1977 had brought them to the point where they had strong hopes of a victory of the left in the parliamentary election due in 1978. With a left government in power, with a "Common Program" that included far-reaching nationalizations in industry, and expenditures on social welfare that would grievously strain the country's finances, the position of President Giscard (whose presidential mandate would still have two years to run) would be most delicate, and the whole constitutional future of France would be in doubt.

One of the main obstacles to the PCF's progress among the French people was its long, almost uncritical devotion to the Soviet cause. Probably as a result of pressure both from socialist-party competition at home and from the Italian party abroad, Georges Marchais, who at the time of his succession to the position of first secretary in December 1972 had been regarded as a safe Moscow man, began to speak more boldly. At least for public consumption, the PCF now supported the principles of independence and equality of all communist parties. On 15 November 1975, after a meeting in Rome, Berlinguer and Marchais published a "Common Declaration" by both parties. It affirmed their determination that under socialism all the liberties resulting from the great bourgeois revolutions would be "guaranteed and developed." These included "plurality of political parties—including the right to existence and to activity of opposition parties—liberty of their formation and the possibility of democratic alternation of majorities and minorities." The two parties attached to these liberties a "value of principle," and stated that their attitude was not tactical, but was derived from "their analysis of the material and historical conditions specific to their respective countries."

PCF spokesmen maintained this line in the following year. Marchais himself did not attend the Twenty-fifth Congress of the CPSU in February 1976, but the PCF representative, Politbureau member Gustave Plissonnier, said in his speech that his party was aiming at a powerful majority movement, a union of parties of the left, and that it would create a "French-style socialism." Marchais attended the conference of communist parties in Berlin in July 1976 and reasserted his party's devotion to democratic liberties, specifically mentioning "the independence of justice and the rejection of any official philosophy." His party, he said, had decided to abandon the principle of "dictatorship of the proletariat" because it "does not cover the reality of political power in the socialist France for which we are fighting." His most striking phrase was: "Socialism in France will be a socialism in the colors of France." During 1977 PCF spokesmen went very far in their criticisms of the Soviet Union, even expressing support for Soviet dissidents who had been persecuted by the security police (KGB).

The prospects for the PCF were limited by the uncertainty of its relationship to the socialists. During 1976 and 1977 there were periodic indications that the PS actually had more support in the country than the PCF. Relations between Mitterrand and Marchais grew very tense. In the late summer of 1977 the PCF began a campaign of direct attacks on the socialists. Attempts by the party leaders to resolve differences of policy within the Union of the Left—especially concerning the extent of nationalization—failed.

Among the opponents of the united left were two opposed views. The optimists believed that the unity would not last, and that if the left should form a government, the partners would soon fall apart. If this were so, then it was important for the opponents of the left to adopt a moderate posture so that they could win moderate socialists away from the communist embrace when opportunity offered. This was, on the whole, President Giscard's attitude. The pessimists believed that the unity was real, because the PS was now dominated by Leninists of one sort or another and "the party of Léon Blum was dead." In this case, the correct tactics for the opponents of the left were to make an all-out attack on socialism as such, to frighten the French middle classes with the prospect of revolution, and so to get the largest possible vote for conservatism. There was no point, they argued, in making concessions to win those who stood on the middle ground. In the last resort, many bourgeois voters would desert the middle ground and vote for the right if they felt themselves in danger. This was basically the attitude of former Premier Chirac, the Gaullist leader.

Meanwhile the communists, taking seriously the lessons of Chile and Portugal, were anxious to show themselves respectable democrats, and fiercely resented the ultraleft, which was strongly entrenched in the socialist ranks. A paradoxical situation was arising: the PCF was trying to win moderate socialists away from the PS, while the PS was trying to seduce the keenest revolutionaries away from the PCF.

Spain

The victory of Franco in the civil war in 1939 found the left forces within Spain exhausted, and also led to the flight into exile of many thousands of

Spaniards of left views. Among these the communists were probably the best organized. The largest number remained in France, and many played an active part in the French Resistance. Others went to Mexico or to the Soviet Union. The hope of Spanish antifascists that the victorious Allies would take action against Franco in 1945 proved illusory, and plans for guerrilla warfare within Spain led to nothing.

In the following years Spain underwent rapid industrial development, distorted by the high priority given to the tourist trade and consequent building, but extending to more complex forms of industry. The centers were largely the same as in the past: the northern provinces and Catalonia, with the two main industrial centers in Bilbao and Barcelona. One effect of this growth was the immigration into the Basque and Catalan lands of thousands of workers from the lands of Castilian speech, especially the south: this was a repetition on a larger scale of trends that had been visible already at the beginning of the twentieth century. This immigration diminished the proportion of Basques and Catalans in their own homelands, but it also served for this very reason to stimulate Basque and Catalan national consciousness.

The social structure of Spain underwent important changes. Between 1950 and 1970, as official statistics show, the percentage of the labor force that was actively employed in agriculture fell from 50 to 25, while that in industry increased from 26 to 38, and in services from 25 to 37. In the same period the percentage of agricultural workers fell from 31.9 to 10.8.[10] The decline in independent landowners and farmers was much smaller (from 17.1 to 10.8 percent). Social groups whose percentages notably increased between 1950 and 1970 were industrial workers (from 23.5 to 35.2), artisans (from 4.9 to 10.1), and administrative employees (from 14.2 to 21.8). In terms of relative weight of agriculture and industry, Spain in 1970 was at the same stage as France in 1950. However, certain special aspects of the Spanish social structure, as a recent most instructive analysis showed[11] deserve brief mention. The industrial labor force was increased mainly by the movement of Andalusian laborers to Barcelona and to the construction sites and new industrial enterprises resulting from tourism on the Mediterranean coast. In these sectors of Spanish industry the proportion of manual workers to the total labor force was very high. In Madrid and the Basque provinces, and in some other centers in Castile, by contrast, there was a much higher proportion of white-collar and administrative

---

10. The percentage of agricultural daily-wage laborers (*jornaleros agrarios*) employed on the large estates (*latifundios*) in Andalusia and Estremadura was 28.6 in 1950 and 8.6 in 1970.

11. Amando de Miguel, *Recursos humanos, clases y regiones en España* (Madrid, 1977). This book by an eminent Spanish sociologist, containing numerous and detailed breakdowns of statistics in tables and appropriate maps, pays special attention to differences of class structure between regions.

workers. This more modern and more "bureaucratized" industry was tending to outstrip the industry of Barcelona. At the same time the main stronghold of both the old urban middle classes and the independent farmers remained Castile north of Madrid, and especially Galicia.[12] Thus, in Spain no less than in Italy and in France, large new social groups were arising with new outlooks, and this was complicating still further the acute problems of competing nationalisms. The Spanish communists, no less than the other parties that emerged after the dissolution of the Franco regime, would have to take careful account of them.

At the end of the 1950s opposition began to stir. In 1956 appeared the first "Workers' Commission," a strike committee set up at a coal mine in Asturias. Further commissions appeared during a wave of industrial unrest in the years 1962 to 1964. These actions seem to have been initiated largely by groups of Catholic workers. The growth of social radicalism, and the consequent opposition to the Franco regime, in the Catholic church was one of the most important political changes of the 1960s. However, once the movement of Workers' Commissions spread, the communists made strenuous and successful efforts to lead them. Communist tactics were to make the fullest use of the government-sponsored *sindacatos*, to penetrate them and use them as genuine organizations to defend working-class interests as well as to spread communist influence. This tactic involved serious risks for militant leaders, and several of the leaders who exposed themselves were arrested. The tactic was also attacked by ultraleft groups (Trotskyist or Maoist) that considered it too cautious and wanted revolutionary action. On the whole, however, the communists had the greatest influence in the incipient illegal strike movement. In 1972 there were clashes between strikers and police in El Ferrol and Vigo in Galicia. In 1973 there were further strikes in the Basque provinces, Seville, and Barcelona, reaching a climax with a general strike in the city of Pamplona in the partly Basque province of Navarre in June 1973.

The exiled leadership of the communist party (PCE) was led by Santiago Carrillo, who became secretary-general in 1960. Exiled Spanish communists were resident in France, Mexico, and several of the East European countries under communist rule. Carrillo traveled frequently between them, and maintained increasingly effective links with the illegal communist movement inside Spain.

Three special problems had to be faced. One was the deep-seated fear in Spain

---

12. De Miguel speaks of "six Spains," the two great cities and four zones (each of which he characterizes by one social group: "northern working class" (*obrera-norte*) in the northern coastal region, including the coastal Basque provinces; "Mediterranean working class" along the coast of Valencia and southward; "middle classes," embracing the interior of northern Spain from Galicia across to Aragon and the interior of Catalonia; and "lordly" (*señorial*), consisting of the interior provinces of the south and southwest where great landowners were still powerful). See de Miguel, *Recursos humanos*, pp. 236–46, and map on p. 242.

of another civil war. Life had improved for almost everyone in the thirty years since the end of the Second World War. This did not mean that Franco was widely popular: he certainly had his fervent supporters, but greater prosperity, as is almost always the case, brought greater expectations and greater frustrations. Millions of Spaniards remembered the horrors of the civil war, including those who had experienced them as children, and it seemed unlikely even that those who had grown up long after it was over would make light of those fears. The communists of Spain were therefore under almost greater pressure than any communists anywhere to persuade their people that they would bring liberation by peaceful means, and would aim at an alliance of democratic forces rather than a dictatorship by their party.

The second special problem was the strength of national movements that, though not necessarily aiming at complete territorial separation from Spain, were determined to obtain far-reaching autonomy for their languages and national cultures as well as to have their own people governing them. There were three main movements—the Basque, the Catalan, and the Galician. The first was the most active. Discontented with the moderation of the exiled leaders of the Basque National Party (PNV), a group of radical intellectuals created in 1959 a new organization entitled Basque Fatherland and Freedom (ETA), which devoted itself to sabotage and terrorism, beginning with the derailment of a train in 1961 and winning its most sensational success in December 1973 by blowing up Franco's premier in his official car in Madrid. The Catalans were less obviously active in the 1960s but they were organizing themselves; they revealed their numbers in the demonstrations at the time of King Juan Carlos's visit to Barcelona in 1975. The official communist line was to support self-determination of the three peoples, and as an interim measure, to reenact the autonomy statutes that had been passed by the government of the Spanish Republic before the civil war.[13]

The third problem was the menace from the ultraleft. It was not clear in the mid-1970s how much support remained in Spain for the anarchists and anarcho-syndicalists who had been so strong in the 1930s and had been such bitter opponents of the communists. Several Trotskyist groups had emerged, however, of which the two most important were the Partido Obrero Revolucionario (POR) and the Liga Comunista Revolucionaria (LCR). Remembering the damage done to their reputation by their destruction of the POUM in 1937, the communists had to be very careful in their dealings with the Trotskyists, opposing their ultrarevolutionary tactics as endangering left-wing unity, yet respecting their right

---

13. See Carrillo's report to the Eighth Congress of the PCE, published under the title *Hacia la libertad* (Paris, 1972); and the proposals of the PCE in early 1974, which are summarized in Carrillo's book-length conversations with Régis Debray and Max Gallo, *Demain l'Espagne* (Paris, 1974), pp. 220–23.

to take part in resistance to the regime. There were also Maoist groups, a Spanish communist party (Marxist-Leninist) (PCE-ML), and a looser organization of Maoist and other ultraleft groups—the Revolutionary Antifascist and Patriotic Front (FRAP), which was linked with a rival illegal strike organization, the Workers' Syndical Organization (OSO). To what extent the old anarchist forces were regrouped under Trotskyist or Maoist names, or would reappear separately, was not clear. However, the experience of Chile and Portugal showed unmistakably that the ultraleft could be a fatal menace to communist plans. Carrillo repeatedly criticized the behavior of the ultraleft in both countries.

Carrillo also laid great emphasis on his party's independence of the Soviet Union. In 1968 he spoke against the invasion of Czechoslovakia; this led to a clumsy attempt by the Soviet leaders to encourage a pro-Soviet splinter communist party under the leadership of Enrique Lister, a famous civil-war veteran, which they did not give up until 1974. Carrillo closely followed the lead of the Italian communists in the repudiation of Soviet control. At the Berlin conference of June 1976 he used stronger language to this effect than any other speaker. Some phrases must have been painfully offensive to Soviet ears:

> Moscow, where our dreams first began to come true, was for a long time a kind of Rome to us. We spoke of the Great October Revolution as if it were our Christmas. This was the period of our infancy. Now we have grown up. . . . We are beginning to lose the characteristics of a church. The scientific content of our theories is taking on aspects of faith and the mysticism of predestination. . . . Yet there is no doubt that today we communists have no leadership centre and are not tied to any international discipline. What unites us are bonds which stem from a joint activity based on the theories of scientific socialism and the fact that we would not accept any return to the structures and conceptions of internationalism, which were to be found in the past.

The man whom the young king Juan Carlos selected as prime minister on 5 July 1976, Adolfo Suárez, showed himself to be an able political tactician: he guided Spain gradually toward a new democratic system, making conciliatory gestures to the opposition, coaxing the moderates of the former Franco regime into concessions, and standing up to the terrorists of both left and right. His Political Reform Bill, providing for the election in 1977 of a bicameral parliament whose lower house was to be responsible, jointly with the government, for constitutional reform, was accepted on 19 November 1976 by a majority of 425 to 59 by the old Cortes, which was composed of persons appointed by Franco. Suárez then put these proposals to the people in a referendum on 15 December. Although the leaders of the left urged their followers to boycott the election, 77 percent of the electorate voted, and of these 94 percent voted in favor.

Suárez conducted a series of negotiations with the leaders of the left to persuade

them to take part in the forthcoming election for the new parliament. Here
one of the main obstacles was recognition of the communist party. The other
left parties had little love for the communists, but it was unthinkable that they
should agree to operate in a political situation in which they were legalized and
the communists were not—even if only because this would enable the communists to accuse them of betraying socialism, and to win their followers away
from them. At the same time Suárez hesitated to accept the communists as a
legal party, since this would infuriate the right and might lead to intervention
by the army. The communists made the best of this situation, but did not wish
to wreck the plans for democratic government. In December 1976 Carrillo returned illegally to Spain, and then publicly announced his presence. He was
arrested for a few days and then released. Communist activity was in effect
permitted. Carrillo insisted on his party's devotion to constitutional methods,
following the line of the Italian and French parties. The communists strongly
dissociated themselves from the left-wing terrorists whose kidnapping exploits
were designed to wreck the peaceful transition to democracy. After several
months of communist good behavior, Suárez took the plunge and gave the party
legal status. No general brought his troops out, and the objections of the right
did not go beyond grumbling.

At the election of June 1977, the rather heterogeneous association of moderate
political groups led by Suárez, under the title of the Democratic Center Union,
won 34 percent of the poll and 165 seats in the parliament. They were followed
by the socialists (Partido Socialista Obrero Español—PSOE) with 28 percent
and 118 seats. The communists won only 20 seats and 9 percent of the poll.
Numerous other parties each obtained a few seats. Among these were the Catalan
and Basque autonomists. However, the demand for Catalan and Basque autonomy had stronger support in the parliament than the numbers of elected autonomists suggested. Almost all the Catalan and Basque deputies, sitting for almost
the whole range of parties, were committed to supporting a statute of autonomy.[14] On 5 October 1977 the old autonomous government of Catalonia, the
Generalitat, was reestablished by royal decree. Exactly two months later Mr.
Josef Tarradellas, returning from nearly forty years' exile in France to be president of the *Generalitat,* presented the twelve members of his autonomous government, which included two communists.

Carrillo expressed himself satisfied with the election results. He had not expected to see a large communist group, but he intended that it should be very
active inside and outside the chamber. Meanwhile he published a book contain-

---

14. At the end of June 1977 it looked as if at least forty-three persons, from four political
parties, would support Catalan autonomy. The Basque deputies, twenty-six persons from five parties,
openly formed themselves into a parliamentary assembly of Euskadi (the Basque name for the
Basque lands).

ing strong criticisms of the Soviet Union, entitled *Eurocommunism and the State*. It was bitterly attacked at the end of June 1977 in the Soviet periodical *New Times*, which accused Carrillo of splitting the European forces of democracy, strengthening the aggressive NATO block, and seeking a "third way" between capitalism and socialism. Carrillo was defended, in somewhat lukewarm terms, by the Italian party's paper *Unità*. The prospects for the Spanish communists were as uncertain as the prospects for Spanish democracy. Among other doubtful prospects were the chances of successful intrigues by the CPSU within the PCE leadership.

Japan

The rapid modernization of Japan after 1868, and the influx of European ideas, had among other consequences the appearance of Marxist socialism, first among intellectuals and then among parts of the working class. From the socialist movement emerged the Japanese communist party, which was founded in 1922, dissolved by its own leaders in 1924, founded anew in 1926, but later reduced by police repression to an ineffective sect. The communists reemerged as a legal party as a consequence of the American occupation in 1945. At first they won only a few parliamentary seats under the new constitution, being completely overshadowed by the socialists. However, the failure of the two coalition governments of 1947 and 1948, in which the socialists were the strongest partner, led to a certain transfer of left support from them to the communists. Communist seats in the lower chamber of parliament increased from four in 1947 to thirty-five in 1949. Hitherto the Japan Communist Party (JCP), led by Sanzo Nosaka, who had recently returned from exile in China, had pursued a moderate policy similar to that of the West European communists immediately after the war. In 1950 they were obliged by Soviet directives to change their policy to active opposition to the American occupation; and when war broke out in Korea, General MacArthur insisted on a thorough purge of communists from public life. The party was not actually banned, but it was subjected to surveillance and repression, and did not dare to hold another congress until 1958. During the 1960s it slowly recovered, and at the parliamentary election of 1972 it made sensational gains, increasing its seats to thirty-nine, compared with fourteen in 1969. It was noticeable that communist strength was greatest in the biggest industrial centers. In the election to the local assembly for the metropolitan area of Tokyo in 1973, the communists won 20 percent of the seats, almost exactly equaling the socialists.

Three aspects of communist policy in Japan will be briefly considered: the relations of the communists with the socialists, their attitudes to the Soviet Union and China, and their posture in Japanese politics in the mid-1970s.

The history of the Japanese socialist party since 1945 in some ways resembles that of the Italian, though the causes of the repeated splits and attempts at reunification, and the ways in which the party was organized, were different. The disappointing election result of 1949 increased internal dissension, and in 1951 the party split in two, with the right socialists accepting the proposed peace treaty and the left opposing it. In 1955 both parties made electoral gains, and meanwhile the two conservative parties united to form the Liberal Democratic party. Better prospects, and the example of their opponents, encouraged them to reunite, and this was achieved in October 1955. However, this only lasted five years. Fierce disagreements broke out in 1959 over the attitude the party should take to the security treaty with the United States, and a minority that was not prepared to go all the way against the United States broke away to form the Democratic Socialist Party (DSP). In the main Japan Socialist Party (JSP), extreme and moderate wings remained, with the former on the whole predominant.

The JSP remained a party that had very little mass organization of its own. In this it differed radically from the Italian and other West European socialist parties. It depended for its electoral organization on the largest single nationwide trade-union movement, Sohyo (the General Council of Trade Unions of Japan). In 1970 only some 34 percent of the Japanese labor force were members of unions, and of these Sohyo had only 38 percent. Most of its members were workers in public services. The same was true of the members of the Japan Trade Union Congress (Zenro, later renamed *Domei*), which had some 17 percent of unionized workers and supported the DSP. The majority of unionized workers were members of small unions that were confined to their enterprises. This form was predominant in private enterprises, and the great bulk of Japanese industry was privately owned. Japanese industry worked, in fact, very largely in paternalist units that cared for their employees, promoted them, saw that they had jobs and provided them with pensions. In return, workers and employees were expected to be loyal to the firm, and usually were. This system, which had its roots in the past, worked very well in the post-1945 decades of continued economic growth and rising prosperity. Thus neither Sohyo nor Domei were very powerful weapons of either socialist party against the ruling conservative governments.

The JCP was not dependent on the trade unions, though it had considerable numbers of supporters within Sohyo. It took great trouble to create a grass-roots organization, and was rather successful. In 1973 it claimed some three hundred thousand organized members, more than any other party in Japan. The only party, apart from the communists, that acted as more than an election-time organization, and had its own permanent apparatus, was the Komeito (Party of Good Government). It was founded in November 1964 and was closely linked with the Buddhist sect Soka-Gakkai (Society for the Creation of Values), a religious group that claimed in the 1970s to have members in eight million Japanese households. Komeito was extremely efficient in choosing the places in which to put up candidates, and in concentrating its organization there. It won forty-seven seats in the 1969 election, but only twenty-nine in 1972. Its main strength was in the big urban centers, where it competed directly with the communists for worker and small-shopkeeper votes, and it held its own with the communists and socialists in the local elections of 1973 in the Tokyo metropolitan area.

In the early 1960s one of the communists' strongholds was the students' federation (Zengakuren). However, they met with growing competition from the ultraleft, and in 1969 there were bloody battles between communist and ultraleft students, both Trotskyist and Maoist. The ultraleftists also had a following within the JSP, one wing of which thus bypassed the JCP on the left. (Here there was a parallel with Chile, and to a lesser extent with France.)

Both communists and socialists were affected by the Sino-Soviet quarrel of the 1960s. Japanese left intellectuals tended to prefer China, and resentment against the Soviet Union for its annexation of the Kurile Islands was widespread in Japanese society. At first the JCP tried to remain neutral, and to maintain correct relations with both communist great powers. However, in 1963 and 1964 the Chinese assertion that Khrushchev was giving in to American imperialism gained ground. The breach came in August 1964 with the JCP's utter refusal to approve the atomic-test-ban treaty. The one prominent Japanese communist who voted for the treaty, Yoshio Shiga, was expelled from the JCP. The Soviet leaders thereafter tried to support a rival Japanese communist party under Shiga's leadership.

The pro-Chinese phase of JCP policy did not last long. The disastrous defeat of the Indonesian communists, who had been China's strongest supporters, after their unsuccessful bid for power in 1965 caused some disillusionment in the JCP about China. Its appeals to the Chinese party for reconciliation with the Soviet party in the interests of support to the Vietnamese communists brought an angry reply in February 1966. The progress of the Cultural Revolution in China brought attacks on the JCP. Its leader, Kenji Miyamoto, was described by a Peking Red Guard newspaper in 1967 as "a leaping little bug emerging from a ditch." In 1968 the official Chinese line was that Japan faced four enemies: United States imperialism, treasonous Japanese monopoly capital, Soviet revisionism, and the JCP. The JCP's relations with China were then about as bad as they could be, but this did not bring much improvement in its relations with the Soviet party. Attempts were made on both sides in 1967, but the JCP condemned the Soviet invasion of Czechoslovakia in 1968, and the Soviet party still continued to support the Shiga faction into the 1970s. The JCP leaders adopted an attitude of independence from both communist capitals, but it would probably be fair to say that the JCP was at least closer to the Soviet Union than any other party in Japan.

Meanwhile the JSP had better relations with China than the JCP. A visit by a group of socialists led by Asanuma to Peking in 1959 did not have much result, but it was retrospectively praised in 1975 when a Chinese delegation came to Japan to sign a joint declaration with the JSP. On 24 June 1976 a JSP delegation, led by the moderate Saburo Eda, visited Peking. The statement jointly signed by Eda and Liao Cheng-chih, the chairman of the China-Japan Friendship Association, referred to "opposing the hegemonism of the two super-powers and consolidation of the fighting friendship between the people of China and Japan." It also stated that "both China and Japan are confronted with the menace from the super-power in the north. The Chinese people resolutely support the Japanese people in their patriotic and just struggle for recovering the northern territory and upholding state sovereignty and territorial integrity."

From 1955 onward the Liberal Democratic party had an absolute majority in the parliament, and formed the government. The only political struggles that affected power were those within the party, between various personal factions. In this respect, the LDP bore a certain resemblance to the Christian Democratic party in Italy. There were, however, important differences. The LDP had no grass-roots organization; it was essentially a parliamentary organization and its factions were formed from members of parliament; it had no connection with any religion; its money came from business alone; and its electoral activity was conducted by local notables without any large mass organization. The Italian DC had a very large grass-roots organization; its influence extended throughout the apparatus of government; its factions were based on persons who had built up their bases of power in sectors of the bureaucracy and in regions of the country; it was closely linked with the Catholic church, whose support of all kinds was no less valuable to it than the support of business; and its electoral campaigns were conducted on a mass scale at the grass-roots level.[15] In 1976 the two parties' fortunes were rather similar. Both were losing ground in public opinion, and both had been affected by public scandals of corruption.

The signs of the decline of the LDP inevitably caused much negotiation and maneuvering among the opposition parties. The JSP, the strongest in parliament, was divided between those who would have been willing to cooperate with the communists alone, and those who insisted on an alliance of all four parties (JSP, DSP, JCP, and Komeito). Since Komeito would not join the communists, and the communists profoundly distrusted Komeito, the JSP had to choose between going with the JCP or with the DSP and Komeito. In practice, it vacillated and spoke with two voices.

---

15. For a comparison at some length of the Japanese and Italian political systems, including the parties of the left and right and certain key economic and social factors affecting them, see the interesting book by Antonio Lombardo, *Il sistema politico del Giappone* (Milan, 1976).

In preparation for the 1976 election, the JCP leaders did their best to present themselves in a respectable light. Their constitutional behavior, and their independence of Moscow and Peking, which antedated the policies of Berlinguer, fitted well with the West European parties' public postures, and were coordinated with them. Carrillo visited Japan at the end of March 1976, and on 1 April a statement was published that was signed by him and Miyamoto. It declared that the JCP's aim was a united front and a democratic coalition government, which would seek the abolition of the U.S.-Japanese military alliance and the realization of a peaceful and neutral Japan; the defense of the people's livelihood; and the protection and development of democracy. The statement then committed both parties to respect for democratic liberties:

> At the stage of democratic reform . . . or under a socialist state, which the two parties envisage, they will respect the plural political parties system, including the change of government based on elections. . . . No "bureaucratic-designated philosophy" in which the state designates a specific ideology as the state's thought, and no ideological compulsion for forcing such thoughts on the people, will be permitted.

A few days later Marchais also visited Japan, and on 11 April a joint statement by him and Miyamoto in more sober language made the same points, stressing "thoroughgoing democratic reforms," "true national independence," and "disbandment of military blocs."

Despite their conciliatory posture, the communists were unable to persuade the other opposition parties to join them in the election campaign. Though their share of the popular vote remained the same at the election of 5 December, in which 72 percent of the electorate voted, the communists won only half the number of seats they had had in the previous parliament (17 instead of 39). The other opposition parties improved their positions: the socialists increased their seats from 112 to 123, the Democratic Socialists from 19 to 29, the Komeito from 30 to 55, and the oppositional liberals from 5 to 17.

Though the number of LDP seats fell from 165 to 149 and they no longer had a majority, they were still in a better position than the DC in Italy. They could count on support from small groups, and there was no prospect of a need for a *compromesso storico*. The communists had little prospect of getting accepted as partners by the JSP, in which the procommunists were a minority, nor did it seem likely that the disgrace of the Gang of Four in China would cause the Chinese leaders to change their minds about the JCP and prefer it to the JSP. Meanwhile the JCP leaders persisted in their European-communist-style posture, and Tetsuzo Fuwa, the prospective leader of the party after the aging Miyamoto, traveled to Rome in January 1977 to consult Berlinguer.

Some Other European Communist Parties

In two northern countries, Finland and Iceland, communists have taken part in parliamentary coalition governments in the last ten years.

In Finland communism had an authentic tradition, going back to the revolutionary socialists of the civil war in 1918. After the Second World War they operated in the form of the Finnish People's Democratic League (SKDL), which was formed in 1944 with the communists as its nucleus and some splinter groups from the socialist ranks. It took part in the postwar coalitions, but was forced out of the government in the crisis of 1948, which was brought about by the other parties' objections to its control of the state police.

The Finnish communists came back out of the cold in 1966 as a result of changing attitudes in the Social Democratic party. The social democrats, who were extremely hostile to the Soviet Union in the 1950s, were forced out of the government in 1959 by Soviet pressure. In their years of opposition they came to regard the Agrarians, or Center Party, who held power with Soviet approval, as their main enemy, and hostility to the communists became less important. Also during these years a more radical trend grew among the younger social democrats, especially in the trade unions. Economic conditions deteriorated notably in the 1960s, affecting especially the industrial workers. At the 1966 election the social democrats made big gains. The party's leaders were divided between those who wanted to form a minority government and those who preferred to enter a coalition with both the Center and the SKDL; they eventually decided on the second.

The coalition government was able to improve the economic situation, but it did so essentially by adopting the policies urged by the business class and conventional economists. The communists found themselves underwriting policies that were arguably more advantageous to the capitalists than to the workers. Within the SKDL younger and more modern-minded persons came to the fore. At the Fourteenth Congress, in 1966, Are Saarinen became chairman of the party. In 1968 the new leadership denounced Soviet action in Czechoslovakia. There still remained a Stalinist opposition, however, led by Taisto Sinisalo, which not only defended Soviet action but made itself the spokesman for widespread working-class discontent with the policies of the coalition. At the Fifteenth Congress, in April 1969, it was clear that the party was split in two. The situation was highly embarrassing for the emissary of the CPSU: the Soviet line at this time favored communist participation in coalitions, but it was the opposition within the SKDL that showed itself most loyal to the Soviet cause. At the congress a formal split was avoided, but in practice the Sinisalo faction began to set up its own organization in several districts. An extraordinary congress had to be called in 1970, which made a compromise, assuring to the Sinisalo faction fifteen out of thirty-five places in the Central Committee, six out of sixteen in the Politburo, and three out of eight in the Secretariat.

At the 1970 election, the SKDL won only 16.6 percent of the votes, the lowest proportion since 1945. In 1972 there was only a slight improvement. After the 1970 election the SKDL left the government. During the next five years of opposition, the division within the party was not healed. In September 1975 the number of SKDL members returned at the election increased to forty (thirty-seven in the previous parliament), and it was invited to join a new coalition, with the Center, the Social Democrats, the Liberals and the Swedish People's Party. The Central Committee decided, by twenty votes to fourteen, to accept. This government, like that of 1966, was forced to take unpopular measures to meet economic difficulties. The SKDL objected especially to a proposed increase in indirect taxation. The trade-union element in the SKDL pressed it to oppose this measure, and the communists were alarmed by the fact that in the Metal-workers' Union, which had long been their stronghold, they now found themselves slightly less numerous than the social democrats. In May 1976 the president of the republic, Yrho Kekkonen, induced the government to allow the communists to vote against government measures while remaining in the coalition. However, in September 1976 the coalition finally broke down, as both communists and social democrats left the government. The new ministry was based on the Center and some small parties.

In the 1970s the SKDL alternated between membership in coalitions and opposition. It was unable to overcome the split within its ranks or to escape the contradiction between its desire to share power and its inability to increase its working-class support if it were responsible for the inevitable unpopular economic measures.

The experience of the Finnish communists was not encouraging for other communist parties. They had retained the allegiance of about half the working class, but had not over a period of thirty years made significant inroads into social democratic positions. Support from the Soviet Union, and from pro-Soviet personalities in the Center Party, had been of some assistance to them at times; but the controversy that the 1968 occupation of Czechoslovakia let loose in all European communist parties had had particularly harmful effects on the Finnish party. In 1977 the Finnish communists were further from political power than in 1945.

☆ ☆ ☆ ☆

The communist party in Iceland derived from a split in the social democratic ranks in 1930. It took part in government coalitions in 1944–1947 and in 1956–

1958, and its share of the poll in elections since 1944 has usually been about 17 percent.

The most important issue for the Icelandic communists was to bring Iceland out of NATO, and to close the American Air Force base at Keflavik (the Iceland Defense Force). The party was, in fact, above all an instrument of Soviet naval expansion in the North Atlantic. The "cod war" with Britain in 1972–1973 and in 1975–1976 gave the communists excellent opportunities to work up hostility to the NATO allies. They were helped by obstinacy on the British side, largely due to pressure from British trade unions, in which communist influence was considerable. In June 1971 they entered the government, but were unable to persuade the Johannesson cabinet to demand the closing of Keflavik, or to prevent the compromise agreement with the British government in November 1973.

☆ ☆ ☆ ☆

The Communist Party of Great Britain (CPGB) could claim a longer tradition of moderate policies than most of the communist parties abroad. Already in 1951 its official program declared that "socialism can be achieved in one country without civil war." In 1968 it criticized the invasion of Czechoslovakia, and at the Berlin congress of 1976 it adopted a posture similar to that of the Italians.

The British party was never a significant force in parliamentary elections, and seemed unlikely to become so. This does not mean that the party was a negligible factor. Communist penetration of trade unions was rather successful. The main strength of the party lay in its factory branches. Hard work and efficient discipline enabled communist caucuses to profit from the political apathy of most trade-union members and get their own nominees into union leaderships. At different times the miners', engineers', transport workers', and various white-collar unions were subject to strong communist influence, which made itself felt not only in strikes but also in the use of union block votes at Labour party conferences. British communist leaders made no secret of their aim to control the Labour party through the trade unions.

During the 1970s in the workshops, in the unions, and in constituency organizations of the Labour party, a good deal was heard of the activities of Trotskyists. It was not always easy to distinguish between Trotskyists and orthodox communists, and the CPGB was certainly much less actively hostile to followers of Trotsky than it had been in Stalin's time. Though genuine Trotskyists detested the Soviet regime, their actions in Britain and other Western countries were "objectively" beneficial to the Soviet cause.

Communist influence was also strong in the Official IRA. Its rival, the Provisional IRA, rejected communism, but received some of its arms from communist states, and by its actions undoubtedly promoted the same cause as the

Icelandic communists—Soviet naval expansion in the North Atlantic. The origins of the IRA, of course, lie deep in Irish history, and the wrongs and rights of Irish Catholics and Protestants are centuries old; but the Irish troubles cannot be seen in perspective unless one also bears in mind that the main object of the IRA is power in the Irish Republic (Ulster being not the end, but a means to attain the end), and that the establishment of a "people's democracy" type of government in all Ireland under the IRA would be a tremendous step toward the Soviet aim of naval supremacy in the North Atlantic.

Finally, in estimating the role of the CPGB, one has to bear in mind the nature of the Labour party. This is not a single party, but a coalition of several. Many who in France or Italy would become communists, in Britain (owing to the electoral system) have to operate within the Labour party. Many prominent members of the Labour party are barely distinguishable from communists in their practical political attitudes. In all parts of the world they support Soviet aims, and they campaign incessantly to deprive Britain of defense forces and of allies. This so-called left wing was in an unusually strong position in 1977. Economic crisis faced the government of the Labour party with hard choices and unpopular decisions. The danger of a split in the party was very real. But a split was viewed differently by the "left wing" and by the leadership. If a division should occur, and Labour be defeated in an election, the "left wing" would not be unduly distressed. In opposition it would have to take control of the party, to radicalize its policies, and to make sure that these were put into practice when its next turn came. For the leaders of the party, by contrast, the preservation of unity took precedence over every other consideration. Obsessed with what one may call a "Ramsay MacDonald complex," determined to avoid the disaster that befell the party in 1931, the leaders would do virtually anything to appease the "left wing" and keep the party in power. The left could constantly blackmail the leadership with the prospect of a party split, but the leadership could not play the same game in reverse. This state of affairs, which was in no sense created by the communists, was "objectively" beneficial to them.

☆ ☆ ☆ ☆

One more communist party that deserves brief mention is the Greek. After defeat in the civil war of 1946–1949, its leaders went into exile, and the illegal organization within Greece suffered police repression. In February 1968 the party in exile split, on much the same lines as the Finnish party, between the faithful champions of the old Stalinist orthodoxy and those who argued for more realistic social and political analysis and for cooperation with other parties fighting the colonels' dictatorship. In contrast to the situation in Finland, a formal split took place; the Communist Party of Greece (KKE) divided into KKE

(Exterior) and KKE (Interior). It was the Interior party that stood for more realism, and that was capable of action inside Greece.

When the dictatorship of the colonels was overthrown in August 1974, the communists were permitted by the Karamanlis government to operate with the same freedom as other parties. For electoral purposes the two communist parties formed a coalition with the left United Democratic Party (EDA), and jointly won not quite 10 percent of the votes. After the election the two KKEs resumed their polemics with each other, were assailed by ultraleftist groups, and were liable to be outbidden in ultraleft slogans by the new socialist party of Andreas Papandreou, which won nearly 14 percent of the votes. At the election of 20 November 1977 Karamanlis was less successful, his share of the poll falling from 54 percent in 1974 to 42 percent. The Center party's share was almost halved, and the communists made a very slight gain. The main winner was Papandreou, whose share rose to 25 percent.

In 1977 Greek communism did not look strong, but in the volatile political atmosphere of Greek politics, with pressing economic problems, national frustration about Cyprus and the national tradition of blaming everything on foreign scapegoats, and with unlimited opportunities for politicians to inebriate themselves with anti-American verbosity, nothing was easily predictable.

☆ ☆ ☆ ☆

In 1977 the prospects of communist victory by the peaceful parliamentary road looked good at first sight, but less good after further reflection. The communists would need the skill of Odysseus to steer between three pairs of Scylla and Charybdis. If they were too revolutionary, they would drive the middle classes whose support they were wooing into the arms of the extreme right (Chile) or the moderate left (Portugal). If they were too conciliatory to the middle classes, they would drive many of their workers and intelligentsia into the arms of the ultraleft, and this would only favor the right (it had happened in Chile and might happen in Spain). If they made a success of participation in a coalition, there would be a risk of feedback on the communists of Eastern Europe. If they defended the Soviet record in Eastern Europe, they would not win voters in their own countries. If they succeeded in reducing their countries' defenses to the vanishing point, they risked occupation by the Soviet army, a fate that Tito had avoided by maintaining his defenses. If they voted for national defense, they made themselves prisoners of the bourgeois parties and of the Americans.

—3—

Communism and Nationalism in the Third World

The expression "Third World," which came into general use in the 1960s, should be treated with caution, since it can be used to cover a great variety of geographical, economic, political, and cultural phenomena. Nevertheless, the word does have some relationship to reality. Two main features characterize the nations of the Third World. The first is that their economies are backward, their people largely agricultural, rural, and uneducated. The second is that they have until recently been ruled by foreigners, and have remained to some degree dependent on foreigners even after their states have achieved the legal status of sovereign independence. Western commentators on Third World problems usually lay the most stress on the first feature, and talk in terms of the ability, or duty, of the economically advanced nations to aid the "underdeveloped," or "less developed," or "developing" nations. Communist commentators lay the most stress on the second feature, insisting on these nations' past misfortunes at the hands of foreign imperialists, seeking to maximize resentments arising from the past, and arguing that their main task in the years ahead must be the struggle against "imperialism" and "neocolonialism," in which only the aid—absolutely disinterested by its very nature—of the "socialist" states headed by the Soviet Union can ensure victory.

Communist parties have existed and still exist in these countries, but it cannot be said that they have played much part in their politics during the last decade, except in Chile, which was discussed in the preceding chapter. Partial exceptions are the Venezuelan, Uruguayan, Sudanese, South African, Syrian, and Iraqi parties. However, it would be quite wrong to deduce from this that communist influence has not been important in these lands. On the contrary, the attempts of the Soviet leaders, assisted by communist leaders in Eastern Europe as well as in the West and in some of these countries themselves, to mobilize the nationalism of Third World nations to their own advantage, to create fear and hatred of an ill-defined monster called imperialism, and to identify this monster with the United States, have been remarkably successful. They have made full use of three particular issues—the war in Vietnam, the Israeli-Arab deadlock, and race conflict in southern Africa. Apart from this, the propaganda attack on neocolonialism has had considerable success in African territories where British or French business interests remain important, and still more in Latin America, where the power of North American capital is both an economic fact and an all-purpose scapegoat.

In the following section I shall confine myself to Latin America, Africa, and the western part of the Muslim World (the "Arab states," or Arabic-speaking lands,[1] and marginally Turkey and Iran). In the case of Latin America, three countries (Argentina, Uruguay, and Chile) did not belong economically and socially to the Third World, since all three had rather high levels of industrialization, urbanization, and popular education; but they could be considered to belong to it politically and psychologically. Their foreign policies were, arguably, "nonaligned," and in all three countries there was a powerful body of anti-North American and anti-"imperialist" nationalist opinion that provided a political climate of opinion within which communists could operate. Hostility to the United States in right-wing circles in these countries, arising from President Carter's advocacy of human rights, might also in effect benefit the communists of those countries, even though the rulers were their bitter enemies.[2]

Southern and eastern Asia, in which some of the same phenomena are found, are discussed in Chapter Six.

Nationalist Intelligentsias

I must begin with some general considerations of the origins and nature of nationalist elites in the three regions, and of the problems created in these lands

---

1. The expressions "Arab states" and "Arab governments" became so widely used from the 1950s onward that I feel obliged to use them too. However, the word "Arab" is ambiguous. Originally it meant persons inhabiting, or descended from inhabitants of, Arabia; Egyptians and Moroccans, to take only two examples, were certainly not Arabs. However, the Arabic language, in the two distinct forms of the classical language of Islam and of the secular language of the modern press, from the Maghreb to Iraq, is a common possession of all these peoples; the belief in the existence of one single Arab nation has become widespread among their intellectual elites; and a vaguer sense of solidarity between Arabic-speaking peoples has been extended to still wider social strata. Readers are asked to bear in mind that there is a large discrepancy between the Pan-Arab ideal and reality; and that "the Arab governments" means no more than "the governments of the Arabic-speaking peoples."

2. Though these attitudes prevail on the political left, and in a very large part of the intellectual elite, the military regimes of all three countries, as well as of Brazil, were comparatively well disposed toward the United States, even if they felt obliged to make occasional anti-*gringo* ritual gestures. This situation might possibly be modified as a result of strong criticism by the Carter administration of the suppression of political liberties by the military regimes in 1977. The formal rejection by the Brazilian government of American military aid was a gesture in this direction.

by diversity of language, religion, and political culture. I shall then consider each region in turn, emphasizing in each case the conditions that favor or hinder revolutionary action, communist-party activity, and Soviet influence.

The beginnings of nationalist movements in the Muslim countries and in tropical Africa must be sought not so much in the condition of the majority of peasants, tribesmen, and workers of various kinds as in the emergence of new elites educated under the influence of modern European ideas. Nationalist movements could never, of course, have made much progress unless they had been able to mobilize for their purposes the resentments of large numbers of peasants and simple people against the conditions in which they lived. It was not the misery of the masses, however, but the acquisition of new ideas by the small educated minority, and the growth in numbers and influence of this minority, that started the movements themselves.

In the Muslim lands of North Africa and the eastern Mediterranean, there was already in the nineteenth century a Westernized secular elite whose members had been educated in secondary schools and universities of the European type in their own countries or in European countries; in these lands modern intellectual professions developed, such as law, medicine, teaching, engineering, and journalism. Among the professions into which members of the new modern-educated elite went must also be included the officer corps of the armies, which enjoyed high prestige in Muslim societies. There were also large numbers of persons who did not reach such high positions in the educational pyramid, but were qualified to be clerks in business or government offices or to be small or middle-level officials in the state machine, first under the Ottoman Empire and then under the various British or French protectorates. The great majority of the peasants and small craftsmen in the cities remained little affected by European culture or ideas. There was thus a profound "cultural gap" between the rising indigenous elite in the modern civil or military professions and most of their fellow countrymen.

In Latin America similar social processes took place, though there were considerable variations. The lands of settlement in the south acquired social structures rather similar to those that arose in North America, as immigrants from Europe came to outnumber the indigenous populations, and as modern industry, urbanization, and education went ahead. However, the political cultures derived from Spain and Portugal were very different from those that evolved in the Anglo-Saxon states: in particular, the social prestige of the military profession remained far higher in relation to civil professions—and so proved relatively more attractive to ambitious young people—than was the case in North America. In this case one might argue that Latin American societies were more similar to Muslim than to North American or North European. In the Andean and Caribbean states the political culture of the elites was similar, but the social structure was quite different since the majority of the population consisted of Amerindians, blacks, or poor *mestizos* (people who were partly European and partly

Amerindian or black), living in premodern economic conditions. Here the "cultural gap" was little if at all less deep than in the Muslim lands.

In Africa south of the Sahara before the Second World War there was no opportunity of a university education for the indigenous peoples in their own lands, but some were able to obtain it in metropolitan France or the United States, and there were schools in which it was possible to acquire modern skills that were sufficient to obtain jobs in the clerical and administrative apparatus of government and business. There were also newspapers managed and written by African journalists, graduates of European schools. Thus in sub-Saharan Africa the new elite consisted of school graduates, officials, clerks, and merchants. To these must also be added men who had served in the British or French armies in the Second World War, some of whom reached noncommissioned officer rank.

In various ways, the new elites in the Muslim, Caribbean, Andean, and African lands became familiar with the social and political ideas of modern Western societies. To put it in simple terms, they became aware of the basic principles of democracy. An essential element in democratic thinking ever since the eighteenth century, if not earlier, has been the concept of the nation. When Muslims and tropical Africans became attracted by the idea that their peoples deserved to govern themselves and that they, as the best-educated members of their peoples, deserved to lead them, they had to ask themselves the question "What is the unit in the name of which the claim for independence must be made?" In nineteenth-century Europe, the answer that had been given to this question had been "the nation." This process of discovery of the nation had taken place in Central and Eastern Europe during the course of the nineteenth century. In those countries, however, the essential characteristic that identified a nation was language. For example, in Bohemia, in the very center of Europe, two languages were spoken—Czech and German. Around these two languages, two rival national movements grew up during the nineteenth century, and as a result of the conflicts between them the modern state of Czechoslovakia came into existence; it was regarded by the majority of its inhabitants, whose language was Czech, as the national state of the Czechs, in which Germans were only a tolerated minority.

In the Muslim lands on the southern and eastern shores of the Mediterranean, a parallel for this nationalism based on language can be found in the role played by Arabic. It is arguable how soon, and to what extent, a pride in the Arabic language became more important for the new modern elite of these lands than devotion to the Muslim religion; but there is no doubt that the idea of a single Arab nation, stretching from the Atlantic to the Persian Gulf, began to appeal to a growing number of educated people before the end of the last century. There was not only an ancient and brilliant literature in the Arabic language, which could be understood by all literate persons in those lands and which was the source of legitimate pride, but there were also modern writers and journalists, and a growing daily and periodical press in a more-or-less standardized modern form of Arabic. Thus, the prospects of an Arab nationalist movement were already quite promising at the beginning of the twentieth century.

In subtropical Africa, there was no parallel to this situation. Few African languages (Ge'ez-Amharic and Swahili being the notable exceptions) had a written literature. The Africans who graduated from French or British schools did not acquire a pride in their literary language, as the Central and Eastern Europeans had done. They felt no need, no mission to develop, enrich, and modernize a written language of their people to be spread among that people, and to be made the basis of a movement for national independence. The movement for independence was based on something quite different—on the territory of a colony as it existed. When the new elite became nationalists, this meant that they demanded independence for their colonies. They demanded that they should take over the government, in place of the Englishmen, Frenchmen, or other Europeans who ruled them. They identified their ambitions, quite sincerely, with the interests of their peoples. They believed that their peoples would be happier and more prosperous under their rule than under foreign rule; and increasingly they were able to persuade the masses not only that their conditions could and should be improved, but also that they *would* be improved once the foreigners were removed from power.

What African nationalists asked for in the first instance was independence for the Gold Coast, or French West Africa, or whatever the territory was, within the boundaries fixed by the European conquerors. But there was also a belief in a wider loyalty than this—a loyalty to Africa as a whole. Thus the African intelligentsia, which emerged as the new claimant to elite status, was nationalist on two levels—on the level of the state in which its members lived and on the level of the whole of Africa.

There is a certain parallel here with the Arabic-speaking Muslim lands. Here too the existing states became the focus of national loyalty. Egypt was a state with some five thousand years of history. Tunisia and Morocco also had long historical traditions; and though Iraq did not exactly coincide with the ancient Mesopotamian empires, yet it could be argued that something of those very ancient traditions had survived. As for the higher level, or broader extension, of loyalty, there was some analogy between Pan-Arabism and Pan-Africanism. However, Pan-Africanism was based on no single tradition or language, but essentially on geography and on the physical appearance of the black peoples: the French version of Pan-Africanism used from the beginning the word *négritude*.

The situation of the Latin American peoples was different, but some essentials were the same. Spanish rule was overthrown on the mainland by the end of the 1820s. There was never any prospect of a United States of all Spanish America, and even the plan for a great Colombia in the whole northwest of the continent broke down. A large number of independent states emerged. The overall consciousness of a common Hispanic culture remained rather weak, though attempts were made by intellectuals to promote it. The alternative attempt to promote consciousness of a common Amerindian culture had some success, at least at the level of rhetoric, in Mexico from the 1930s onward, but it was a failure in the Andean republics. A similar attempt, associated with the doctrine of *Indoamérica* proclaimed by Victor Raúl Haya de la Torre, the founder of the Peruvian APRA (Acción Popular Revolucionaria Americana), was a failure, since APRA suffered years of persecution and then disintegrated from within. However, the military regime of General Velasco paid public tribute to Peru's Indian past, and gave its two main economic plans the evocative names of "Plan Inca" and "Plan Tupac Amaru."

More effective was the growing resentment among the elite within each state at the extent to which their economies (their foreign markets and their mineral resources) were owned by foreign businesses—at first British and then North American. This anger became the basis of a nationalist doctrine that argued that independence was a fiction, and that the reality was a "semicolonial" status. A growing solidarity came into existence between nationalists of this type within the different countries, and from the 1930s their resentment was above all directed against the United States. However, it could hardly be said that there was an ideology of "Spanish-Americanism" that was comparable to Pan-Arabism or Pan-Africanism. In Brazil similar phenomena existed, but anti-North American nationalism was less widespread. This may be explained partly by the fact that the Brazilians were aware that they were different from the Spanish Americans and partly by the peaceful winning of independence, the continuity of the institutions of the Brazilian state from monarchical times, and the vast size and resources of Brazil, all of which operated to give Brazilians a less defensive and hostile attitude toward North Americans than was created among the Spanish Americans by their history.

The wider doctrines of Pan-Arabism and Pan-Africanism were affected by worldwide ideologies that were current at the time when the elites obtained their education, and the same is true of the "anti-neocolonialist" nationalism in Latin America. Nationalists in Latin American countries were naturally attracted by radical doctrines, which promised a drastic transformation of political and social life. They were also naturally attracted by those doctrines that treated as enemies the nations under whose rule, or semicolonial domination, they were.

In the 1930s the ideology that met these requirements was fascism. In pursuit of his Mediterranean imperial aims Mussolini encouraged Pan-Arabism, which was hostile to Britain and France, the two nations that stood in his way. Later, the Germans adopted a similar propaganda line. In the years when fascism seemed to be winning all over Europe, not only by brute force but also by a certain attractive revolutionary romantic rhetoric that won over millions of young people, it was natural that Arab nationalists, and to a lesser extent the much smaller numbers of aspiring sub-Saharan African intelligentsia, should be attracted to fascism. Fascism also won a great deal of support in South America, especially under the regime of Vargas in Brazil in the 1930s and under the Argentine military regime of 1943–1945 from which Perón's dictatorship emerged.

However, Hitler and Mussolini were defeated in the Second World War, and among the victors (besides the British and French, their old masters and enemies) there emerged the new great power, the Soviet Union, which stood for a new ideology that was capable of appeal to the whole human race—Marxist-Leninist communism. Thus in the 1950s, and still more in the 1960s, both Pan-Arabism and Pan-Africanism adopted a great deal of the style of communist rhetoric; the still small but very rapidly growing number of young Africans who were now able to attend universities not only in the capitals of the colonial powers but also in some of the colonial territories themselves—where the colonial governments began to establish universities after the Second World War—became seriously interested in Marxism and began to learn something about it. Some accepted orthodox communism, but a larger number merely felt that aspects of communism could be adapted to their countries, and began to speak of a new "African socialism," whose specific features were, however, obscured by clouds of rhetoric so that they could appeal to widely varied social groups and mentalities. The attraction of Marxism to the Latin American intelligentsias was even greater—both in the Andean and Caribbean states where the "cultural gap" was still deep, and in the southern states where socialist and communist movements grew in the same way they had grown in Europe some generations earlier. The romantic and insurrectionary versions of left-revolutionary doctrine became still more attractive after the victory of Fidel Castro in Cuba in 1959 and his later public adoption of Marxism-Leninism.

The Soviet leaders, and Soviet ideological experts, could not possibly accept Pan-Arabism or Pan-Africanism or African socialism as serious answers to the needs of the peoples of those countries; they were also not very happy about Castro's conversion, though they accepted it with enthusiasm in public and went so far as to endorse his "takeover bid" for the leadership of the Cuban communist party. For them, there could be no doubt that the course of human society had been foreordained—and must follow the lines which it had followed in Russia, and which had been laid down first by Marx and then by Lenin. However, insofar as African socialism and Pan-Arabism were damaging to the interests of the governments in Western Europe and North America that were Soviet Russia's chief enemies, they deserved support. The situation was not unlike that of China in the 1920s, when the Kuomintang appeared to deserve Soviet support because it was anti-British, although the ideas its leaders propounded could not possibly be taken seriously by communists. In China at that time there was a conflict between the supporters of anti-Western nationalism and the supporters of communist revolution; and the same sort of contradiction was latent in the African situation in the 1960s. Nonetheless, for the time being the Soviet government found it convenient to support nationalist causes. Soviet doctrine also emphasized the need to preserve existing state frontiers. The aim had to be independence for each territory.

New States and New Elites

With regard to the great mass of the population, a competition developed in the last period of colonial rule between the colonial rulers and the new elites for its support. The masses had been accustomed for centuries to poverty and to autocratic rule; the idea that they should govern themselves was virtually unknown. The colonial rulers believed that they had benefited the subject peoples by their years of domination, and that the peoples were basically loyal to them. They regarded the indigenous intelligentsia, who were applying European democratic ideas to African conditions, as trouble-making agitators who were only making things worse for everybody. However, whatever may be maintained about the benefits or the exploitation brought by colonial rule, what is historically clear is that in a competition between two elites, each with its own arguments and rhetoric, the elite that appears closest to the people is likely to win. The new African elites were Africans, whereas the imperial rulers—benevolent or not—had white faces and spoke different languages. Inevitably, the elites succeeded more and more in mobilizing the people—that is, first in making them actively discontented with their lot (as opposed to passively submitting to it as they had done for centuries) and second in persuading them that they would have a better future only when foreign rule was removed.

In the independent states that emerged, for the most part with very little resistance on the part of the colonial rulers except the Portuguese, the intelligentsia became bureaucrats. This was partly a matter of promotion: the NCO became a colonel, the office clerk became a high administrative official. Partly it was a matter of a radical change in activity; the journalist or teacher or member of some other independent profession now became a diplomat or a minister of state. Most members of the aspiring elite enjoyed this promotion and adapted themselves well to it. There were, however, a minority who fundamentally disapproved of power. Such people wished always to criticize and always to oppose, and they found themselves opposing the new paternalistic and dictatorial governments that followed independence. In the new states the universities produced a rapidly growing number of graduates, and these young people tended to pick up the most radical ideas that were around, which made them critical of the new regimes. Thus the members of the earlier generation of intelligentsia found themselves in the position of the former colonial rulers or the former Ottoman pashas—that of repressing seditious ideas—while those in the next generation found themselves performing the same functions their predecessors had, with the difference that instead of fighting against a colonial power they were fighting against a new ruling class from their own people. This process had occurred in the independent Balkan states in the nineteenth century, and is very familiar to historians of that period and that part of the world. Also similar to the Balkan experience was the fact that the members of the new generation of African, Muslim, or Latin American intelligentsia were torn by a conflict between their interests and their ideas. Their interests led them to serve the apparatus of government of the independent state; their ideas caused them to revolt against the practices of the indigenous rulers and to become at least radical critics and possibly revolutionaries.

There need not be a complete contradiction between the pursuit of career ambition and the acceptance of a progressive left-wing ideology. It was possible to argue that the new bureaucratic apparatus of government in the independent state was an agency of enlightenment, spreading the joys of modernization and social welfare to the masses—even if the particular group of politicians who controlled the apparatus at any particular time seemed at least equally interested in enriching themselves and in satisfying their greed for power, glory, and public adulation. It was also possible to believe that some new group of army officers who seized power from the previous government by force, although not themselves progressive intellectuals, nevertheless stood for a more progressive form of government, and that it was therefore the task of the progressive intellectuals to serve them, incidentally thereby obtaining promotion in their careers.

It should also not necessarily be assumed that even those members of the newer generation of intelligentsia who gave themselves up to uncompromising revolutionary activity, becoming communists or possibly following some "ultraleft" movement, were actuated by absolutely pure idealism. In the new government they expected the revolution eventually to create, there would certainly be plenty of important posts for them, and rapid promotion. Indeed, an argument can be made that if the regimes in the new independent states are to be considered as representing the interests of a class, then this class is the graduate and diploma-bearing educated elite. It is they who get the jobs in the bureaucracy; the greater the bureaucracy, the more jobs for them; and thus ever more "progressive" policies of state intervention will meet the needs and class interests of ever larger numbers of graduates. This is not the whole story, but it is an important aspect of the history of the last decades, not only in the new states but also in the relatively old states of Latin America.

Ethnic Diversity in Africa

Most of the independent states faced serious problems as a result of the diversity of languages, religions, and customs within their boundaries.

This problem existed in those Spanish American states in which large Amerindian populations remained, and in which a large proportion of the Spanish-speaking *mestizos* still lived in what might be called an "Amerindian political culture," whether in rural areas or in the slums of such sprawling conurbations as Mexico City or Lima. The states most affected by these problems were Mexico, Guatemala, Peru, Bolivia, Ecuador, and Paraguay, but they were of some importance even in Chile and Argentina. Around the Caribbean the "ethnic" problem of Amerindians was replaced by the "racial" problem of blacks, though the social implications were more similar than the difference of adjective would imply. Brazil and Venezuela suffered especially, while in Guyana the fact that East Indian immigrants formed nearly half the population was an added complication. In the Arabic-speaking Muslim lands the diversity was more religious than linguistic or racial, though the Berbers in North Africa and the Kurds around the upper Euphrates formed large non-Arabic-speaking elements, the latter extremely resistant to Arabization. The Arabic-speakers themselves were divided between Sunni and Shi'i (the latter forming the largest community in Iraq, though the Sunnis had the political power), while numerous Christian communities and numerous sects of Islam or of Muslim origin were scattered between the Atlantic and the Persian Gulf.

It was in Africa that "ethnic diversity" was most dangerous. Whether one speaks in a specific context of "ethnicity," "tribalism," or "nations" often depends less on "scientific" criteria than on the sympathy of the observer. Some of these groups were sufficiently conscious and proud of their culture to deserve the use of the word "nation"; plausible examples are the Amhara, the Somali, and the Yoruba. Others were very small, primitive tribes. Many were in an intermediate position, however, and their quality could not be clearly pinpointed by the use of any convenient term of Western social science. The task of governments was inevitably to hold these groups together. This was what the colonial governments tried to do; it is what the independent African states set as their aim. The task proved significantly more difficult in the new states, all of which were committed to a much greater degree of intervention in the economy, than it had been in the colonial governments, which had left much more to private enterprise. The need to distribute powerful and prestigious jobs in the economic administration intensified ethnic rivalry. Every individual holding such a job had an incentive to distribute lesser jobs to members of his ethnic group, and every ethnic group that had a small share of such new economic potentates felt itself victimized by the government. However, the priority of welding all groups together into one nation was proclaimed by all. It was also the aim approved by communists and in particular by Soviet specialists writing on the subject.

There was thus an impressive degree of agreement as to what should be, but that is far from saying that reality was going to conform to these wishes. Nigeria was the pride of the British empire-builders. When they granted it independence, with a federal constitution they hoped would keep the different peoples (or in this case perhaps "nations") in harmony with each other, they had great hopes for its future. For almost anyone in British political life, it was a matter of dogma that the unity of Nigeria (created by pure chance as a result of frontier agreements between European powers at the end of the last century), must and could be preserved. This was also the view held by the military rulers of Nigeria in 1967 and taken by the governments of both the United States and the Soviet Union. None of this prevented the breakdown of Nigeria and the outbreak of a civil war that cost between one and two million lives.

The fact that the emerging intelligentsias of different African peoples did not, like their predecessors in Central and Eastern Europe, show great interest in their own languages, or develop literatures and cultures out of them, has already been noted. The independent governments for the most part sought to maintain the unity of their states, and to educate their subjects both in knowledge and in political loyalty, through the medium of the language of the former imperial power. There were some exceptions. In Sudan the ruling northern politicians sought to impose the Arabic language on the whole population; this was one of the main causes of the protracted conflict between the northern and southern peoples, which ended in 1972 in an agreement that optimists considered a settlement and skeptics only an armistice. In the East African states, Swahili became the official language, and was used to some extent parallel with English in administration. In Ethiopia Amharic had been the language of governments for centuries. In the greater part of western, central, and southern Africa no African language was so well developed, and known to so large a population, that it seemed capable in the predictable future of replacing English, French, or Portuguese—though the possibility existed that new and different forms of those three European languages might eventually evolve.

It has often been claimed that urbanization is likely to remove ethnic conflicts. The experience of other countries of multilingual populations—for example, Quebec, pre-1918 Austria-Hungary, or Imperial Russia—does not confirm this view. The experience of great cities in the United States is not likely to be very illuminating. Immigrants from Europe, seeking a new home in America and separated by thousands of miles from their former homelands, were fairly quickly absorbed into an American society and culture that already had a character of their own. The Africans pouring into new cities were living, like the peoples of old Hungary, in the midst of compact rural populations of their own kinsmen whose forefathers had been there for centuries past. They were not uprooted from their homelands, and they remained in contact with their own cultures. The ethnic diversities of the surrounding regions were imported into the cities.

The histories of most independent African states from the early 1960s have consisted of a series of coups d'état installing military dictatorships, few of which have lasted long. Six states, however, have been exceptions: they enjoyed a fairly stable leadership for a good many years. Two of the rulers in this category were generally regarded as "progressive"—that is, they spoke a more or less Marxist terminology and built up their political apparatus on lines rather similar to those of communist-party-ruled states. They were Sékou Touré in Guinea and Julius Nyerere in Tanzania. The other four, while maintaining in effect authoritarian governments on a one-party basis, were not inclined toward communist models; they allowed individual enterprise, both indigenous and foreign, to operate fairly freely and sought to maintain good relations with Western countries as well as with communist and "Third World" states. These were Jomo Kenyatta in Kenya, Houphouet-Boigny in the Ivory Coast, Kenneth Kaunda in Zambia, and Hastings Banda in Malawi. What was characteristic of the policies of all six of these successful African leaders was that they managed very carefully to balance the representation of different ethnic interests in their governments and in their bureaucracies.

Until 1974 one would have added Ethiopia to this list of states with stable regimes. The imperial regime in Ethiopia differed from all other African governments in that it had a long traditional history behind it, and was, in fact, one of the earliest states in the whole world. In 1974 the imperial regime was at last overthrown and replaced by a military clique that defied classification, though it was noteworthy that in mid-1977 it adopted a more and more "Marxist" posture, and increasingly sought Soviet protection.

It is possible that to the six should be added the regime of General Mobutu in Zaire. However, the extreme complexity of the ethnic pattern in the Congo, the dependence of the regime on foreign aid, and the new situation created by the victory of the MPLA in Angola made the regime of Mobutu extremely vulnerable. This was shown in the spring of 1977 by the invasion of the Shiba (formerly Katanga) province by Angola-based armed bands, which were, however, repelled with the aid of troops sent to help Mobutu by the sultan of Morocco.

During 1977 the conflict between Ethiopia and Somalia in the Horn of Africa increased. While the Ethiopian regime was torn by growing dissension, the province of Ogaden became the scene of guerrilla action by its Somali inhabitants, reinforced by the regular army of Somalia. During this period Soviet support was transferred from Somalia to Ethiopia, while Somalia obtained new patrons in the oil-rich Arabian rulers. Somali forces, equipped with Soviet war matériel, won victories over the Soviet government's new favorites, whose equipment was American, but the Soviet rulers strove to reverse the fortunes of war by cutting off spare parts and ammunition from the Somalis and rushing in more modern weapons for the Ethiopians.

The new regimes that emerged from the collapse of Portugal seemed likely to be somewhat different. In Angola and Mozambique there was a strong communist influence, which had gained ground during the course of the struggles of the previous decade. It is important to note that the colonies of Britain and France in Africa obtained their independence without any significant armed struggle (the so-called Mau-Mau insurrection in Kenya in the early 1950s was the only exception). The situation was quite different in the Portuguese colonies, since Portugal itself was ruled by a dictatorship that permitted no free political discussion, and since the rulers of Portugal were committed to the dogma that the Portuguese colonies formed part of a single indivisible Portuguese cultural community. Nationalists therefore had to act conspiratorially, and guerrilla warfare was the only course available to them. In this guerrilla war they received aid from communist countries. It was inevitable that when Portuguese rule collapsed, the "freedom movements" of guerrilla fighters should present themselves as the heirs to power, since the old regime had not permitted the formation of nonviolent democratic parties in the way that had occurred in the old British and French empires. It was also inevitable that the governments set up by these "freedom fighters" should contain very strong elements of communist or Marxist thought, since the whole course of the revolutionary struggle had made communist ideas attractive to the leaders, and since the communist governments had trained many of the fighters and had given them military aid. This was fairly clear in the case of Mozambique, and still more in that of Angola, where the end of Portuguese rule was followed by war between conflicting freedom movements, one of which received massive aid from the communist countries in the form of twelve thousand Cuban combat troops provided with modern military equipment and flown in Soviet or Cuban aircraft across the South Atlantic to place the Soviet Union's favorite—the MPLA—in power.

The government of the MPLA (the Popular Movement for the Liberation of Angola) was bound to encounter the same problem of ethnic diversity the other independent states in Africa had faced. The MPLA derived its leadership from an intelligentsia that thought in super-ethnical terms, and aimed to create mass loyalty to a single Angolan state in which no ethnic group should discriminate against any other. That this was the genuine desire of many urban intellectuals from Luanda was beyond doubt; and it seemed that among a detribalized urban element in that city, especially among the persons of mixed Portuguese and African origin, the MPLA had effective support. However, the great majority of the subjects over whom it ruled belonged to different ethnic groups, and the new leaders had to satisfy and balance them. It seemed likely that in attempting this they would follow the lines of the "nationality policy" that had been developed in the Soviet Union from the doctrines of Lenin and Stalin. Both FRE-LIMO—the Liberation Front of Mozambique—and the MPLA called themselves Marxist-Leninist parties and claimed to be founded on the principles of "democratic centralism." Whether the MPLA leader Agostinho Neto would go beyond the practice of other "progressive" African one-party state leaders and follow the example of his patron Fidel Castro in proclaiming himself a Marxist-Leninist and turning his party officially into a communist party remained to be seen. The fragility of Neto's position was shown by a revolt against him, led by one of his ministers, in May 1977. The links of the rebels with Cuban or Soviet advisers formed the object of widespread but obscure discussion in the Western press.

The case of the former Portuguese colonies showed that a policy of denying political liberties to African nationalists seems not only to make guerrilla movements inevitable, but to promote the attractions of communism to intelligentsias and to serve the purposes of the Soviet government. In the autumn of 1976 it looked as if the same forces were operating in Rhodesia and in South Africa. In Rhodesia the African nationalist parties that had existed before the "unilateral declaration of independence" of 1965 were suppressed by the government of Ian Smith. Several of their leaders were interned, and others fled abroad to seek guerrilla training. Tanzania and Mozambique became their operational bases, and African guerrilla groups became very active in adjacent parts of Rhodesia in 1976, continuing their actions during the long period of alternating negotiations and mutual insults between white and black politicians. These negotiations were initiated by the United States and South African governments and continued by the British, whose role as universal whipping-boys for white and black nationalists had become one of the permanent features of an otherwise constantly changing international scene. In South Africa itself, black African nationalists were denied political activity. Guerrilla activity by blacks had not developed in 1976, but widespread riots in black quarters of South African cities were an alarming indication for the future.

In both Rhodesia and South Africa the blacks were divided into a number of ethnic groups. In Rhodesia the divisions between nationalist political parties were due, in considerable measure, to ethnic divisions, sharpened by conflicts between rival personalities. This was bound to make it more difficult to reach a lasting agreement on independence, even if one could assume goodwill on the part of both white and black politicians. In South Africa the government favored ethnic divisions by its policy of creating separate "homelands" or "Bantustans." The pursuit of a policy of "divide and rule" was no proof that the divisions were not real. In particular, it was arguable that in view of their distinct traditions and culture, and of their pride in them, the Zulus deserved to be considered not so much a "tribe" as a "nation."

Communists in the Western and Central Muslim Lands

During the 1960s and 1970s the political life of this whole region was dominated by the Israeli-Arab conflict. There were wars in 1967 and 1973, and in 1977, despite the patient diplomacy of Dr. Kissinger and Mr. Vance, the conflict seemed little nearer a solution. Rivalries between political groups and ideologies, as well as between governments, in the Arab states continued to complicate things still further. Only in the easternmost part of the region—in Iran—was there comparative political stability. Israel itself remained a stable state, despite political divisions, though the victory of the Likud party in the election of May 1977 might be expected to make the government less amenable to American pressure than governments of the Labor party that had ruled Israel ever since its foundation.

It is difficult to avoid the conclusion that in 1977 and for the immediately predictable future, the minimum requirements of any Israeli leaders likely to obtain power, and the minimum demands of any Palestinian Arabs capable of commanding the support of their compatriots, were likely to remain irreconcilable. Israelis of moderate opinions would have been willing to return most of the lands occupied in 1967; but all would insist on the preservation of the sovereignty of the state of Israel over the territory acquired in 1948, and most would also insist on retaining the city of Jerusalem and the key strategic points of the Golan Heights. No Palestinian spokesman with a substantial following would renounce the claim of all Palestinians (whose numbers naturally increased to 1.5 million by 1976) to the right to return to their original homes and recover their property. This could not be done without the transformation of Israel from a sovereign Jewish state into quite a different kind—with about half its citizens Jews and half Arabs, and surrounded by Arabs on its land borders.

The Israeli communists claimed to believe that some sort of joint Jewish-Arab popular democracy was possible, but the Jewish and Arab sections of the party could not agree; in any case there was no prospect of the communists obtaining power. The argument that Jewish and Arab workers had common enemies—imperialism, Zionism, and capitalism—and that their actions should be directed against these rather than against either the Jewish or the Palestinian Arab people had a certain abstract beauty, but it was not politically convincing. Who was to be counted a Zionist, or an agent of imperialism? Who was to decide? Jews might be forgiven for remembering the phrase quoted, for his own use, by

Reichsmarschall Hermann Göring from the words of Karl Lueger: *Wer Jude ist, bestimme ich* ("It is for me to decide who is a Jew"). Individual Jewish and Arab communist intellectuals undoubtedly believed in a fraternal socialist Palestine, but the Jews' memories of the holocaust and the fanaticism of their enemies made the vision unreal.

The governments of neighboring states had a different perspective. To the Egyptian, Syrian, and Jordanian leaders it might make much better sense to accept a sovereign Israel within the old frontiers, though it was virtually impossible for any of the three governments publicly to renounce Jerusalem. Some Arab government spokesmen spoke with guarded approval of the idea of a small Palestinian state comprising the west bank of the Jordan and the Gaza strip, but they could not bring themselves to abandon explicitly the demand for complete restitution to the Palestinian Arabs. King Hussein fought and crushed the Palestinians in Jordan in 1970; President Assad fought and defeated Palestinians in Lebanon in 1976; and President Sadat did not lag behind these two in his opposition to the Palestinian extremists. But to fight Palestinian extremists was one thing, to abandon the Palestinian cause another. The genuine convictions of the Arab rulers, their knowledge of their own subjects' emotional sympathies, and the fear of assassination by some fanatic combined to forbid it.

A sensational change in the situation came with the visit of President Sadat to Jerusalem at the invitation of Israel's Premier Begin at the weekend of 19-20 November, and the decision of both governments to negotiate for peace. Sadat undoubtedly wished for a settlement involving all Arab states, but the bitter hostility of Algeria, Libya, Iraq and unfortunately also Syria, and the unwillingness of the rulers of Jordan and Saudi Arabia to express openly the approval of the Egyptian initiative which they undoubtedly felt, made it likely that the most that could be achieved would be a separate peace between Egypt and Israel. Even this would not be easy, since Sadat certainly did not intend to abandon Syrian or Palestinian claims. However, the fact that the leader of the most powerful single Arab state had given up the sterile refusal to admit the existence of Israel, and had met the Israeli leaders as human beings, had a tremendous, if imponderable, influence—not least on the emotions of the Israelis.

The notion of Israel as a Middle Eastern state, a component part of the eastern Mediterranean region, belonging not to Europe but to the part of the world in which Judaism and the two succeeding monotheistic religions had arisen, was attractive to many Israeli intellectuals. It also had much to recommend it to some Muslims—perhaps especially to Egyptian intellectuals who could appreciate the tremendous economic and cultural contributions the Jews would make to the life of the whole region, and who could believe that in the long term the Arab Muslim mass would quietly absorb the Jewish island. In this longer perspective the attractions of the notion might seem to thoughtful Jews less real than the dangers. It was not only that they too must consider it possible that in the long term a peaceful Israel in a peaceful Middle East might be absorbed in an Arab world; it was also true that many Israelis still felt themselves to belong to European culture, and could never bring themselves to turn their backs on Europe in order to face the Euphrates and the Nile. Also, despite a certain amount of mutual irritation and incomprehension, the ties between Israelis and American Jews remained numerous and strong. Thus, though many younger Israelis passionately wished to be accepted by their neighbors as a Middle Eastern nation, they could not be content to be *only* a Middle Eastern nation.

Not only was the communist attitude in the Israeli-Arab conflict unconvincing, but the interests of the Soviet Union were far from simple. The Soviet government was one of the first to recognize Israel in 1948. For the next decade Soviet policy was neutral: Soviet spokesmen declared that the conflict had been created by "the imperialists," and watched with glee the confusion in which it involved their enemies, first Great Britain and later the United States. It was only after the Suez crisis of 1956 that the Soviet government decided to take sides in the dispute and to support the Arab cause. This decision increased the prestige of the Soviet Union in all the Arab states, especially among the intelligentsia. However, the purposes of the Soviet leaders remained different from the purposes of Pan-Arab intellectuals—and still more, of Arab governments. The Pan-Arabs wished to destroy Israel, the Soviet rulers to keep it in existence as a means to occupy the political attention of the United States, and also to bind the policies of the Arabic-speaking countries to the Soviet Union. If Israel ceased to exist, the Arab governments would have much less reason to support Soviet policy. Israel was also useful to the Soviet leaders in their internal policy: a certain amount of anti-Semitism, in the officially approved form of "anti-Zionism," provided a useful scapegoat for internal discontents in Russia, and was an important ingredient of the type of Russian national arrogance that formed the essence of the official Marxism-Leninism of the 1970s. The dislike of the Russian public for bureaucrats, and the resentment of the uneducated toward intellectuals, could usefully be canalized against the Soviet Jews who were still numerous enough to be visible in both categories. The Soviet rulers were continuing, in a more sophisticated and more effectively controlled manner, the policies of Nicholas II. For these reasons, the Soviet government continued to desire not a solution of the Israeli-Arab conflict, but its maintenance and controlled aggravation. At the same time there were limits to the use that could be made of this festering wound in the body of the Middle East; there was no prospect of bringing the region as a whole under Soviet control.

Much the same could be said, in general terms, of the balance of advantage to the Soviet Union and to the communist cause of the persistent rivalries between Arab states and of the ideological divisions between Arab nationalists. Throughout most of the 1960s and 1970s Morocco, Saudi Arabia, Jordan, and the Gulf sheikhdoms continued to have "reactionary" monarchical regimes, while the governments of Algeria, South Yemen, Egypt, Syria, and Iraq were regarded in varying degrees at varying periods as "progressive." The regime of Colonel Qadaffi in Libya was in a special category. On the ideological level, it stood for Islamic fundamentalism and was bitterly anticommunist, but Qadaffi's encouragement of terrorism and subversion in the Arab lands and Africa was helpful on balance to the Soviet cause, and by 1977 his official relations with the Soviet Union had greatly improved. In Egypt, Syria, and Iraq communist parties exercised some influence at times; these deserve a brief mention.

President Nasser had one close friend who had communist sympathies, Khalid Mohieddin, but he refused to tolerate a communist party as such. In 1964 he made a gesture before Khrushchev's visit by releasing 600 communists, and this move was rewarded by Soviet instructions to the Egyptian communists to disband their party, which they formally did in March 1965. Members of the former party were told to join Nasser's Arab Socialist Union (ASU), and to make themselves felt there. Soviet and international communist spokesmen began to write more favorably of the ASU. They could not, of course, admit that it was a "socialist" organization, but they went so far as to say that "a channel for spreading socialist ideology (in countries where there are no effective Marxist parties) is the revolutionary intelligentsia—in the case of the UAR the military officer corps." Nasser was urged to transform the ASU from a mass party into a vanguard revolutionary-cadre party, and to make Egypt a new center of socialism; it looked as if the Soviet and communist leaders had hopes that Egypt would become a sort of Cuba of the Muslim world. However, Nasser refused to become a Castro, refused to denounce religion, and had a statement inserted in the ASU charter, that "the real solutions of any people cannot be adopted from the experiences of other peoples." After the death of Nasser on 28 September 1970, his successor Sadat showed himself more hostile to communists. In May 1972 he dissolved the "Socialist Vanguard" group within the ASU and made some arrests. Communist-inspired riots in January 1972 probably increased his resentment against Soviet influence, which culminated in his dismissal of Soviet military advisers in July 1972. His decision in November 1976 to permit the formation of three political parties, loosely connected under the umbrella of an ASU with diminished functions, appeared to be a sign of confidence in his political strength. However the riots of January 1977 that raged through the Egyptian capital, while undoubtedly reflecting popular economic discontent, looked as if they were inspired by communists and still further increased Sadat's hostility.

In Iraq the communist party, which had flourished under Qassim's government of 1958, was suppressed after his overthrow in 1963. In its illegal struggle it split into three factions and gave support to the Kurdish struggle for self-determination. The Ba'athist military coup of July 1968 released communists from prison and allowed exiles to return. In May 1972 two communists joined the government, presumably as a consequence of the Soviet-Iraq treaty of friendship and cooperation signed on 9 April. In July 1973 the communist party was given legal recognition in return for its adhesion to the official National Front and its acceptance of the National Action Charter. At this stage the communists, who had hitherto supported Kurdish demands, transferred their support to the government, which was not prepared to grant effective self-government in the Kurdish regions. In the war between Iraqi and Kurdish forces that broke out in 1974, the communists gave wholehearted support to the government, which enjoyed Soviet approval, while the Kurds received help from Iran. However, on 16 March 1975 the Iranian and Iraqi governments reached an agreement: in return for Iraqi recognition of Iranian claims to secure use of the Shatt-al-Arab for their seaborne trade the Iranians abandoned the Kurds to their fate. It seemed possible that Iraq might now become less dependent on the Soviet Union, and that the communists would have fewer opportunities. However that might be, experience seemed to show that Iraq, with its unsolved Kurdish problem, continuing Shi'i-Sunni division, and frequent military coups d'état, was of doubtful value as an ally.

The Syrian communists were allowed to operate as a party after the seizure of power by left Ba'athists on 23 February 1966. Khalid Baqdash, the most eminent communist in the Arab lands, was allowed to return from exile. Individual communists or near-communists became ministers, but the communist party was not represented as such in the government. The coup d'état of November 1970 by General Hafez al-Assad improved the situation of the communist party, which was represented by two ministers in the government from 1971 onward. It was doubtful how much influence they exercised, however, or how successful they were in placing communists in key positions in the state apparatus. In November 1973 the Syrian communist party split. The section led by Baqdash continued to follow in general terms the Soviet party line; the rival party, led by Riyad al-Turk, put Pan-Arabism above "proletarian internationalism," rejected the U.N. Resolution 242 on Israel and Palestine, urged the complete destruction of Israel, and favored the creation of a single Arab communist party.

Assad, who had taken the most extreme anti-Israeli posture during the October 1973 war, moved in the following period to a more moderate position. Like Sadat in Egypt, he was concerned with developing his country's economy; and this development, especially in agriculture, appeared to be following more capitalist than socialist lines. Assad's military intervention in the Lebanese civil war of 1975–1976 in practice favored the Maronite Christian side, while the Lebanese communists (a party small in numbers but with a rather long history and some high-quality support among the intelligentsia) supported the Palestinian guerrilla forces who provided the main military strength on the Muslim side.

Reviewing the period as a whole, one is tempted to conclude that the communist parties of the Arab lands were a very weak force, with small prospects of growth; that the cooperation of Arab governments with the Soviet government was based on little more than the short-term material interests of the former; and that Moscow gave more than it got in return. However, this may be a hasty conclusion. Though the Soviet leaders still had very little prospect of getting a Middle East political-social system that was firmly based on their principles or interests, it is arguable that this was not in fact the aim of their policy. Rather, they seemed to be aiming at the preservation and intensification of a state of chaos that could dangerously weaken their American enemies, and promote the more important Soviet plans for the domination of all Europe. Disruption of Western oil supplies may be expedited no less by the actions of "reactionary" sheikhs than by those of "progressive" democrats. The oil sheikhs were widely regarded in the United States as good friends, but the value of such friends was questionable. Not only were they vulnerable to assassin's bullets, but by policies of rapid industrialization (enthusiastically recommended by American or European advisers) they were helping the assassins, and not even in such a very long term. Arabian bedouin could not provide sufficient manpower for modern industries; not only expert engineers and managers but even the labor force had to be imported, mainly from other Arab lands. Mass production of intelligentsia and mass production of skilled workers doomed to work in frustrating circumstances amounted to mass production of future revolutionaries. As for the already existing revolutionaries, who were mainly Palestinians, though the great majority were certainly not communists, it did not follow from this that they were not accessible to material assistance, or manipulation, by the secular arm of the Soviet regime, the KGB.

The remaining country in the Middle East, besides Israel itself, that looked as if it had fair prospects of material progress on fairly solid foundations was a non-Arab state, Iran. The shah's regime seemed to have combined economic development, political organization, and police repression in an intelligent and ruthless—if from a liberal point of view disagreeable—manner. The Iranians are a numerous people with great natural abilities as well as a long cultural tradition. On such people, if education and material conditions were rapidly increased, a modern state could be built: Iranians were not Saudi nomads. The shah's land reform not only benefited many (if not necessarily most) Iranian peasants, but also replaced the landowners, as the basis of local power, by government officials and army officers who owed their allegiance to the central government and the monarch. The Iranian communists were active in exile throughout these years, and recruited many Iranians studying in the West (whose ranks were also penetrated by the security police, SAVAK), but within Iran they appear to have had little success. Even so, the shah, like the oil sheikhs, remained vulnerable to assassins' bullets; and he, like the leaders of Arab governments, found it necessary to disarm criticism by rhetorical tirades against the West and by economic actions that could weaken the Western economies, thus freely serving Soviet purposes.

Communists in Africa

Something has already been said of the social structure and the political climate of African nationalism, in which African communists and Soviet emissaries had to operate, and especially of the role, both in the struggle for independence and in the new sovereign states, of the urban intelligentsia influenced by European radical ideas.

By the mid-1960s, almost all of the former colonies of Britain, France, and Belgium had become independent sovereign states. The Portuguese colonies were a theater of guerrilla war from the early 1960s; the discontents created in the Portuguese army by the guerrilla war were largely responsible for the overthrow of the Salazar regime in April 1974; and the revolutionary regime in Portugal gave independence to the former colonies. In 1977 the attention of Pan-Africans and of their non-African well-wishers was concentrated on three objectives, all in southern Africa: Rhodesia, southwest Africa, and the Union of South Africa itself.

The rulers of independent African states gave vocal support to Pan-Africanism in the same way the Muslim rulers gave vocal support to Pan-Arabism and Latin American rulers to anti-Yankee rhetoric. They applauded the African guerrilla war against Rhodesia and advocated armed rebellion in South Africa, as the Muslim rulers applauded Palestinian acts of violence against Israel and threatened renewed war; yet in reality they entertained mixed feelings. The victory of the MPLA in Angola was a clear menace to the regimes of Mobutu in Zaire and of Kaunda in Zambia, but both men recognized the Angolan victors and joined in the demand for intensified action against Rhodesia and South Africa. The destruction of those uniquely evil regimes, they publicly agreed, must be the first aim of all Africans, taking precedence over the interests of any individual African state. Such pious statements did not, however, cause Mobutu, Kaunda, or other rulers in analogous predicaments to neglect the repression of their opponents or the development of their economies; in this they resembled the Egyptian or Jordanian rulers faced with the Palestinian terrorists.

For a Marxist-Leninist of the Soviet persuasion Pan-Africanism was as objectionable as Pan-Arabism in principle, but it seemed less likely to harm Soviet interests in practice. It has been suggested above that there were limits to the willingness of the Soviet government to support Arab nationalists against Israel. No such consideration applied in southern Africa. The Soviet rulers could have no objection to the complete destruction of the white Republic: they intended that South Africa's mineral resources and the strategic key to the oceans at the Cape should be held by themselves. Having imposed the MPLA in Angola, they were well placed, with the help of their Cuban conscripts, to develop that country's extraordinary mineral wealth. In Angola there seemed to be good prospects of creating an African Cuba, the first people's democracy on the continent; in

Mozambique, a land less naturally rich but strategically perhaps even more important, something similar might be achieved. Magnificent vistas opened before the planners in Moscow: Zimbabwe and Namibia liberated by freedom-fighters led by Cubans under Soviet guidance; the popular masses rising to crush their oppressors on the Rand; other popular masses overthrowing the imperialist lackeys in Zaire and Zambia; all mineral resources south of the Congo denied to the European capitalists; the Indian Ocean a Soviet lake; and the Soviet navy, carrying out the doctrines of the modern Tirpitz, Admiral Gorshkov, dominating the Atlantic from north and south.

Whether even the brilliant leaders of the great Soviet Union, equipped with a profound understanding of Marxist-Leninist science, could do all these things at the same time was rather doubtful, but no single one of them could be considered absurd. It is worth briefly considering the forces that impeded or favored Soviet aims.

The first obstacle was lack of skilled manpower. To create a modern state and party apparatus of the Soviet type in an African country with a population lacking modern skills could be no easy task. Skilled Soviet administrators who were at the same time specialists in African affairs must still be very few, even after many years' development of African studies in Soviet universities. Even in Angola alone the creation of a modern "people's democracy" would require much time and effort; it was improbable that the Cuban troops and policemen were adequately qualified for the task.

The second obstacle, which was present not only in Angola but in all the other African states that were objects of Soviet imperialist appetite, was the ethnic diversity of the populations; these could be kept in passive awed submission to the Soviet empire, as they had been to its predecessors, but it was a task of a different order of magnitude to weld them together into a united nation and a skilled labor force. The Soviet imperial rulers were likely to find them even more intractable material than their Turkish subjects in central Asia.

The third obstacle was the determination of the political class of white South Africa to resist even against superior force. As long as the white South Africans were resolved to defend what they felt to be their own country (even if many of them disliked its government), as long as they could recruit obedient and efficient Africans into their armed forces and police, could overawe their African subjects as a whole, and could mobilize their great economic resources and their industrial and technological skills, they appeared capable of holding out for many years against African nationalists, even if the latter were armed by the Soviet government.

The principal force favoring Soviet aims, other than their own military resources and political will, was the worldwide hostility to South Africa. That educated blacks should hate the regime that denied them opportunities to pursue their own talents, insulted them day-by-day in numerous ways, and treated them as insolent upstarts from a helot race that should accept permanent helotry is easy to understand. That this hatred should extend to the political class of all African states and to blacks in other parts of the world was also to be expected. However, the peculiar fact about worldwide hostility to South Africa was that millions of nonblack non-Africans and noncommunists became convinced that in a world overflowing with injustice and tyranny, the South African regime was so exceptionally unjust and tyrannical as to form a special class all on its own, to deserve a loathing and condemnation different in kind from that which might be provoked by any other regime in the world.

For this state of affairs the South African nationalists had mainly themselves to blame. It was not so much the way they treated their African subjects (many black African governments were probably more oppressive and more brutal) as the doctrine which they proudly and loudly proclaimed to the world. The idea that blacks should be considered permanently and inherently inferior because they were born black and should be doomed to perpetual inferiority in their own country profoundly shocked European and American opinion. It was rejected as absolutely incompatible not only with the predominant liberal outlook but also with Christianity, as it was understood by most European and American Christians.

There were also two further reasons for special revulsion. One was that the West had only just emerged from war with Hitler, who had proclaimed a doctrine of inborn race inferiority (in his case applied mainly to Jews) and had applied it in his extermination camps. There were no Auschwitzes in South Africa, nor did Afrikaner nationalists intend to create any, but the association of ideas was made, and the accusation of ''genocide'' against South Africa became a cliché of Western rhetoric of the left.

The second reason was that South African racial dogmatism hit like a raw nerve the latent guilt complexes of Americans and British. The American guilt complex concerned the treatment of blacks in American society, the British complex the supposed bad record of the British Empire. The brash imperialist arrogance, so widespread in Britain earlier in the century had been replaced by a strange inverted imperialism. Not only was past British imperialism denounced by the British left intelligentsia, but most of the woes of the world were attributed to it. Whereas a previous generation had proudly shown every continent on the globe marked red for British, the inverted imperialists would not admit that any crime could be committed anywhere in the world without laying the blame for it on the defunct empire. To persons of such mentality it was natural not just to denounce the injustices and oppressions practiced by the South African regime, but to elevate them to a solitary pinnacle of wickedness.

The South African government showed no great interest in acting to diminish worldwide hostility. The Soweto riots of 1976 were not followed by serious improvement in the condition of the urban black population. In September 1977

Steve Biko, the leader of the Black Consciousness movement, was killed in prison. This was not only a crime but a blunder. It was generally agreed by the white South Africans who knew him that Biko was the one black leader with qualities of an outstanding statesman—the one man who, while defending his own people's cause, also understood the white people's case and worked for peaceful solution by mutual agreement. His death could only strengthen those who called for black violence and increase the detestation of even moderate foreign democrats for the South African system.

The result of all this was that in 1977 it seemed almost inconceivable that any Western government would assist South Africa against its enemies. It was especially difficult to imagine that any American president would do so, both because of the importance of the black vote in the American electorate and because of the reflex action of the American public against "another Vietnam." What was not understood in the West was that if this position were pushed to its logical extreme, it would mean that the United States would do nothing to prevent Soviet domination of the Indian Ocean and the South Atlantic. This in turn would make possible two results, either of which was frightening to contemplate. One was that the Soviet Union would succeed in controlling the Cape route and in denying to the West (either by taking it for itself or by creating such chaos that it would be available to no one) the mineral wealth of central and southern Africa. The other was that before the Soviet triumph was finally consummated, the American government would suddenly realize what was happening, would react in a panic with improvised measures, and would set off a conflict that could produce a third world war. There could be no easy answer to these problems for any American leadership. The Nixon-Ford administration neglected Africa. President Carter, and his advisers Vice-President Mondale and Andrew Young, were certainly aware of the problems. Of their good intentions there could be no doubt, but political and strategic facts remained intractable realities. The Soviet leaders were in a more fortunate position: they could gleefully watch Western statesmen floundering in the mire, and make the best use of the opportunities this spectacle afforded to them.

These prospective dangers and conflicts in Africa had much less to do with communism than with Soviet imperialism. However, though communist parties appeared insignificant in Africa in 1977, it would be wrong to dismiss communism as a force for the future. There were two countries in Africa in which a communist party had been, or might seem likely to become, a significant political force: the Sudan and South Africa. Sudan was geographically a part of tropical Africa, but culturally a borderland between the Arab and Nilotic regions. In the 1950s and 1960s the Sudanese communist party gained a good deal of support within the small educated elite. General Nimeiry, who seized power in Khartoum in May 1969, allied himself with the party and appointed communists to some ministries in his government. In July 1970 the communists attempted to overthrow Nimeiry and were defeated. Their party organization was broken, but it seemed unlikely that communist inclinations among a part of the intelligentsia had disappeared. However, in 1977 it looked as if Soviet plans for the Horn of Africa were based no longer on Sudan, but on Ethiopia.

The second country in which communism seemed likely to find support was South Africa. The merit of communism, at least as a doctrine and a program, was that it stood above distinctions of race or nation. Black nationalism was a great potential force among the black majority in South Africa, but it was alarming not only to the four million whites but also to the two million Coloureds and the near-million Indians. Communism, however, offered a place to all who accepted it and devoted themselves to the revolutionary struggle. Coloureds and Indians had much larger intelligentsias, in proportion to their total numbers, than blacks; and communism was likely to appeal to them, especially to their younger members. To members of the white intelligentsia of radical outlook, communism might seem the one remaining hope of avoiding mutual slaughter between the races. Thus the South African communists might in time acquire valuable cadres from the nonblack educated classes, as well as mass support from Coloured and Indian workers—though little from white workers, who, as a class, were more thoroughly infected with antiblack racialism than were the white bourgeois. The South African communists in exile included persons of ability, as was shown by the high quality of their review *African Communist.*

For any potential future popularity of the communist party, the South African government would have itself to blame. The endless denunciations of "communism" by its spokesmen, and the use of the word in legislation and in public life in general to describe all active opponents of the regime, inevitably created, among blacks and Coloureds, a predisposition in favor of communism. They were unlikely to be dissuaded from this attitude by the arguments of official spokesmen based on the record of Soviet behavior, even were these arguments true.

It was the difficult task of American statesmen to steer between the Scylla of South African official white racial obstinacy and the Charybdis of growing Soviet influence. Their aim was to promote rapid but peaceful change. The Americans believed that the necessary drastic reforms could only be brought about by strong pressure on the South African government. Mr. Vorster and his colleagues had to be convinced that if they refused drastic reforms, they would receive no help from the West, however desperate their plight might become and however deeply Soviet or Soviet-sponsored military forces might be engaged against them; that it would be useless for them to rely on any feeling of solidarity with South Africa in the United States, whether on grounds of common "Christian civilization" or of strategic necessity. But if Vorster were to be persuaded of this, then the American attitude could not be intimated to him merely through diplomatic channels: it must be proclaimed *urbi et orbi.* But others besides the

South African government would be listening. Among the listeners would be the Soviet admirals, and all those in the Soviet Union who were professionally or emotionally inclined toward a forward policy. American statements might be taken as a green light for Soviet expansion in the South Atlantic. Such a green light had once been assumed, in the time of that much more cautious and much more powerful Soviet leader Joseph Stalin, as a result of Dean Acheson's statement about American lack of interest in Korea in 1950.

Moreover, it was quite possible that the policy would be counterproductive even in its immediate aim. Pressure might increase the obstinacy of the Afrikaners. Mr. Vorster might remain convinced that whatever the Americans said and believed, they would in the end become involved. Thus American policy might strengthen both white South African extremism and Soviet inclinations to meddle in the South Atlantic. The conflict might steadily escalate.

Communists in Latin America

The one substantial victory already achieved by communism in Latin America—the establishment under Fidel Castro of a communist party dictatorship in Cuba—was consolidated during the 1960s, but the limitations of this victory became clearer. From the orthodox Marxist-Leninist point of view, the style of the Castro regime was not entirely acceptable: it smacked of *caudillismo,* with Fidel enjoying a type of personal glamor that was very different from the drab pontifical infallibility of Stalin, let alone the bureaucratic mediocrity of Brezhnev and his team. Castro's glamor had the advantage that it appealed to hitherto uncommitted radicals outside the ''socialist camp,'' especially to young revolutionary zealots looking for a model that remained untainted by the legacy of Stalinism. To some extent, therefore, the peculiarities of Castroism were objectively useful to the Soviet cause. A serious practical disadvantage was that Castro gave encouragement in Latin America to types of revolutionary activity of which orthodox communist parties strongly disapproved.

It was probably economic realities that determined the extent of Castro's ability to remain independent of Moscow. The attempts of the first years to diversify the Cuban economy did not succeed. In order to make them effective, Castro would have required substantial assistance from the ''capitalist world,'' but the price would have been a diminution of his hostility to the United States and to private enterprise, and this he was not willing to concede. Castro was forced to accept a return to the former concentration of the Cuban economy on sugar production, and this was made possible only by Soviet willingness to buy a very large part of the Cuban sugar output at favorable prices. He was thus completely dependent, from about 1961 onward, on Soviet economic help, for which the political price was greater support for Soviet policies. The original hope of making Cuba a third center of world communism, equal to Russia and China, appeared less and less realistic. The First Afro–Asian–Latin American People's Solidarity Conference, held in Havana in January 1966 and known as the "Tricontinental Conference," produced little but rhetoric. In January 1967 China and Cuba withdrew their ambassadors, and in the following years Castro periodically expressed his support of the Soviet Union in its controversies with China. In the summer of 1968 Castro's public support for the Soviet action in Czechoslovakia showed beyond doubt where he stood, and opened a new phase in Cuban alignment with the Soviet Union in world politics. The culmination of Castro's pro-Soviet policy, and the most sensational repayment of his debt to his protectors, was the Cuban airborne invasion of Angola at the end of 1975.

Nevertheless Castro did not abjure his voluntarist, heroic, romantic doctrine of guerrilla action as the best way to revolution, and his disciples in Latin America did not willingly give up their struggle.

In Peru there was a tradition of small guerrilla actions, and two groups existed in the mid-1960s that professed to be Castroite. Neither was very effective, and both were held in check by the combination of repression with left-wing pronouncements favored by the military government of General Juan Velasco Alvarado, who was established by the coup d'état of 3 October 1968. The mass invasions of landed estates in northeastern Brazil by militant peasant unions led by Francisco Julião had already been crushed by the military dictatorship of 1964.

In Venezuela there emerged an ultraleft party, Movimiento de la Izquierda Revolucionaria (MIR), which became increasingly divided during the 1960s into those who preferred "peaceful methods" and those who favored guerrilla warfare. The Venezuelan Communist Party (PCV) split in December 1970 as a result of arguments about the events in Czechoslovakia, and a new group was subsequently formed, the Movement toward Socialism (MAS). The leaders of the two parties hurled abuse at each other: Trotskyist, Marcusian, petty-bourgeois leftist, on one side, and Stalinist and "mothball Marxist" on the other. In 1966 a member of the PCV Politburo, Douglas Bravo, who was in command of a mixed guerrilla force of PCV and MIR followers, formed a force of his own that was independent of the PCV, from which he was then expelled. Both the Bravo force and the rival force that remained loyal to the PCV received a small stream of recruits, largely students, and for some years there was in fact a safe base for guerrilla recruitment in the University of Caracas (from whose campus the police were excluded);[3] but their operations in the state of Oriente achieved very little. The attempts of the extreme left to use legal channels were hardly more impressive; in the election to the Venezuelan congress in December 1973 the PCV, the MAS, and the MIR won a total of over 7 percent of the poll,

---

3. In December 1966 President Leoni broke the principle of the inviolability of the campus by sending police in, and there were occasional police raids in subsequent years.

the MAS being the strongest with 5 percent. This disappointment led to yet another split, in June 1974, with the formation of Communist Vanguard (VC). The total effect of the continuing admiration of young Venezuelan revolutionaries for Fidel was disappointing. Venezuelan controversies, however, bulked very large for some years in Latin American Marxist discussions, and received considerable attention in intellectual communist circles in other parts of the world as well.

The MIR in Chile also looked to Castro as its model, and Fidel found himself in an embarrassing position, as he was obliged, after Allende's election to the presidency, to express public support for the Allende coalition and to some extent for the orthodox Chilean communist party line. (The disastrous effects of ultraleft, especially MIR-ist activity on the fate of the Allende regime have been discussed in Chapter Two.)

At the end of the 1960s it was clear that rural guerrilla warfare in the Caribbean and Andean republics had failed. The best hopes of moderates for peaceful social change seemed to lie with democratic government in Venezuela, while more radical spirits might put their hopes on the military regime in Peru, which might play some such "objectively progressive" role as Nasser's regime had in Egypt. However, in 1977 the danger that Nasserism might be replaced by Sadatism in Peru was not to be ignored. Meanwhile there had appeared a new form of ultraleftism—urban guerrilla warfare—which flourished for a time not in the economically underdeveloped regions of Latin America, but in the modern industrial cities of the south and east.

The best-known manual of urban guerrilla warfare is a book written by a Brazilian, Carlos Marighella, whose Action for National Liberation put it into practice in 1968. It was practiced still more successfully in Uruguay, by a group that called itself Tupamaros (from the name of the leader of the Indian insurrection against the Spaniards in Peru in 1780, Tupac Amaru), and by two other groups in Argentina. Kidnapping, robberies, and assassinations were the urban guerrillas' methods, together with temporary seizure of radio stations, factories, or cinemas in order to harangue large audiences with revolutionary propaganda. They paid special attention to foreign diplomats, whom they held to ransom in return for large sums, the release of imprisoned revolutionaries, and the publication of their propaganda. The American ambassador in Brazil, Burke Elbrick, and the British ambassador in Uruguay, Geoffrey Jackson, were two eminent victims.

The Brazilian military rulers did not hesitate to reply with violence. Marighella was killed at the end of 1969 and his successor a year later, and mass arrests brought the movement to defeat by the end of 1972. In Uruguay the democratic government proved unable to crush the Tupamaros within the limits of civil government, and in April 1972 a free hand was given to the armed forces, which by the end of the year had crushed the guerrillas. Thus the main achievement of the Tupamaros was to destroy Uruguayan democracy—the oldest and most continuous in Latin America. In Argentina in 1970 two movements emerged: the Montoneros, who were recruited from the left wing of the Peronista movement, and the Trotskyist Ejército Revolucionario del Pueblo (ERP). These groups preferred foreign businessmen to diplomats as their kidnap victims, and for a time did well. The advent to power of the Peronistas, under Hector Cámpora, then Perón himself, and then his widow Isabela, increased the political confusion from which these movements profited. In March 1976 the Argentine army took power under General Jorge Rafael Videla, who proceeded vigorously against both groups, first the ERP and then the Montoneros. Both were very seriously weakened, but it would be premature to assert in 1977 that they had been destroyed.

During these years the orthodox communist parties of these countries played no significant part. The Brazilian communists were crushed by the military dictatorship in 1964; in Uruguay communists dominated the trade unions between 1964 and 1973; the Argentine communist party, which had been a promising party in the 1930s, dwindled during the Perón era and did not recover any importance after Perón's overthrow.

The preservation of the Cuban base appeared to have been a useful investment of substantial Soviet economic resources from the point of view of Soviet expansion in Africa; but elsewhere in Latin America communists did not fare well in the 1960s and 1970s. Their major effort, in Chile, was a disastrous failure, and elsewhere they remained ineffective. Nevertheless, plenty of explosive human material remained in Spanish America and Brazil, and both local communists and Soviet political-warfare planners could hope that they would be a source of continuing trouble for their North American adversaries.

Strangely, in view of its earlier heroic revolutionary traditions, Mexico was the most stable country in the region. With sixty million inhabitants, considerable resources, and quickly growing industries, it seemed to face a comparatively promising futu..e. The Mexican form of government, a combination of bureaucracy and capitalism, embellished by a rhetoric that extolled social revolution and the superiority of Indian culture, and reinforced by the maintenance of a rather high degree of social mobility, seemed to satisfy a rather large political class and to be at least passively accepted by the majority of the people, even though millions continued to live in squalor in an age of rising expectations. The most gifted and sensitive intellectuals might resent the hypocrisy, but their hostility did little to weaken the regime. The Mexican rulers seemed to have discovered a workable balance between ritual denunciations of Yankee imperialism and practical cooperation with the United States government and businessmen.

In the Caribbean and Andean regions prospects of economic and social progress, without revolutionary upheavals, appeared better than in the past. It was true that in both Jamaica and Guyana governments of more-or-less Marxist out-look might prove difficult partners. Still more dangerous was the growth of anti-North American feeling in Panama, which might threaten the future of the Canal. On the other hand, the democratic regime in Venezuela seemed to be using its oil wealth to good effect; no doubt fortunes were made, by politicians as well as by businessmen, and corruption was not unknown, but movement was perhaps toward greater liberty and justice. In Peru the Velasco regime professed its love for the peasants and the urban slum-dwellers of Indian origin, and possibly brought them some material benefits, even though great poverty still existed. The replacement of Velasco by his defense minister General Francisco Morales Bermúdez in 1976 brought some diminution of radical rhetoric (though not nec-essarily any abandonment of effective reform), and a less anti-North American attitude.

It was in the most developed states, in the south, that the democratic cause suffered the heaviest blows, but without bringing visible advantage to the com-munists. The anarchy of the Allende regime and the crimes of the Tupamaros brought the end of free institutions in Chile and Uruguay, the two countries in which they had been most deeply rooted for the longest time. In Argentina and Brazil, the two countries most favored in natural and human resources, it seemed that the age of Perón, Vargas, and Goulart, the age of demagogic euphoria and of wastage of both manpower and material wealth, had ended in military dic-tatorships more ruthless than those of earlier tradition. All four southern military regimes set themselves to defeat the extremists of the "left"; and the communist parties, which had to be considered relative "moderates" by comparison, faced a bleak future. There were, however, differences between them. In Chile in particular, repression seemed to be more widespread and more severe than could be justified by the need to render powerless the subversive elements of the Al-lende regime. In Argentina President Videla was under pressure from some of his officers to act in a more dictatorial manner than he would prefer, yet he was able to offer some resistance to these pressures. President Geisel of Brazil also adopted milder methods than his predecessors. All four regimes faced massive hostility from the Third World orators in the United Nations and from the spokes-men of the Soviet bloc; in the case of Chile, and to a lesser extent Argentina, this hostility was shared even by persons of mildly liberal opinion in Europe and North America. Whether the military rulers would be able to improve their coun-tries' economic conditions, to restore their resources after decades of profligacy, and to create a consensus of support from a large part of their citizens, remained uncertain.

In the longer term the communists, seeking consolation for their failures, might count on two factors. One was the built-in hostility to North America. The superior wealth and efficiency of the northerners, their predominance in the industries and markets of the Latin American peoples, and the deep gap between the Anglo-Saxon and the Spanish-American or Portuguese-American political cultures were inescapable facts. The rulers might understand that it was necessary to cooperate with the United States, and the United States government might try very hard not only to help its southern neighbors but (which was more difficult) to persuade American businessmen to behave with tact and generosity; nevertheless, the pressure of latent hostility would remain for a long time, and the governments would have to make concessions to it by the ritual rhetoric of anti-imperialism. In this their predicament resembled that of the governments of Egypt, Saudi Arabia, and Syria with their ritual Pan-Arabism, or of the governments of Zaire and Zambia with their ritual Pan-Africanism. And it was not entirely a matter of ritual, because Latin American generals and conservative politicians too felt a deep resentment against the Yankees. The implications of President Carter's campaign for human rights could not fail to worry them. It was the task of the communists to work incessantly to maximize this resentment in all classes, and even to exploit the resentments felt by their bitterest domestic opponents against the foreign enemy.

The second factor was the alienation of the intellectual elite. For half a century Latin American universities had been mass-producing an intellectual proletariat, larger than the opportunities for their employment in the law, journalism, literature, or other congenial professions; its members were filled with the latest radical and utopian ideas from Europe or North America, washed down with immense floods of the superfluous verbiage in which the Spanish-American political culture is so rich. The combined pursuit of dignified jobs for themselves and of a political and social order that would be more consonant with the noble but abstract principles their education had instilled in them made successive generations of Latin American intelligentsia a source of constant unrest. A penetrating observer of the Latin American scene, with rich experience of revolutionary movements both in that continent and in Western and Central Europe,[4] has made a fascinating analysis of this phenomenon, standing Marx on his head and arguing that the interests of the intelligentsia as a class form the foundation of Latin American social and nationalist revolution. He argues that the populist movements of the 1950s, and their successors of the ultraleft in the 1970s, were based not, as orthodox communists maintain, on a "national bourgeoisie" (businessmen were conspicuous by their absence from them), but on this materially and mentally frustrated intelligentsia. The essential aims of Latin American intelligentsia nationalists were, in Halperin's words, "administrative positions for educated persons in need of employment, and social and economic development

---

4. Ernst Halperin, author of several works and articles on Latin America, himself fought in the Spanish civil war, and later published a perceptive book on Tito's Yugoslavia. His theory is presented, in brilliantly clear language and without any social-science jargon, in his booklet *Terrorism in Latin America*, published as no. 33 of the Washington Papers of the Center for Strategic and International Studies (Beverly Hills and London: Sage Publications, 1976).

to create still more such positions. . . ." To provide such jobs became a high priority for Latin American politicians for whom "100 unemployed university graduates pose a greater threat . . . than 100,000 unemployed illiterates . . . . Poverty cannot be administered out of existence, but in Latin America as elsewhere, the administration of poverty does provide employment for numerous sons and daughters of the educated classes." This same motive was a driving force not only behind official programs of social reform but also behind the drive to confiscate foreign enterprises. "Maximisation of profits, the guiding principle of private enterprise, is replaced by a new principle: maximisation of administrative employment opportunities. The demands of the administrative class— educated persons pressing for administrative employment—have precedence over the demands of the exchequer."[5] But in the 1960s and 1970s, the pressure increased faster than the opportunities, governments found it impossible to satisfy the demands, and the frustrations of the young intelligentsia became more and more intolerable. Meanwhile the conditions of the peasants and workers, who were desperate but inarticulate, remained almost unchanged. Politicians, intelligentsia, and masses could be united only by ever more frantic rhetoric directed against one object of hatred, one force that was believed to be responsible for all their misfortunes—the hideous monster of North American imperialism. This obsession, this "vampire complex" as Halperin calls it, made it impossible to deal with real economic problems and real class conflicts precisely in those southern republics that had the highest literacy rates and the human and material resources that would lead one, judging by European and North American experience, to expect that there were the best prospects for stable and socially progressive democracy. The reality proved to be the opposite of this expectation: in the Spanish political culture the high proportion of educated people was a force not of democratic leadership but of anarchy; the resulting discontents could not be managed within a democratic framework; and military dictatorship was the result. However, repression would not remove these disruptive forces unless drastic social and economic reforms were undertaken. The communists might therefore take comfort from the belief that though they had been repeatedly defeated, yet their countries would continue to cause trouble for, and to occupy the attention of, the leaders of the United States, the principal adversary of their protector the Soviet Union.

5. Halperin, *Terrorism*, pp. 23, 24, and 30.

−4−

The Soviet Empire

From Tsars to Bolsheviks

The Soviet Union is the successor, in terms of its territory, to the Russian Empire of the tsars. Within the Union, the Russians formed in 1970 slightly more than half the population, and in 1977 almost certainly slightly less than half. In addition, the governments of the Soviet Union exercised most of the attributes of sovereignty over the peoples of five, arguably of six, European states and of one Asian state on its boundaries.[1]

The Russian Empire was formed by the expansion, spread over nearly six centuries, of a small state situated close to the watershed between the great rivers leading into the Baltic, Black, and Caspian seas—the Grand Duchy of Muscovy. Successive rulers of this state conquered the Muslim Tatars of the Volga valley and the peoples of the southeastern Baltic coast and of the Lithuanian and Ukrainian borderlands with Poland, while an unplanned process of colonization brought Russian hunters and peasants through sparsely populated Siberia to the Pacific. In the nineteenth century Russian armies conquered the Caucasus, Transcaucasia, and the central Asian valleys north of the Asian mountain massif. When war and revolution brought the empire of the tsars to collapse, many of the conquered nations tried to become independent. Some succeeded for a time, but most were brought back under Russian rule in its new Bolshevik form, and most of the rest were incorporated once more in Russia with the encouragement of Adolf Hitler, and later with the acquiescence of Roosevelt and Churchill. Only the core lands of Poland and Finland remained outside, and there were serious limitations on their independence.

This brief summary would be scornfully rejected by Soviet spokesmen. They might accept what I have written of the events before 1917, but would add the

---

1. The arguable case is Romania, which is discussed later. The Asian state is Mongolia. It should also be noted that the Soviet Union later annexed some lands the tsars had never ruled: Khiva and Bokhara in Central Asia, Tannu Tuva on the borders of China, the Kurile Islands in the Sea of Okhotsk, and a portion of East Prussia with its main city Königsberg, renamed Kaliningrad—the last two by virtue of its victory over Germany and Japan. The annexation also included two regions that before 1917 had been Austrian, not Russian—eastern Galicia and northern Bukovina.

comment that however brutal the tsars may have been in their conquests, incorporation in the Russian Empire proved a great blessing for these peoples. It spared them the terrible fate of being subjected to the odious British imperialists, or from being snapped up by the Ottoman Turkish or Chinese empires, and it brought them into contact with the superior culture of the great and noble Russian people, which was fated in the course of time (though nobody knew this at the time of most of these conquests) to give birth to the most progressive thinkers and the most intrinsically revolutionary working class in human history, and above all to the greatest genius known to the human race, the incomparable Vladimir Ilich Lenin.

As for the events after 1917, Soviet spokesmen would maintain that they were utterly different. What happened was that the great Lenin proclaimed the principle of self-determination up to the point of separation, while stressing that no non-Russian nation *need* separate from Russia; and that the broad popular masses of these nations, with few exceptions, joyfully declared themselves for membership in the young socialist republic, which soon afterward was renamed Union of Soviet Socialist Republics. As for the few exceptions on the western borders, their peoples rectified their errors in 1939 and 1940, when the people of western Belorussia and western Ukraine—till then subject to reactionary rule by Polish landowners—and the people of the three Baltic states, northern Bukovina, and Bessarabia all manifested their desire to join the Soviet Union in the same joyful and almost unanimous manner.

The truth, however, is that none of the peoples who remained in the Soviet Union after 1920, or were incorporated later, were ever given the chance to choose, by a free election preceded by free competition between different political groups, whether or not they wished to form independent sovereign states. It is arguable that the nationalist movements of 1917–1920 were actively supported only by minorities of their peoples, but this does not mean that preservation of Russian rule was the positive desire of the majority. It is also arguable that incorporation in the Soviet Union brought them material benefits in the long term, but this is, of course, an argument that can be used on behalf of any "more advanced" empire, and that was, in fact, used by the "imperialists" of the Western colonial empires in the days of their strength and self-confidence.

The Legitimacy of Empire

The legitimacy of government in the great multinational empires of the past was based on the duty of obedience to the reigning monarch, deriving from the divine right of kings. This was true of the Russian Empire of the tsars and of the Habsburg monarchy, which proclaimed it in the one word *Kaisertreue* (loyalty to the emperor). This was also truc of the origins of the legitimacy of government in the Western countries whose rulers created colonial empires in the nineteenth and twentieth centuries, though in the metropolitan lands popular sovereignty had replaced the divine right of kings, and some had become republics.

The legitimacy of the Soviet empire is based on a doctrine that attributes universality to what its spokesmen consider to be the greatest event in human history, dividing history in two in a more radical sense than the birth of Christ or the *Hejira* of the prophet Muhammad—the Great October Socialist Revolution. The successful seizure of power by Bolshevik troops in Petrograd on 25 October/ 7 November 1917 was considered by Lenin to be the first socialist revolution in human history; the subsequent victory in civil war convinced him that the Central Committee of the Bolshevik party (later the CPSU), in which he was the leading figure, was unique in the world in its possession of a "correct" grasp of Marxist theory—that is, of the scientific laws governing human society. After Lenin's death the exclusive and complete understanding of what came to be known as Marxist-Leninist[2] science—a completely scientific and sufficient explanation of the essential laws that have determined the past and present, and will determine the future, of human society—was passed down, by a sort of apostolic succession, to the persons appointed as members of the Central Committee up to the present time.[3]

Admittedly, there were some little difficulties. The great purge of 1936–1939 removed about two-thirds of the Central Committee, as well as hundreds of thousands of members of the party at lower levels. There were two possible explanations for this process. One was that these persons were indeed enemies of the people, wreckers and agents of foreign powers, in which case some doubts might arise concerning the validity of the apostolic succession. The other was that they were good communists, innocent victims of "the cult of personality of I. V. Stalin"; in which case the question arose, how was such a monster able to make himself master of a Central Committee consisting of persons endowed with the exclusive wisdom conferred by the apostolic succession? However, such doubts were officially cast aside by Stalin's successors: though there had been "mistakes," the Central Committee remained the inner shrine, the sole fountain of Marxist-Leninist science. Outside observers have often asked themselves whether the leaders of the CPSU in the 1970s really believed this. Nobody except they themselves can answer this question, and perhaps not even they. Does the pope really believe in his infallibility? Who knows? It should be noted, however, that the pope's infallibility extends only to matters of theology; Marxist-Leninist scientific infallibility covers all aspects, however trivial, of man's secular life and thought.

---

2. Lenin, who was not personally a vain man, did not encourage the use of the word "Leninism."

3. Central Committee members are elected by each congress of the party, but their election is a formality, since they have been chosen in advance by the party leaders.

What is certain is that the completely scientific quality of Marxism-Leninism, and the final and complete possession of this knowledge by the leadership of the CPSU, are proclaimed day in and day out to the peoples of the Soviet Union—and to all in the outer world who will listen—by the CPSU's vast propaganda machine. In this respect there was no change during the decade with which this book is concerned. The leaders of the CPSU alone understood the immanent interests of the workers of the whole world—which the workers themselves were not usually capable of understanding.

One point on which Marxist-Leninists and old-style Russian imperialists could unite—and there was a good deal of both these outlooks combined in the minds of most Soviet citizens of Russian nationality—was that what was good for the CPSU and the Soviet state was also good for its non-Russian citizens.

The "National Question" in Theory and Practice

There is a vast official literature on what is called "the national question," and its volume increased during the last decade. The official view was clearly summarized by Secretary-General L. I. Brezhnev in his speech on the celebration of the fiftieth anniversary of the formal establishment of the Soviet Union, on 21 December 1972: "Summing up the heroic accomplishments of the past half-century, we have every reason to say that the national question, as it came down to us from the past, has been settled completely, finally and for good. . . . A great brotherhood of working people, united irrespective of their national origins by a community of class interests and aims, has emerged and has been consolidated in this country, the relations between them have no equal in history, and we have every right to call these relations the Leninist friendship of peoples." Later in the same speech, however, the Soviet leader warned his listeners that "nationalistic prejudices, exaggerated or distorted national feelings, are extremely tenacious and deeply embedded in the psychology of politically immature people. These prejudices survive even when the objective premises for any antagonisms in relations between nations have long ceased to exist."

Recent Soviet literature on this subject is replete with rhetoric and also with semantic disputes of Talmudic subtlety relating to the definitions used in Stalin's famous and partly (but it is rather risky to guess how far) discredited article.[4]

---

4. "Marxism and the National Question," written in 1913 at Lenin's request and subsequently made the sacred text of communists the whole world over. It has been reprinted in a series of expanded editions of Stalin's works on this subject, entitled *Marxism and the National and Colonial Question* and translated into dozens of languages. Since Stalin's death it has lost its sanctity, but has not been officially repudiated, and it is discussed from time to time in Soviet publications on problems of nationalism.

The essence of the official doctrine is that the Soviet Union is composed of brotherly "socialist nations." This proposition is considered to be proved by two assertions and one fact. The assertions are that the class factor is always the determinant element in national culture and national consciousness, and that the dominant class in the Soviet Union is the working class. The fact is that during sixty years of the Soviet regime the material conditions of life and the cultural opportunities of non-Russian citizens have greatly improved. From the two unproven assertions and the historical fact the conclusion is drawn that the non-Russians are "socialist nations" united by mutual brotherly love, proudly devoted to the Soviet motherland.[5]

Yet the experience of all other colonial empires casts doubt on this conclusion. In all other cases, it was precisely the good things the colonial rulers did that raised up opposition to them among their subjects. As long as they ruled them with a rod of iron, there was no nationalism to be seen. When they gave them civil liberties, schools, universities, and factories (even if on a limited scale, and with many anomalies and injustices), new elites came into existence whose members became more and more discontented with what they had because it was less than their rulers enjoyed, and explained all the continued poverty and backwardness of their less fortunate compatriots, as well as their own "relative deprivation," by the fact that they were ruled by members of another nation. Improved conditions do not diminish but increase national discontent in multinational empires; this is the Law of Colonial Ingratitude. It is flying in the face of all historical experience to claim that the Soviet Union is exempt from the operation of this law. The fact that far less nationalist opposition is publicly expressed there than was expressed in the African colonies of European powers can be very easily and simply explained: the system of repression by the Committee of State Security (KGB) is immensely more ruthless and comprehensive than was any modern European colonial repression, and it was not and is not subject to undermining by any liberal public opinion in the metropolitan country, as was the case in colonial Africa.[6]

Such doubts, of course, are not admitted, and possibly not even felt, by Soviet spokesmen. Complete brotherhood having already been achieved, the time has come to advance to a higher stage. This will, however, take time, and Soviet spokesmen reject the word "assimilation." What will occur after the victory of communism on a worldwide scale is something else: "the flowing together

---

5. This argument is developed at length in M. I. Kulichenko, *Natsionalnye otnosheniya v SSSR i tendentsiya ikh razvitiya* [Relations between nations in the USSR and the trend of their development] (Moscow, 1972).

6. The second condition applied also to Portugal under Salazar, but the Portuguese repressive system, though doubtless brutal, was infinitely less comprehensive and sophisticated than the KGB.

(*sliyanie*) of nations will take place without anyone's deliberate efforts, in a completely natural way."[7]

If we turn from the doctrine to the practice of "national policy"[8]—that is, of the treatment of the non-Russians by the Soviet government—we must first note some general features and then consider some individual cases.

The USSR is often described as a federal state. This is a misuse of words. The essence of federal government is that powers are shared between the central government and the constituent units (states in the United States, provinces in Canada, cantons in the Swiss Confederation). Each is sovereign in its field. The governments of the constituent units are coordinate with, not subordinate to, the central government. This is true of the U.S., Switzerland, and Canada, even though in the course of time, the addition of new powers to the central government has caused it to overshadow to a greater extent the governments of the constituent units. The government of the USSR is not federal since the authority of the republics is not *coordinate* with the authority of the central government but *subordinate* to it. The purely republican ministries handle matters of trivial importance. All matters involving significant political decisions are handled by the republican branches of central ministries, or by purely central ministries. The most that can be said of the republican structure of the USSR is that it provides for administrative decentralization. The practical extent of this decentralization is, however, limited by the fact that the CPSU, which is responsible not only for deciding all matters of policy but also for seeing that they are carried out at every level, is highly centralized.

The Soviet constitution gives every republic the right to secede from the USSR. The well-understood fact that any public advocacy of secession would cause its authors immediately to be arrested for offenses under the criminal code (especially under the all-purpose clause forbidding "anti-Soviet propaganda") sufficiently explains why no secession has taken place. It no doubt remains true that if all citizens of a republic woke up one morning with an identical supernatural revelation that their republic was about to secede, and simultaneously proclaimed it, the Soviet government would be in an embarrassing situation. One must doubt whether that resourceful organization the KGB would let its embarrassment last long.

---

7. M. I. Kulichenko, "Protiv burzhuaznoy ideologii i revizionizma" [Against bourgeois ideology and revisionism], *Voprosy Istorii KPSS,* 1976, no. 2.

8. This is a translation of the Russian words *natsionalnaya politika.* The word *natsionalnaya* is derived from *natsiya,* meaning nation. Soviet doctrine also uses the word *natsionalnosti,* translated "nationalities," implying a community of somewhat lower status than a "nation": it is, of course, the members of the dominant nation who decide to which category a community belongs. This depreciatory use of the word "nationality" derives from the practice of the pre-1918 Habsburg monarchy.

The Soviet economy (with the not unimportant exception of collective farmers' private plots) is managed by the state, and the plan that determines the allocation of resources is made in Moscow. The planners are guided by what they consider to be the interests of the economy of the whole vast country. If the plan for Uzbekistan was made in Tashkent, the results would be different. It is quite possible that Moscow planners are more enlightened than Tashkent planners would be, and beyond doubt that economic development has benefited many inhabitants of most non-Russian regions. It is arguable that the specialization of central Asian agriculture in cotton growing, to the neglect of food crops that have to be brought there from outside, has been good for the central Asians; similar specialization with similar results in Egypt under British rule was justified by similar arguments. Such arguments, however, never commend themselves to nationally conscious persons living under foreign rule, who have never been allowed to decide whether or not they wish to be independent.

Sixty years of Soviet rule were marked by increasing penetration of Russian culture into non-Russian areas, which to the historian who is not content to repeat the boastful rhetoric of Soviet ritual incantations looks very like a continuation of the tsars' policy of Russification. Policy was carried out by Russian officials, though in certain regions this has been resisted with increasing success in recent times, as will be noted below. Settlement of Russian populations took place in some non-Russian territories in irregular spurts at various periods, but without reversal. Colonization by Russians and Ukrainians in Kazakhstan, and to a lesser extent in the central Asian agricultural regions, was begun under Tsar Nicholas II, resumed after the mass famine of the Kazakhs in the collectivization years, accelerated by Khrushchev's "virgin lands" agricultural plan, and continued more slowly thereafter. Its effects were, however, increasingly mitigated by the fact that the rate of natural increase of the Asian peoples remained very much higher than that of the Russians, as will be noted later. Large numbers of Russians were settled in the Estonian, Latvian, and Moldavian republics soon after the second reincorporation of these countries into the USSR, being accompanied by large-scale deportations of the indigenous peoples.[9] Similar processes took place in the Crimea and in parts of the northern Caucasus.

The problem of the Russian language is rather complex. It is to be expected that there should be one official language in a vast empire, and that this should be the language most widely spoken. The census of 1970 showed that of a total population of 241,720,000 in the Soviet Union, 141,830,000 had Russian for their first language and 41,938,000 persons spoke Russian fluently as their

---

9. These lands were part of the empire of the tsars until 1918, and were reincorporated by the Soviet government with Hitler's encouragement in the summer of 1940. During the following year there was plenty of deportation, but not much time for settlement of Russians before Hitler invaded. The second reincorporation was completed in 1945.

second language. However, this knowledge of Russian was unequally distributed, being higher among those nationalities that were geographically mixed up with Russians, or whose native tongue was of the Slav group, and lower among the Asian peoples—though there were some exceptions.[10] Russian was not only the language of higher administration and of economic management, but also of higher education, in most parts of the Union; the Transcaucasian republics of Georgia and Armenia were partial exceptions. This makes it difficult to evaluate the official Soviet figures for students in higher education in individual republics, and among individual nations. In the first category, persons of the indigenous nation are not differentiated from resident Russians, and in the second category are included persons of the nationality who reside outside their republic and may receive their education at a purely Russian institution.[11] The extent to which instruction in Russian is made an instrument of Russification is a matter of controversy, and neither side can prove its case. It may well be that the Soviet leaders do not wish deliberately to attack non-Russian cultures or to "Russify" other peoples, but it does not follow from this that these peoples do not see things this way, or that that is not indeed a reasonable description of what happens on the spot.

The increased use of Russian throughout the Soviet Union can be defended on practical grounds; but the language used by Russian writers to describe the process often goes beyond mere utilitarian aims. One recent writer, after noting the value of Russian as one of the most developed and richest languages of the world, works himself up to a climax in listing its virtues. Russian literature is "the grandest achievement of world culture. This language is the active bearer of the most advanced scientific thought. This is the language of Lenin."[12]

---

10. The percentages of Russian-speakers in three nations whose peoples are very much mixed up with Russians, because of either Russian immigration or their own dispersal among Russian populations, are: Tatars, 62.5; Latvians, 45.2; and Kazakhs, 41.8. The percentage of Russian-speakers among those Armenians living outside the Armenian republic (about one-third of all Soviet Armenians) is also high: 41.2, but among Armenians in the republic it is only 23.3. Among the five main Muslim nations it ranges from 14.5 for Uzbeks to 19 for Kirghiz. The percentage of Ukrainians who speak Russian is surprisingly low: 36.3. Source: *Handbook of Major Soviet Nationalities,* Z. Katz, R. Rogers, and F. Harned, eds., (New York, 1975), pp. 32, 150, 198, 225, 247, 270, 297, and 332.

11. Take the Uzbek SSR as an example. In 1971 there were 27,199 students at universities in the Uzbek republic; 1609 of them graduated in that year, but how many of these were Uzbeks and how many Russians we do not know. In higher educational institutions in 1970–1971 there were 134,300 Uzbek students and 43,600 Russians. The number of Uzbek students in all such institutions in the USSR was given as 150,700. These figures undoubtedly show a picture of great educational opportunities for Uzbeks, but we would need to have more detailed information on the types of education subsumed under "higher" to be able to compare opportunities for Uzbeks and for Russians.

12. A. M. Gindin, "Protiv burzhuaznoy ideologii i revizionizma-o nekotorykh sovremennykh burzhuaznykh falsifikatsiyakh natsionalnoy politiki KPSS" [Against bourgeois ideology and revisionism—some contemporary falsifiers of the national policy of the CPSU], *Voprosy Istorii KPSS,* 1975, no. 10.

If there is much to be said for non-Russians learning Russian, it is more questionable whether it is beneficial that their history should be rewritten to glorify Russian national pride. Yet this is what has been happening ever since the 1930s. Conquest by Russia, at various times from the sixteenth century onward, is depicted in official Soviet historical literature as a blessing for each people that in the course of time has come under Russian rule. Admittedly, the process itself may have been painful, and the original conqueror may have been an odious reactionary tsar, but the consequence was beneficial because it brought each people in turn into contact with the culture of "the great[13] Russian nation," which was destined in the course of time to give birth to the noble army of nineteenth-century revolutionaries, and to the great Lenin. Annexation to Russia also benefited the Asian peoples by expediting their progress toward socialism, whether first through capitalism, or in one heroic leap. The rebellions of the Kazakhs and of the north Caucasians against the tsars in the nineteenth century were instigated by British or Turkish imperialists. Had they succeeded, these peoples would have suffered the hideous fate of falling under those empires; mercifully the tsars prevailed, and so these peoples were kept together with the Russians until the great Lenin arose.

In this interpretation of the history of the non-Russians there is the mixture of truth and fiction that characterizes all imperial mythologies. For the more backward Asian peoples, conquest by Russia did bring progress in the sense in which progress is understood in the modern industrializing world. Exactly the same, of course, can be claimed for all the other European empires. The language of Russian falsifiers of the histories of non-Russian peoples strikingly recalls the language of the spokesmen of Victorian British or Wilhelminian German imperialism, or of Presidents McKinley and Theodore Roosevelt; and this, to use a Marxist cliché, "is no coincidence," for the Soviet Russian mythmakers are one more in the line of upstart imperial elites glorifying their supremacy over lesser breeds. This basic truth is in no way disproved by the equally valid truth that the spokesmen of the Soviet regime do not see themselves this way.

Some of the more absurd and insulting details of this falsification of history, as it was practiced in Stalin's time, were abandoned under his successors, but the arrogant assumption of the superiority of Russian culture over the cultures of the non-Russian nations continued. Recent Soviet writers have stressed that when the process of *sliyanie* is completed, in a future no longer considered remote, the "ethnical marks of nations" will "die away"—especially "language, the specific features of national culture, way of life, traditions, national

---

13. It should be noted that the word "great" is here used in a laudatory moral sense. The Russian language is known to philologists as "Great Russian"—in Russian a single word *velikorusskii*. In this context two words are used—*velikii russkii*: this constantly repeated ritual phrase refers not to distinctions of linguistic categories but to moral excellence. Note also that before 1956 the great Lenin's name would have been coupled with that of the still greater Stalin.

psychology.''[14] A single language of all humanity will be formed. It is not difficult to guess which language the author expects that to be.

Stalin once used a phrase that became famous, that the culture of all the peoples of the Soviet Union was "national in form, but socialist in content." In his December 1972 speech, Brezhnev added to this that it was "internationalist in spirit and character." It would be more accurate to say that the culture promoted by the Soviet government, for all the nations of the USSR alike, was "socialist in form, and imperialist in content."

Attitudes of Non-Russian Nations

It is not difficult to trace the official policy of the Soviet government toward the non-Russian nations of the Union, but it is difficult to estimate the responses of these nations to it. There have been periods of opposition, and from time to time there are denunciations in the Soviet press of "bourgeois nationalism" in different regions. These too are difficult to estimate. The adjective "bourgeois" has no sociological connotation; it is simply a vituperative epithet. It does not even necessarily indicate real national opposition to Soviet policy; it may be no more than a term of abuse used by one party clique to denounce its rival. Granted these difficulties, all that can be attempted here is to look briefly at certain facts or trends visible in some of the non-Russian regions that seem significant for the last decade, and may be important in the future.

One general point should be noted at the outset: the differences between different nations of the USSR in the rate of population increase and in the age structure of the population. Between the two censuses of 1959 and 1970 the population of the whole Union increased by 15.8 percent. The two nations whose percentage of increase was smallest were the Estonians (1.8) and Latvians (2.1). Higher than these but still well below the USSR average were the Ukrainians (9.4). Three nations were a little below the average in rate of population increase: Russians (13.1), Belorussians (14.4), and Lithuanians (14.6). Another three were substantially above it: Tatars (19.4), Georgians (20.5), and Moldavians—more correctly Romanians— (21.9). The Armenians, with a rate of increase of 27.7 percent, were considerably ahead. Finally, the six main Muslim nations had approximately the same, very much higher, rate of increase: Kazakhs (46.3), Azerbaidjanis (49), Kirghiz (49.8), Uzbeks and Tadjiks (both 52.9).

The much faster growth of the Muslim nations was likely to continue, since they had much younger populations. The available figures relate to republics, and so are approximate. In the four central Asian republics and in Azerbaidjan,

---

14. Kulichenko, *Natsionalnye otnosheniya v SSSR.* . . .

more than half the population was less than twenty years old, while in the Russian republic (RSFSR) the proportion was 36 percent. When one takes into account the fact that the RSFSR contained large non-Russian minorities, and that there were substantial Russian minorities in the Muslim republics, it is clear that the discrepancy between Russians and Muslims is a good deal larger, with perhaps 33 percent of Russians and 55 percent of Muslims less than twenty years old. Two other nations that had young populations were the Armenians in their republic (with slightly less than half under twenty) and the Moldavians.[15] The two nations that had the lowest percentages of young people were the Latvians and Estonians.

The Ukrainians

The Ukrainians, with a population of more than forty million, make up the second most numerous nation in the Soviet Union. It has always been difficult to estimate the strength of Ukrainian national consciousness because the majority of Ukrainians have belonged to the same religious community as the Russians—Orthodoxy—and the two languages are very close to each other. These facts made Ukrainians, in the eighteenth and nineteenth centuries, more accessible to the influence of the growing Russian culture than any other people of the Russian Empire. It is, however, also true that their legal and social institutions had been much more subject to Polish than to Russian influence; and that in those Ukrainian lands annexed by Austria in 1772 and 1795 the people were not Orthodox, but belonged to the Uniate branch of the Roman Catholic church. In this territory, usually known as Eastern Galicia, Ukrainian nationalism developed into a powerful force, supported by the overwhelming majority of the Ukrainian-speaking population. Its main enemy after 1918 was the Polish state, which attempted to Polonize Ukrainians. After the Soviet government annexed Eastern Galicia in 1939, the main enemy became the Soviet state. Ukrainian nationalism was first used by Hitler against the Soviet Union and then repressed; and after the Soviet army came back in 1945 there was armed resistance for some years. The Soviet government deported hundreds of thousands of Ukrainians to other parts of the USSR, but in Eastern Galicia (now known as Western Ukraine) national consciousness remained extremely strong even among those born after 1945.

---

15. The presence of Russian minorities in the Asian republics lowers the overall averages for these republics, while the presence of non-Russian peoples in the Russian Socialist Federated Soviet Republic (RSFSR) raises its average. The figure for Armenia gives a more precise picture of the Armenians living in that republic, since they form almost 90 percent of its population. Data covering all Armenians (including the third who live outside the republic) would show a lower percentage for those less than twenty years old.

Further east, it was probably less intense. Nevertheless Ukrainian nationalism, advocated mainly by the intelligentsia, had won growing support from the peasants in the last decades of the rule of the tsar, had formed the basis of strong resistance to the Bolsheviks in the Civil War, and had obtained at least theoretical recognition from the government of Lenin and then of Stalin. In the great crises of Soviet history, the collectivization of agriculture in 1928–1933 and the great purge of 1936–1939, Ukrainians suffered still more than Russians, and their discontent inevitably took the form of nationalism: while a Russian peasant might hate the government, a Ukrainian peasant would tend to direct his hatred against all "Muscovites." The Second World War and the postwar years of Stalin's repression strengthened Ukrainian nationalism. It was Khrushchev who first tried to win over the Ukrainians, by flattering Ukrainian national pride and putting Ukrainians in important jobs at high government levels. Conditions of living also steadily improved for the Ukrainians, from the late 1950s onward, as for all Soviet citizens. Some foreign observers concluded from this that Ukrainian nationalism was diminishing. The small increase in the Ukrainian population between 1959 and 1970 might also suggest not so much a decline in fertility by comparison with Russians as a decline in the numbers of those who considered themselves Ukrainians.

This view could plausibly be supported by the fact that in the cities of the Ukraine the Russian language predominated. Yet too much stress should not be placed on this. In 1970, 51.5 percent of Ukrainians were still rural, and the peasants still spoke Ukrainian. Second, it does not follow that the Ukrainian city-dwellers whom foreign visitors hear speaking Russian in their offices and in the street do not speak Ukrainian when they go back to their families at home. Third, one need not necessarily speak the national language in order to feel that one belongs to the nation (many who speak only Castilian consider themselves Basque nationalists, and Scots and Irish express their nationalism in English). It seems more likely that a double process is at work: Russian culture reaches the Ukraine through the cities and Russifies some of those who live there, but the influx from the villages also Ukrainianizes the cities. As for material progress, this is just as likely to increase discontent through rising expectations as to win gratitude from Ukrainians to a government whose seat of power is in Moscow.

The Soviet press in the late 1960s and early 1970s had evidence of Ukrainian nationalist discontent, and information also reached the West about Ukrainian dissidents and illicit literature (*samizdat*). In 1965 and 1966 several Ukrainian writers were arrested for their nationalist activities, especially the journalist Vyacheslav Chornovil, the literary critic Ivan Dzyuba, and the historian Valentin Moroz.[16] The attitude of the communist party's first secretary of the Ukraine,

---

16. See *The Chornovil Papers* (New York, 1968); Ivan Dzyuba, *Internationalism or Russification? A Study in the Soviet Nationalities Problem* (London, 1968).

P. Shelest, was ambiguous. He spoke fiercely against "bourgeois nationalism," but to some extent protected the nationalist intelligentsia and made efforts to increase the use of the Ukrainian language in official business and the publication of works in Ukrainian. When he was removed from office in January 1973, the official hostility to Ukrainian national aspirations stiffened, but it was most unlikely that these had been, or could be, crushed.

The Baltic Nations

The Estonians and Latvians suffered from mass deportation and large-scale Russian immigration in the late 1940s, and the rapid transformation of their economies along Soviet lines was a brutal process. In the 1960s they began to recover, and their higher cultural level and greater natural and acquired skill enabled them to move ahead of the Russians. In the mid-1970s these two republics had some of the qualities of a Scandinavian enclave on Russian soil. The Estonian and Latvian republics had the highest industrial output per head of population of all the Soviet republics, and most available indicators of economic and cultural achievements and medical services placed their people at or near the top of the list. This does not, however, prove that they were content; rather, the indications were that the presence in their cities of great numbers of Russians,[17] and the dominant role in political life played by a small number of Estonians and Latvians who had grown up in Soviet Russia as communist exiles and whose first loyalty was to the Russians, were sources of irritation. The best defense against this situation seemed to be to live separate lives of their own, associate only with fellow Estonians or fellow Latvians, ignore the Russians, and even pretend not to understand Russian. Sometimes this passive hostility gave way to active protest, as in the case of the Letter of Seventeen Latvian Communists protesting against Russification in Latvia, which became known in the West in January 1972.

The Lithuanians, though speaking a language similar to Latvian, had a different historical background from their two northern neighbors. They were Catholics, not Protestants; their cultural traditions followed the Polish, not the Scandinavian model; their social structure was predominantly rural; their natural rate of increase was higher, and their population younger. Another peculiar feature of the Lithuanians was that a very large proportion of their people had emigrated at the beginning of the century, so that in 1970 there were 2.6 million Lithuanians in the Soviet Union but about 2 million persons of recent Lithuanian origin abroad, of whom 1.6 million were in the United States. The knowledge of the existence of this diaspora was important for educated Lithuanians, and

---

17. Russians formed 25 percent of the population in Estonia and 30 percent in Latvia. Only 41 percent of the population of Latvia's capital city of Riga in 1970 were Latvians.

the direct influence of diaspora opinion, though obviously not quantifiable, was probably important. In the first years after 1945 there was armed resistance in Lithuania against the Soviet regime. In the following decades the mutual hostility between the Catholic church and the communist party strengthened national consciousness and opposition to Russification. When several priests were arrested in 1970, a spate of letters of protest to the authorities occurred. In January 1972 a petition with seventeeen thousand signatures was sent to the United Nations secretary-general. On 14 May 1972 a Lithuanian student publicly set fire to himself, and this was followed by street demonstrations of several thousands in Kaunas at his funeral four days later and on the day after.

The Armenians and Georgians

At the other end of the Soviet Union the Georgians and Armenians, peoples with a Christian culture half a millennium older than that of the Russians, were more successful in preserving their national identity. Not only did they live a collective life of their own, but they were able, unlike the Baltic nations, to keep the numbers of Russians in their midst very small. The Soviet government in the 1960s in effect tolerated this state of affairs, perhaps because it was confident that communist-party rule would not be affected if the local parties were run by indigenous people and perhaps also because it knew that both nations, surrounded by Muslim nations that were traditional enemies and themselves mutually antipathetic, were unlikely to wish to break away from the Soviet Union. They even reckoned that if the Armenians were well treated, the Armenian diaspora abroad might be expected to support Soviet policies.[18]

The Georgians played an ambivalent part in Soviet political life. Stalin had his own Georgians whom he used for his own purposes, while treating Georgia with his customary brutality; it is even arguable that his Georgian origin caused him to overcompensate through excessively Russifying attitudes—a phenomenon rather common among members of small nations who become assimilated into a bigger nation.[19] During Beria's direct or indirect control of the security-police apparatus (1939–1953), Georgian security policemen were to be found in key positions in other republics. When Stalin was denounced by Khrushchev, even those Georgians who had suffered from his tyranny felt affronted by the

---

18. Two diasporas should be distinguished. In 1970 there were 2,204,000 Armenians in the Armenian SSR, 1,049,000 in other Soviet republics, and about 1,700,000 in other countries. This last group is the diaspora abroad. About 400,000 of its members lived in the United States, and another 500,000 in states of Arabic speech much courted by Soviet policy.

19. Other examples of this phenomenon are the numerous persons with Polish, Czech, or Slovene names to be found among German or Austrian Nazis.

insult to the memory of an outstanding Georgian. In the following years there were periodic purges in the Georgian party leadership, but these appeared to have been caused not so much by any national resistance to Russian domination as by the exposure of corruption scandals and by infighting between rival party cliques. This appears to have been the reason for the replacement in September 1972 of the party's first secretary Vasilii Mzhavanadze by the security policeman Edward Shevardnadze.

The Central Asian Nations

The people of the four central Asian Muslim republics have been profoundly affected by sixty years of Soviet rule. They have experienced great economic and cultural progress—though it is arguable that this has benefited the Russian minorities living among them more than the Asians. Their Muslim religion and culture have been subject to various forms of discouragement, discrimination, insulting propaganda, and, at times, active persecution, but they appeared in the 1970s to be still very strong. With regard to national consciousness, the policy of the Soviet government from the late 1920s onward was to combat two perceived dangers, Pan-Islamism and Pan-Turkism.[20] In order to destroy the idea that there was such a thing as one Turkistani nation, united by one Chagatay Turkic language, the Soviet rulers set themselves to create several distinct written Turkic languages, and to base on them several distinct Turkic nations, of which the most important were the Uzbeks, Kazakhs, Turkmen, and Kirghiz. They also set themselves to separate the Iranian people of Soviet central Asia from those of Iran or Afghanistan by creating a Tadjik language distinct from Persian, and a Tadjik nation. By manipulating vocabularies, writing these languages in the Russian Cyrillic script, and importing Russian words, they hoped to break up the cultural unity of the Turkic and Iranian peoples.

In this they were rather successful, but the operation boomeranged: instead of causing each new nation to dislike its Muslim neighbors, it created in each a national consciousness that was directed against the Russians. This became steadily more visible in the 1960s and 1970s. Instead of gratefully bowing before their Russian benefactors who had brought them economic and cultural progress, they tended to argue that the progress was due to their own hard work and skill, and would have been greater if they had not had the Russians breathing down their necks. It seemed that they accepted the system known in the USSR as

---

20. Pan-Islamism was the movement to unite all Muslims all over the world; in modern times it has never been very effective. Pan-Turkism was the movement to unite all peoples speaking a language of the Turkic group; it has also not been very effective, though it had some following in the first two decades of this century.

"socialism," because they had known no other, but that their aim was "socialism without Russians." Meanwhile the much more rapid growth of their populations gave them added confidence, and also increased their resentment of the Russian colonists in their midst.

This was equally true of the Kazakhs, a people who spoke a Turkic language but were not strictly a central Asian people, since they inhabited the steppe lands lying to the north. The Kazakhs had suffered terrible losses during the 1930s,[21] had experienced a new wave of Russian settlement as a result of Khrushchev's "virgin lands" plan for agriculture, and in 1970 formed only 32.6 percent of the population of "their own" republic, though their numbers were increasing very rapidly indeed.

In the mid-1970s the central Asian peoples were aware that they were dominated by Russians, both by the central government in Moscow and by the Russians in their midst. There was a general pattern to which there were few exceptions: the top positions in the party and state apparatus were held by Asians (premiers, most ministers, first secretaries of the party at republican and provincial—*oblast*—level), but there were Russians in the posts immediately below (deputy premiers, high officials in the ministries, second secretaries of republics and *oblasti*), and it was widely believed that it was these Russians who acted as the real executants of central-government orders. Relations between Russians and Asians in their places of work were usually smooth, but each went back at the end of the day to his family, his culture, and his quarter of the city. Social intercourse between the two cultures was sparse and intermarriage very rare— especially between an Asian girl and a Russian man.[22] It was peaceful segregation, but still segregation.

The overall situation was that of an empire and its colonies. The intentions of the rulers of the empire might have been benevolent, and the material achievements impressive, but the same could be said of most modern colonial empires. Unfortunately the perspective of modern Western liberals has been distorted by decades of Soviet boastfulness and anti-imperialist demonology. Soviet propaganda has created a grotesque dreamworld of blissful brotherhood among socialist nations: judged by this standard, Soviet reality is shameful and oppressive. The word "colonialism" has become accepted not only by all communists and

---

21. Between the censuses of 1926 and 1939, if the natural rate of increase of previous years had continued, there should have been an increase of 600,000; instead there was a decrease of 869,000. About 1.5 million Kazakhs, a number equal to half the total Kazakh population recorded in 1939, had perished or failed to be born. This was a result of starvation through loss of about three-quarters of the livestock of these pastoral peoples in the collectivization of agriculture and "settlement of nomads."

22. It is possible that there are more mixed marriages outside the central Asian republics. An Asian working permanently in Moscow or Kiev might marry a Russian or a Ukrainian; such a person would be lost to his or her culture and nation.

by African nationalists, but also by millions of educated liberal-minded Europeans and Americans as denoting a hideous hell of exploitation and cruelty; judged by this imaginary standard, the Soviet reality is idyllic. But colonial empires were not like that (though cruelty and exploitation sometimes resulted from their policies, as from the policies of virtually every government known to history), nor was the Soviet regime ever like what the rhetoric of its admirers suggested. The Soviet colonial empire was in many respects benevolent, but it was still an empire.

Unfortunately for the Soviet rulers, as for the rulers of the empires that have disappeared, the twentieth century is not a period in which colonial empires are popular. Just because the non-Russian peoples of the USSR are becoming more skilled and better educated every day, they are becoming less content to be colonial peoples. The Law of Colonial Ingratitude is making itself felt in the Soviet empire. It is difficult to see why if the Zaireans or Zimbabweans are entitled to independence, the Uzbeks or Estonians or Ukrainians should not be. Soviet central Asians have become aware of the achievements of Turkey and Iran, in which at last in the 1970s, after decades of stumbling and errors, real progress on a massive scale is at hand. They have also become aware of China. Turkic peoples might have no more wish to live under Chinese than Russian rule, and there has been little reason to suppose that the Chinese wish to rule them; but it seems unlikely in the long term that the central Asians will not find ways to exploit the Sino-Soviet conflict to promote their national independence.

—5—

Communists in Power in Eastern Europe

Soviet Neocolonialism

The Soviet empire was not confined to the republics of the USSR. The conquests of 1945 enabled the Soviet rulers to establish their domination over a hundred million Europeans—a domination much more comprehensive than that once exercised by Western "capitalist" empires over "semicolonial" lands like the old China and Turkey. Eastern Europe became an area of indirect rule, or of Soviet neocolonialism.

In one country only—Finland—the Soviet rulers were content to limit themselves to an old-style "sphere of influence"; they made a treaty of alliance that gave them a veto over Finland's foreign policy, but left the Finns to rule themselves as they pleased. In six other states (Eastern Germany, Poland, Czechoslovakia, Hungary, Romania, and Bulgaria) they imposed a form of government closely modeled on their own, including the same type of economic planning and the same type of party purges. In Stalin's lifetime everything was directly controlled from Moscow, largely through Soviet "advisers" attached to various ministries in the subject states. The purpose was to exploit their economic resources, and their military and civilian manpower, for the purposes of the Soviet state. Direct domination extended also to the cultural field: national histories had to be rewritten and falsified, as those of the non-Russian peoples of the USSR had been rewritten and falsified, for the greater glory not only of the CPSU and the great Stalin but also of the great Russian nation, from the time of Peter the Great or earlier.

After Stalin's death these controls were substantially loosened. The communist party leaders were given some freedom of maneuver for the management of their parties, though the general lines were laid down in Moscow. At first Moscow favored greater freedom of opinion, but when this led to a dangerous trend toward independence in Poland, and to a violent revolution in Hungary (both in 1956), the reins were again drawn tighter. In the early 1960s the conflict between the Soviet Union and China, and the need of Brezhnev and his colleagues for a support from their East European comrades whom they could no longer simply command, led to a further strengthening of the sovereignty of the individual communist regimes. Nevertheless the essentially colonial dependency of these regimes on Moscow remained.

It will be convenient briefly to examine the trends of the 1960s and 1970s in each country, noting the considerable variety among them. A few words are also needed on the two states ruled by communists that escaped from Soviet domination—Yugoslavia and Albania.

Romania

Romania was the country in which in the 1950s the process of destruction of national culture went furthest; the national hatred of Romanians against Russians was second only to that of Poles.

The whole process of Romanian national revival in the nineteenth and early twentieth centuries had been based on the myth of Romanian Latinity. Like all myths, this had large elements of truth in it: the Romanian language was Latin in its basic structure, and the Latin words in its vocabulary were more numerous than the Slav words. In addition, both the diplomacy and the cultural influence of the Latin Western powers France and Italy had greatly contributed to the emergence of an independent Romania, and French and Italian military efforts had helped to bring about the union of Romanians in 1918. In the 1950s the Soviet rulers forced the Romanian communists not only to break off cultural relations with France and Italy, but also to rewrite Romanian history and to remold the Romanian language. The aim was not merely to extol communism and the Soviet regime, but also to show that Romanian culture was mainly Slav, and that the chief historical benefactor of the Romanians had been ''the great Russian people.'' Russian was also given first place among the foreign languages taught in Romanian schools.

The results were profoundly counterproductive. Romanian children learned very little Russian and quickly forgot it, while many of them learned French from their parents and their friends. The new myth of Slav culture was universally rejected, and the old myth of Latinity actually reinforced, even in comparison with precommunist times. In 1963 conflict between the Romanian and Soviet communist leaderships was brought about by economic causes: the Romanians bitterly opposed a plan for economic specialization within the ''socialist camp'' that (whatever its merits in economic theory) would have frustrated the Romanian communist plans for large-scale and diversified (even if economically less rational) industrialization. They were able to resist Soviet pressure because the Soviet leaders were preoccupied with their quarrel with the Chinese communists, with whom the Romanians succeeded in maintaining independent contacts. Once the conflict had broken out for economic reasons, it developed cultural and political aspects, which were tolerated by the government. Writers and literary critics busily re-Latinized the language, and historians rectified the re-writing of history. There were even occasional public mentions of the Bessarabian question. In the Moldavian SSR, as this territory—divested of the regions of Ukrainian population at its northern and southern extremities—was called, the Soviet authorities had fostered the myths of a separate Moldavian nation and Moldavian language. These absurd historical distortions[1] infuriated all thinking Romanians, and suitable quotations were found from Karl Marx to show that he had considered Bessarabia a victim of the Russian tsars.

The outlets given by the communist leaders, first Gheorghe Gheorghiu-Dej and then his successor Nicolae Ceauşescu, to Romanian national feeling made the government comparatively popular for a good many years. Romania's foreign policy diverged from time to time in not unimportant details from that of the USSR. In 1968 Ceauşescu came out very strongly against the Soviet invasion of Czechoslovakia, and for a time there appeared to be a danger of war. In the following years tension was reduced, and the popularity of the government diminished, though it still remained far greater than any of its immediate predecessors had enjoyed. The internal political regime remained very strict, though there was much more freedom in nonpolitical and cultural matters, which made life more endurable to intellectuals. On the other hand the growing "cult of personality" of Ceauşescu aroused a good deal of derision from Romanians, whose nation was one of the most irreverent in Europe. The economy continued to be badly mismanaged, probably more so than the economies of any neighboring "socialist states." However, despite an undoubtedly more polite tone on both sides, Soviet-Romanian relations continued to be fragile, and knowledge of this fact tended to rally Romanians, whether communist or not, behind Ceauşescu.

Bulgaria

The Bulgarian communist leaders continued throughout the 1960s and 1970s to behave as faithful satellites: theirs was the only East European country in which there was no major overt challenge to Soviet hegemony. After the purge trial of 1949, the only mild disturbance to the smooth surface of Bulgarian po-

---

1. Bessarabia is simply the eastern half of historic Moldavia. It was annexed from the Ottoman to the Russian Empire in 1812; half was ceded to independent Romania in 1856 but taken back in 1878; the whole was united with Romania in 1918. It was reannexed to Soviet Russia with Hitler's blessing in 1940; reannexed by Romania, also with Hitler's blessing, in 1941; and recovered by the Soviet army in 1944. The Moldavians had the same written language as their southern neighbors from the early nineteenth century, and indeed earlier; differences between spoken dialects were small. Romanian was the common language and common national identity.

litical life was an unsuccessful military plot in 1965, in which officers and party officials were involved but whose real purpose and scope remained obscure. Bulgarian communists liked to recall in their speeches the profound gratitude of the Bulgarians to the great Russian people, whose armies had twice liberated them within seventy years; Soviet leaders liked to bask in this warm glow of gratitude, and Soviet historians to see to it that their Bulgarian colleagues were generous with their ritual kowtows. This outward picture suggested that the Bulgarians were just waiting for the day when their country would be made into the West Black Sea *guberniya* of the Soviet empire.

A foreign observer might perhaps be allowed to preserve a little skepticism. The Bulgarian people's gratitude after the first liberation (of 1878) was not very profound or very lasting. After the second liberation, and the installation of the communists as rulers, the latter did rather well for themselves. In particular, the recalcitrance of the Romanians in 1963 enabled the Bulgarian government to extract large-scale Soviet aid for its industrial projects. Bulgaria, like Cuba, was subsidized in a big way. The Bulgarian workers and peasants, more efficient and industrious than the Cubans, made better use of the aid. Education and culture also greatly advanced, and if the Bulgarian intellectuals who began to appear in Western countries from the late 1960s onward were at all typical, it was by no means evident that educated Bulgarians were enamored of the superior culture of the great Russian people or contemptuous of Western ways of life.

Even the briefest discussion of Bulgaria must note its geographical position, as the nearest to the Mediterranean of the "socialist states," surrounded by three states that are independent of Soviet control: Yugoslavia, Greece, and Turkey. Most Bulgarians, whether communists or not, believed that Macedonian Slavs were Bulgarians, that the official doctrine of Tito's Yugoslavia that there was a distinct Macedonian nation was untrue, and that Macedonia should be united with Bulgaria. Relations between the Bulgarian and Yugoslav governments, and the press polemics between Sofia and Belgrade, or between Sofia and Skopye (the capital of the Macedonian republic), fluctuated during the postwar decades. When the polemics became intense, one was inclined to assume that Moscow was encouraging Sofia to attack Belgrade for its own reasons; but the possibility of a Bulgarian lobby influencing Soviet policy also should not be ignored. As for Greece and Turkey, their mutual hostility in connection with Cyprus and with oil prospecting in the Aegean enabled Soviet policy to exploit anti-Western reactions in both, and Bulgaria was an important instrument in this diplomatic game. However, this made it necessary to favor a friendlier attitude by the Bulgarian government toward its two southern neighbors, which in turn involved a risk that Western cultural influences might contaminate Bulgaria. If, from a Western point of view, rapprochement between Bulgaria and Greece or Turkey looked like a maneuver to undermine NATO in the eastern Mediterranean, from a Bulgarian point of view it looked like an opportunity for ampler contacts with

Western culture, which seemed desirable to Bulgarian intellectuals but suspect to the Bulgarian, and still more to the Soviet, leaders.[2]

The essence of this argument is that in Bulgaria things have not necessarily been what they have seemed; Bulgarians have an almost inborn capacity, after centuries of Ottoman rule, to conceal their thoughts; it would be unwise to write off Bulgaria as forever a Soviet satrapy.

East Germany

Second only to Bulgaria in its devotion to the Soviet Union was the government at the other end of the bloc, the East German.

One obvious difference separated the German Democratic Republic from all the other "socialist states." Whereas the others included virtually the whole of their respective nations within their boundaries, or at most had minorities from their nation ruled by other communist governments,[3] the Germans were divided between the Soviet bloc and the West, and three-quarters of them were in the West.

In the first postwar years most East Germans probably both hoped and believed that they would be united with their kinsmen under a Western democratic form of government. The outburst of revolt by the East German workers in June 1953, and its suppression, dimmed this hope. The building of the Berlin Wall in 1961 destroyed the hope, at least for any foreseeable period.

The final enclosure of the East Germans behind the former zonal boundary was followed by major efforts to get the economy going, and the population soon responded vigorously. In the mid-1970s East Germany had become one of the leading industrial states of the world, and both output and income per head were the highest in the "socialist camp." This achievement was a source of understandable pride to the people of East Germany. A certain puritanical sense of superiority over the West Germans, those privileged cosseted inhabitants of *Wirtschaftswunderland,* with its permissive society, became fairly widespread, even among people who were far from being communists. However, it is very doubtful whether these emotions outweighed, in the minds of most East

---

2. There is some inevitable confusion here. Disappointment with American attitudes toward the Cyprus crisis of 1974 made both the Greeks and the Turks react against the West and against NATO; but in both countries Western cultural influences—political democracy, modern trends in literature, culture and life-style—were completely dominant. It was these things Bulgarian intellectuals sought, as forbidden fruit.

3. For example, the Hungarians in the Romanian, Yugoslav, and Czechoslovak states. There were a few small minorities of Soviet bloc or of Yugoslav peoples in Western states, such as Macedonians in Greece or Croats in Austria, but they form an insignificant exception to my statement.

Germans, the sense of belonging to a single German nation, artificially divided by the superior force of foreigners.

It remained official doctrine in the Federal Republic of Germany (FRG) that there was a single German nation in two states, but the East Germans denied this. In a press conference on 19 January 1970 Walter Ulbricht spoke of the German Democratic Republic as "a socialist German national state," whereas the FRG was "a capitalist NATO state . . . with limited national sovereignty."[4] This corresponded to the views being elaborated at this time by Soviet ideological experts on "the national question," to the effect that "socialist nations" can have no community on a national basis with "bourgeois nations." However, the amendment to the German constitution enacted on 27 September 1974 removed all references to a German nation. It stated that the GDR was "a socialist state of workers and farmers," that it was "linked irrevocably and for ever with the Soviet Union," and was "an inseparable part of the socialist community of states." East German communists appeared to be seeking compensation for their lost German nationality in emphasizing a higher international level of loyalty to the "socialist camp." Paradoxically one may argue that fanatical subservience to the Soviet concept of "proletarian internationalism" was a kind of *Ersatz* patriotism. It is even arguable that there was some analogy between this attitude of the leaders of the GDR in the 1970s and the enthusiasm for "the European idea" that spread among leaders and people of the FRG in the 1950s, when it was a means of finding a collective loyalty untainted by the memory of Hitlerism.[5] Whether it had much real popular appeal is more doubtful.

There was, however, another potential basis of loyalty, of which very little was heard in the 1970s. This was the aim of a future single German nation, united under "socialism." The GDR was not intended by German communists to remain forever a rump state. There was little prospect of unification under communist-party rule in the mid-1970s, but this did not mean that the idea was abandoned. The FRG looked less likely than any other West European state to disintegrate, West German communism was weak, and the American commitment to Western Europe was still taken seriously. However, these things could change. It is, of course, obvious that a united communist Germany would be most objectionable to Western noncommunists, but it is also questionable what would be the Soviet attitude to it. Clearly it would increase the total strength of communism in the world; and indeed ever since the foundation of the Comintern in 1919 a communist Germany was the main aim and the long-term expectation of the best communists, Lenin included. However, even though a united Germany would have little more than a third of the population of the Soviet Union,

---

4. Quoted in Melvin Croan, *East Germany: The Soviet Connection,* Washington Papers no. 36, 1976, p. 25.

5. This point is forcibly argued by Croan in *East Germany,* pp. 41–42.

its level of efficiency would be so immensely greater that it might grow into a formidable competitor. Devotion to "proletarian internationalism" in the minds of comrades in the GDR was by no means incompatible with deep-rooted contempt for Russians, and indeed long-suppressed resentment against, or hatred of, them.

Meanwhile the best policy for GDR leaders was to seek, within the framework of the Soviet bloc, a "special relationship" with the Soviet Union. This was Ulbricht's line, and he reached his greatest success with the invasion of Czechoslovakia. After 1968 a "normalized" Czechoslovakia could be patronized by Ulbricht, but Poland was less easy to handle, even though Ulbricht and Gomułka had shared a common hatred for Dubček. Ulbricht fell when the Soviet government, for its own economic reasons, decided to improve relations with Bonn. He was replaced in May 1971 by Erich Honecker, who was obliged to make the Basic Treaty with the FRG, which was finally ratified in June 1973. This could, however, only be a temporary stage in an evolving and unpredictable political situation. Within the GDR, economic prosperity and hard-line political dictatorship coincided, and the tasks of the Soviet rulers, who had to coordinate their relations with three unmanageable and intractable units—the GDR, the FRG, and Poland—were not simple.

Czechoslovakia

In Czechoslovakia, people over forty years old were still aware, in the late 1960s, of a historical experience that differed in two important respects, both relevant to the subject of this book, from that of any of the other communist-ruled countries. The Czech people had a long experience of freedom of opinion and the rule of law, and in Czech political life a strong social-democratic party had played a leading part.[6] It was for this very reason that the purge of the communist party between 1949 and 1952 had been most severe in Czechoslovakia: the directors in Moscow of the puppet show in Prague had considered it especially important to destroy social-democratic vestiges, as a good dentist takes pains to remove every particle of decay from the roots of a tooth on which he is to build a new structure capable of bearing strain.

The country in which the nearest approach to this historical heritage existed was Hungary, though the rule of law and the influence of social democracy had

---

6. It could be argued that the Czech tradition of freedom of thought goes back to Hussite times (with the obvious modification that the authorities in those times did their best to repress it). The rule of law derives at least from the mid-eighteenth century, and is a legacy of the Habsburgs. So is social democracy. Democratic institutions, in the sense of responsible parliamentary government, were achieved only in the Republic of 1918, in which they struck deeper and more healthy roots than in any neighboring countries.

never been very strong outside the capital city of Budapest.[7] In Hungary, too, the Moscow producers had insisted on an unusually drastic purge, though it did not last as long or affect so many categories of persons as the purge in Czechoslovakia.[8] In Hungary pressures from within the party, encouraged for a time by the post-Stalin "liberalism" of Malenkov and then of Khrushchev, led to a public rehabilitation of purge victims, and this played its part in sparking off the revolution of October 1956. This fact was almost certainly used by the leaders of the Czechoslovak party as an argument against the rehabilitations that Moscow apparently favored in the early 1960s. Whatever the cause, Czechoslovakia remained for ten years after the events of 1956 the most "conservative" or unreformed of the communist-ruled East European states, with the possible exception of Bulgaria.

In the late 1960s pressures within the party grew too strong to be ignored. Perhaps the most important were economic. The economy of industrial Bohemia and Moravia, the most efficient and most complex of the whole communist-ruled area except Eastern Germany, could be less and less easily fitted into the Moscow-type straitjacket of centralized doctrinaire planning. Managers and economists joined in calling for reforms that were designed to give individual firms initiative in buying, selling, and pricing. These demands were also associated with the different demand (which was in potential future contradiction with them) for the participation of workers in the management. The man who emerged as the chief spokesman for economic reform was the director of the Institute of Economics, Ota Šik. His proposals were received with kind words by the party leaders, but as time passed and nothing was done, he and other economists

---

7. The ingenuity of Hungarian officials in bending the law and inflicting repeated pinprick penalties and disabilities on their opponents was developed to a fine art in the age of parliamentary government from 1867 to 1918; both then and in the interwar residual Hungarian state the small peasants and agricultural laborers received little, if any, protection from the law.

8. A superficial but probably instructive impression of the relative severity of the purges of the late 1940s and early 1950s may be obtained from the figures showing the percentage of members of each party's Central Committee before the purge who had disappeared from public life (not necessarily from this world) by the time of the first postpurge congress. These were: 55 percent in Czechoslovakia, 50 percent in Hungary, 29 percent in Bulgaria, 22 percent in Poland, and 20 percent in Romania. I have discussed this subject at greater length in an article in the *Annals of the American Academy of Political and Social Science*, May, 1958, which was reprinted in my collection of essays entitled *Nationalism and Communism*, (London, 1964). Some readers may feel that what I have said about the element of similarity between the Czech and Hungarian heritages might also be said of the Polish. My reply would be that though this is true of the medieval and early modern periods, it is hardly true of the post-Partition era. The greater part of Poland came under Russian rule, and in imperial Russia there was not much to be seen either of freedom or of the rule of law. It is true that social democracy was a powerful force among the Poles, but this was very largely a nationalist movement (owing to circumstances for which the Poles were not responsible), whereas in the Czech lands and in Budapest it was essentially a social movement, based on the class demands of the working class, formulated—as almost everywhere in Europe—by the section of the intellectual elite that espoused its cause.

found themselves driven to the conclusion that nothing could be achieved without political reform, without changes in the operation of political power through the party.

A second force pressing on the leadership was Slovak national feeling. Though the communists had come forward in 1945 as champions of Slovak national identity—in contrast to the fictitious "Czechoslovakism" of the interwar years[9]—once they had achieved power they made nonsense of the self-government nominally granted to Slovakia. It is probably true that the ruthless centralism of the Prague government in the 1950s and 1960s was exercised on behalf not of Czech nationalism, but of Moscow-type totalitarianism—which had its Slovak no less than its Czech servants—yet at the receiving end there seemed little difference, and "anti-Czech" Slovak nationalism grew.

The third pressure came from the intellectuals, both Czech and Slovak, especially from those who were members of the party and thus able to some extent to express their discontent. What they demanded was literary and artistic freedom, the right to tell the truth about their culture and their history, the removal of the suffocating blanket of official lies, and above all the rehabilitation of the victims of the past decades, both communists and others. Some concessions were made. Victims were released quietly, and official inquiries were made into the judicial murders of the 1950s, but the results were not published. Historians were allowed to write the truth about the recent past, and novelists were given more liberty by the censors.[10] But this was not enough for the Czechs, a dour obstinate people for whom the motto "Truth will prevail" was more than an empty slogan.[11] At the Fourth Congress of the official Union of Czechoslovak Writers in June 1967 there was an open clash with the party's chief spokesman, and the whole editorial board of the union's periodical was dismissed. Discon-

---

9. Many, probably most, Slovaks desired to live together with the Czechs in one state between the wars. But the official "Czechoslovakism" that was prevalent among Czech politicians and officials in those years was not content with this. These people would not admit that there were two nations, Czechs and Slovaks. They believed in a single "Czechoslovak nation," and their idea of it was to transform the Slovaks, whom they considered simply as "backward Czechs," into modern Czechs.

10. This is seen especially in the treatment of T. G. Masaryk, founder of the republic in 1918 and president from then until 1935. In the course of a very long and intellectually and politically fruitful life, Masaryk spent six months in Russia in 1917. During this period he, and the Czech deserters from the Austrian army who were fighting on the Russian and Allied side, fell foul of the Bolsheviks. This is the only fact about Masaryk that mattered to the Soviet conquerors; once the communists had seized power in 1948, they had to expunge his name from the history of the Czechs and Slovaks as taught in the schools. In the late 1960s, however, Novotný removed this veto, and several good books were written by Czech and Slovak historians that put Masaryk in historical perspective.

11. The Republic's motto *Pravda zvítězí* is an abbreviation of the medieval Latin *Magna est veritas et prevalebit.*

tent was also acute among students, and this welled up in a demonstration on 31 October 1967 that was brutally repressed by the police.

The first crisis came (as in Poland and Hungary in 1956) in the form of hostility within the party to its leader. Antonin Novotný, who had been first secretary since September 1953 and president of the republic since November 1957, had become a symbol of all that was most hated—though it is only fair to him to say that in his last years his regime was much milder. The crisis was resolved on 3 January 1968, when he resigned his party office and was succeeded by a compromise candidate between reformers and "conservatives," a little-known Slovak named Alexander Dubček. On 21 March Novotný also resigned from the presidency.

In the next months events moved fast. At the plenary session of the Central Committee of the party, held in the first days of April, only three members of the precrisis Presidium (Politburo) of the party remained, one of whom was Dubček, and the party's Secretariat was almost completely new. On 10 April it published an Action Program that embodied most of the demands made by the critics of the past several months. At the end of April, elections were held to the party's regional committees, at which almost all the former first secretaries were replaced by new people. Party members clamored for the convocation of an extraordinary congress of the party to reconsider policy and organization; at the next plenary session of the Central Committee (31 May to 7 June) this was conceded, and the date of 9 September agreed on. In Slovakia greater emphasis was placed on the demand for a new federal constitution placing Slovakia on a level of equality with the Czech lands than for measures of political liberalization, but the latter also received support. Press censorship virtually disappeared throughout the country by the end of March. At the end of June a rehabilitation law was passed by the National Assembly with the full support of the communist party leadership. It provided legal procedures for the compensation of victims and for inquiry into illegalities and the dismissal of officials responsible for them.

All this was understandably viewed with alarm by the communist parties of neighboring countries, especially those of the Soviet empire. On 23 March a conference of their leaders was held in Dresden, which Dubček attended. Strong criticisms were made of the Czechoslovak communists' new policy, but the public tone was still restrained. During the summer it grew much fiercer, and the possibility of action against Czechoslovakia by her allies began to be taken seriously both at home and abroad.

Dubček and his colleagues were determined to minimize the offense to the Soviet leaders. They were at pains to avoid the errors committed by Imre Nagy in Hungary in 1956. These they took to be the renunciation of the alliance with the Soviet Union in favor of neutrality, and the restoration of multiparty rule in place of a communist-party political monopoly.

Unlike Hungarians, Poles, and Romanians, the Czechs and Slovaks had no traditional hostility to Russians; on the contrary, they regarded them as their natural protectors. The alliance with the Soviet empire was genuinely popular among both peoples, both in itself and because it provided a defense against any future revival of German power, and against any desire that Germans might one day have to revenge themselves for the cruelties inflicted by the Czechs on innocent Germans in 1945—which were, of course, acts of revenge for the cruelties inflicted by the Germans on innocent Czechs between 1938 and 1945. Dubček spoke for both Czechs and Slovaks when he insisted that Czechoslovakia intended to remain faithful to her alliance with Moscow, and to remain in the "socialist camp."

In Czechoslovakia under Novotný parties other than the communists existed, but they were fictitious: their policies and their leadership were determined not by their members but by the communist leaders. In the spring of 1968 there were some signs that a few members of these parties wished to breathe new life into them, and their official newspapers began to write outspokenly, but this was true of the whole press after March. It is also true that a new organization had come into being, the Club of Committed Non-party Persons (KAN). However, this was not intended to be a political party, a rival to the communist party, but an organization designed to rally persons of no party in support of the new policies. There were perhaps some indications that it would throw up new leaders who might be future competitors, but this was no more than a hypothesis for the future, as was the revival of the permitted parties. New parties were not permitted, and the request to revive a social-democratic party was refused.

Dubček and his colleagues, who firmly insisted on their loyal foreign policy and on the "leading role of the communist party," did, in fact, avoid the two main known errors of Imre Nagy. Unfortunately they were guilty of two other errors, which were equally alarming and unforgivable in the eyes of the Soviet rulers.

The first was that they were allowing democracy of the Western, or "bourgeois," type to operate within the communist party. Party members were being allowed to choose their leaders and to propose and carry through their policies. This looked to the Soviet leaders like sheer Menshevism. The communist party was turning itself into a social-democratic party. The political original sin of the Czech comrades was manifesting itself. If this were tolerated, ghastly effects could be expected in the communist parties of both Western and Eastern Europe, and even the CPSU was perhaps not entirely proof against infection.

The second "error" was that the demand for punishment of the judicial murderers of the 1950s was being tolerated. For the Soviet rulers, the implications were too ghastly to contemplate. Brezhnev and Kosygin personally, not to mention thousands of lesser luminaries, owed their careers to their skill in getting in their denunciations of their colleagues and friends before the latter had denounced them, in the great purge of 1936–1939 in the Soviet empire; in comparison with that purge what had happened in Czechoslovakia was as a children's school treat. Khrushchev's speech of 1956, which had for a short time lifted a corner of the blanket, had shown a little of the nightmare that would be upon them if the full truth about the victims were revealed; and even Khrushchev had never suggested, as the demented Czech comrades were now suggesting, that the *guilty should be punished.*

A further point was that these dreadful things were happening in a western outpost of the "socialist camp," reaching into the heart of Germany. How much this worried the Soviet leaders, one may speculate: knowing, as they did, how insignificant was free Germany's power, and how determined the rulers of the United States were to avoid any unpleasantness, one may doubt whether they had much fear. What is sure is that the rulers of East Germany and Poland were intensely worried. It was clear that Dubček and his team neither felt, nor had any reason to feel, hatred for West Germany, and that the Bonn government would soon establish friendly relations with them. This prospect was bound to distress Ulbricht beyond endurance; for Gomułka, whose increasingly detested regime could only rally a residual minimum of support from Poles by ever more frantic hate propaganda against Germany, the specter of good relations between Bonn and Prague was even less endurable. There is no doubt that both satraps urged their Moscow patrons to act, though it is probable that the latter made up their own minds independently.

The invasion of Czechoslovakia by half a million troops from the "socialist camp," including the touching sight of Polish soldiers marching *Schulter an Schulter* with both Russians and Prussians, provoked another unexpected spectacle: the united passive resistance of two nations, in uniform or in civilian clothes. Most extraordinary of all was the communist party congress which was held illegally in a Prague factory while the city was patrolled by the armed forces of several communist-ruled countries. Moving though this sight was, the resistance could not last long, nor could the personal heroism of the arrested Czech and Slovak communist leaders prevail against the stolid militarism of the Soviet imperial proconsuls or the studied indifference of the spokesmen of the "free world." Repression was introduced by slow stages, but in less than a year personal victimization and refalsification of history were such as to bring nostalgia for the good old times of Novotný.

The effect on the communist cause in the wider world is a matter for argument. In West European communist parties the invasion was ill received, and even the leaders condemned it, some in more convincing terms than others. This condemnation may have made the parties more popular, in which case one could argue that by invading Czechoslovakia the Soviet leaders *strengthened* their position in Western Europe—though the contrary remains the widespread opinion among political commentators. The Yugoslav, Romanian, Chinese, and Albanian communist leaders denounced the action with obvious conviction; Castro with equal conviction approved it. To Arab and African nationalists, the spectacle of European armies invading another European country, and of a people whose sympathies tended toward the Western type of democracy being crushed, was more likely to bring pleasure than distress.

One change was wrought by the action: Czechs and Slovaks seemed to be cured of the sentimental affection for the distant and little-known Russians that had inspired them for two centuries. Though repression continued, and efforts were made at the same time to improve living standards, neither threats nor bribes prevented Czechs and Slovaks from thinking their own thoughts. Their continued devotion to liberty was dramatically revealed by the emergence of the "Charter 1977" action: hundreds of Czech intellectuals and workers signed a statement on the suppression of liberty intended for the Belgrade conference of June 1977, whose task was to check the fulfillment of the obligations accepted by the governments that had signed the Helsinki agreement of 1975.

Hungary

The East European country of which there was least to say in this period was Hungary. By 1966, ten years after the revolution he had betrayed, János Kádár had established his new regime, based on the slogans of "a state of the whole people" and "who is not against us, is with us"—a regime milder, more tolerant of nonpolitical varieties of opinion, than any other in the region; in 1977 he was still set on this course.

The main achievement was the introduction, from the beginning of 1968, of what was known as the New Economic Mechanism. Central control over enterprises was reduced, managers were given much wider choices, and taxation was to be based not on the fulfillment of centrally determined plan targets but on the profits achieved. Some prices continued to be fixed centrally, others were allowed to range between centrally fixed limits, and others were left free to fluctuate. The policy was, in fact, a milder version of that which Šik had recommended in Czechoslovakia. For this reason the events in Czechoslovakia worried and distressed the Hungarian leaders, whose support of Soviet policy was based on the assumption that complete political acquiescence was the necessary price for their own limited progress. The economic policy was rather successful. Productivity in industry and in construction, and real income per head, rose with some fluctuations from 1968 through 1975, and both inflation and unemployment were kept fairly well under control. The policy attracted criticism, however. It inevitably brought greater inequality in real incomes, which was resented by large numbers of workers and was exploitable by the "conservative" section of the communist party. It also came under attack from the Soviet Union, where similarities to the earlier trends in Czechoslovakia were detected and the increasing trade with "capitalist" states was viewed with suspicion. Concessions were made by slowing the progress of reform, and by demoting individual leaders especially associated with it, at the plenary session of the Central Committee of the party of 19–20 March 1974, and again after the Eleventh Congress of the party in March 1975. Nevertheless, for the average factory worker, collective-farm member, or intellectual, Hungary was a pleasanter place to live in, with a better combination of material comfort and personal privacy, than any other state in the Soviet bloc.

Poland

In Poland in 1966 the compromise effected after the crisis of 1956 was still in force: agriculture remained based on private peasant holdings; the Catholic church retained its supremacy in the spiritual sphere; and the communist party leaders retained their political monopoly. The previous decade had been a period of declining liberty and growing discontent. Władysław Gomułka, who had risen to leadership of the communist party in 1956, utterly disappointed his most ardent supporters of those days by systematically whittling away the small liberties extracted at that time. He maintained himself, apart from his monopoly of force and dependence on Soviet power, by a certain improvement in material conditions and by endless harping on the theme of the danger of German *revanchisme* and Soviet defense against it. The more conciliatory the tone of West German public life became, the more violent were official Polish denunciations.

In April 1968 the events in Czechoslovakia found an echo in the Polish intellectual elite. There were demonstrations in Warsaw University, with a clear anti-Russian flavor. However, the students awoke no support among the workers: the authorities transported truckloads from the factories, and these loyal proletarians gladly beat up young people accused of wasting the resources contributed by the working class to their education.

Two years later, when the Soviet government decided that it needed better relations with the Federal Republic of Germany, the Poles were ordered to stop their anti-German hate campaign and sign a treaty with Bonn. This must have been embarrassing enough for Gomułka, but it was followed by something worse. Economic conditions were deteriorating, and the government found it necessary to raise food prices. The result was an outbreak of violence in the Baltic ports of Szczecin and Gdańsk. The shipyard workers took over the cities for some hours, and their violent suppression cost dead and wounded on both sides. Gomułka was forced to resign in January 1971, and his place was taken by Edward Gierek, former party secretary in Silesia, who had spent a large part of his working life in France and was known as an efficient administrator and supporter of milder methods.

For the next five years Gierek was rather successful. He obtained large credits from Western countries, with the approval of the Soviet leaders; the general standard of living rose; important new industrial enterprises were undertaken;

and the intellectuals were allowed more freedom of expression provided they kept out of politics.

However, the improvement was only temporary. In 1976 the government decided to introduce a new constitution that was to contain a reference, modeled perhaps on the phrasing of the East German constitutional amendment mentioned earlier, to the ''unshakable fraternal bond with the Soviet Union.'' This childishly inept attempt to make an unpopular foreign policy more acceptable by putting it into the constitution[12] infuriated patriotic Poles, and was openly opposed by the leaders of the Catholic church, whose relations with the government had been deteriorating for some time. Public protest enforced a modification but not an abandonment of the reference to Poland's ally: the new wording was that Poland ''strengthens its friendship and cooperation with the Soviet Union and other socialist states.''

Following the controversy about the constitution came a more immediately pressing crisis. In June 1976 Gierek found that economic pressures (the world oil crisis, West European inflation, and Poland's heavy indebtedness to Western creditors) compelled him to do what Gomułka had done in 1970: raise food prices. The result was the same: mass-scale riots in industrial centers, this time in Gdańsk, in Radom, and at the Ursus factory south of Warsaw, beginning on 24 June. The riots were suppressed with casualties on both sides, numbers of workers were beaten by the police, and the government withdrew the decree. When calm was restored, police arrested the alleged ringleaders, some of whom were condemned to terms in prison. This combination of vindictiveness, brutality, panic, and incompetence succeeded in discrediting Gierek and his team and in uniting the people against the government. Unlike 1968 when the students were isolated, or 1970 when only workers protested, now all the main classes of the population were united, and the church was behind them. A Committee for the Defense of the Workers, which was created by the intellectuals, operated publicly, made contact with foreigners, including West European communists, and campaigned against government policy. Like the Charter 77 Group in Czechoslovakia, the Polish committee refused to be intimidated by arrests.

The government's predicament was painful. Surrender to the workers on prices could not solve the real economic problems, and there was no visible alternative leader to replace Gierek as he had replaced Gomułka in 1970. All classes were discontented, frustrated, and anxious (even the peasants feared collectivization, though there were few grounds for believing that it was imminent). Discontents were flowing together into the best-known phenomenon of modern

---

12. This strange faith in the power of paper seems to be more Russian than communist. In February 1810 the foreign minister of Tsar Alexander I proposed that a draft Franco-Russian treaty should contain the words: ''The kingdom of Poland shall never be restored.'' Napoleon's comment was: ''Divinity alone can speak as Russia proposes.'' (Documents are in Grand Duke Nikolay Mikhailovich, *La France et la Russie*, vol. 4 [St. Petersburg, 1905], pp. 407–19.)

Polish history—hatred of Russia. An open letter to Gierek by the octogenarian economist Professor Edward Lipiński probably expressed what most Poles felt:

> The imposition of the Soviet system has devastated our social and moral life. It represents a great misfortune in the history of the nation. We are being compelled to support Soviet foreign policy unconditionally, and we have ceased to be an independent element in world politics. This is often contrary to Polish national interests . . . Today there is no more important goal for Poland than the reassertion of its sovereignty. Only after regaining political independence will it be possible to undertake systematic economic reform and to restructure the political and social system, which will release the creative potential of the nation.[13]

All thoughtful Poles realized that they could not hope to drive the Russians out of their country; yet the state of affairs, more than thirty years after the German conquerors had been driven out of Poland, was felt to be intolerable. Soviet Russian rule was living up to the worst traditions of the imperial Russian rule that Poles had endured and hated for a hundred and fifty years. Both the Polish communists and their Soviet patrons certainly desired to avoid further bloodshed; yet the agents were at the mercy of the masters, and the masters were unwilling to consider removing the causes of discontent. An explosion was avoided, and in July 1977 the Polish government—probably with an eye on the preliminary international conference on "Helsinki" held in Belgrade—released those workers, and those leaders of the Committee for the Defense of the Workers, who were still in prison. Nevertheless, a condition of simmering unrest continued.

Yugoslavia and Albania

Yugoslavia ceased to belong to the "socialist camp" in 1948. As a state ruled by the dictatorship of a communist party, however, and as a multinational republic, it faced many similar problems, and its presence on the border of the Soviet bloc influenced, and was influenced by, events inside the bloc. For these reasons it must be discussed at this point.

In the decades that followed the breach of 1948, the Yugoslav communists tried new policies, and sought to formulate them in a series of constitutions, each more complex than the last. The main principle that emerged from Yugoslav doctrine was "workers' self-management," whose practical operation, and whose relationship to the chain of command in the League of Communists

---

13. This passage from the open letter is taken from the interesting article by Adam Bromke, "A New Juncture in Poland," *Problems of Communism,* September–October 1976, p. 13.

(as the party was renamed), remained obscure to most external observers, and probably also to most Yugoslavs. There is no doubt, however, that in the 1960s there was a substantial devolution of power from the central to the republican authorities. Also beyond doubt is the country's economic progress. Yugoslavia in the mid-1970s had many of the outward features of the "consumer society," and this was increasingly reflected in the way of life and of thinking of its citizens, including party members. Yet the prosperity was rather precarious: it depended on the employment of about a million Yugoslavs in Germany and Switzerland, and it was limited by the very inefficient use of the resources available for agriculture, especially for livestock farming.

Decentralization meant that not only the governments of the six republics, but also their communist parties, enjoyed a good deal of independence. In most republics the trend was toward more individual initiative and freer discussion. In Croatia, this greater freedom brought a revival of nationalist rhetoric. President Tito tolerated this for a time, but then became convinced that the leadership of the Croatian communist party was being dangerously lenient, at a time when Croatian fascist exiled groups were active, and one of these even enjoyed some Soviet support. The Croatian party was purged, there were arrests, and a bitter climate of repression and resentment was created during the winter of 1971–1972. It soon became clear that Tito's reaction was directed not so much at nationalism as at liberalism. The Croatian purge was followed by a purge in both the Serbian and the Macedonian republics, whose leaders were guiltless of any disruptive nationalism but stood for more liberal policies in general. In the following years repression was relaxed again, but the hopes of the early 1970s had received a serious setback.

Yugoslavia had another national problem, which grew every year. There were a million Albanians in the Kosovo region of southern Serbia, and several hundred thousand more in the Macedonian republic, Muslims by religion, with a birth rate about twice as high as that of their Slav neighbors. In the postwar years they had been brutally repressed by the Yugoslav police, but beginning in the late 1960s conditions greatly improved. The principles of equal status of the Albanian with the Slav languages, and of employment of Albanians in both government service and industry in proportion to their numbers, were genuinely carried out in Kosovo. Indeed, Albanians began to take over the local administration, and it was the Serbs who were now persecuted, threatened, or even forced out of jobs and homes.

The adjacent Albanian republic, in which Chinese influence had replaced Soviet in the 1960s, was less hostile to Yugoslavia after the Soviet invasion of Czechoslovakia in 1968. Diplomatic, economic, and cultural relations developed, and the new Yugoslav university of Priština, designed for the Kosovo Albanians, not only published books in Albanian but was able to export them to Albania. The two governments took some pains to treat each other with respect. The future evolution of relations between the Albanians on each side of the border was of some importance. It was more likely that Albanians in Albania would be attracted by conditions in Kosovo than the reverse, since the Tirana government's policies remained extremely harsh; but the determination not to be ruled by others was as strong in Kosovo as in Tirana. Four million Albanians could not be ignored as a future factor in Balkan politics. If Enver Hoxha, the autocrat of Albania since 1945, were to disappear, competition for influence in Albania between Balkan governments and communist parties was likely to be acute, and the Soviet rulers, too, would have their plans. There were signs of change in July 1977, when Albanian spokesmen criticized Chinese policy as beneficial to Western imperialism. This offered the Soviet leaders new opportunities.

The problem of succession seemed likely to arise sooner in Yugoslavia than in Albania, for Tito at eighty-five was an older man than Hoxha at sixty-nine. Certainly no individual of comparable authority was available. This did not mean that, as writers of sensational articles in Western newspapers sometimes suggested, his death would bring the disintegration of the state. Undoubtedly national antagonisms remained strong; there were also rivalries between the party leaderships and the economic and political bureaucracies of the six republics (which is not quite the same thing). It was also certain that all the leaders knew very well that if they did not hang together, they were likely to hang separately. One strong uniting factor was the army, which without doubt felt that its duty was to preserve Yugoslavia, not the hegemony of any one Yugoslav nation over the others. At the same time both the soldiers and the civilians wished to avoid military government, which had played an important and disastrous part in the earlier histories of Yugoslavia and Serbia. It was unlikely that Tito's successors would incline toward closer association with the Soviet bloc. Though Tito had maintained independence ever since 1945, it is probably true that he was the least anti-Soviet person in his government. It was also most unlikely that the Soviet army would invade Yugoslavia after Tito's death. What was, however, possible was that serious internal disorders might give an excuse for intervention, or that some group within Yugoslavia might appeal to the Soviet leaders for help. None of these things would happen quickly, but it would be unwise to assert that they could never happen: either obstinate refusal of liberalization, or too rapid or uncoordinated attempts to liberalize in different republics, might conceivably lead to a crisis, and the crisis might be exploited by the Soviet leaders, for whom the recovery of a dominant influence in this strategically important Mediterranean country would be a great prize.

What could be predicted with fair certainty is that the Yugoslavs, like the Poles, would fight if the Soviet army attacked them; and if large-scale fighting developed in the vicinity of the line between the NATO and the Warsaw Pact states, who could say what the consequences would be?

−6−

Communism and Great-Power Politics in the Far East and Southern Asia

This chapter is concerned with the two vast semicircles of land mass that extend roughly from the Red Sea straits to the Strait of Malacca, and from the Great Barrier Reef to Kamchatka.

In the lands lying north of the Indian Ocean communist parties fluctuated in strength during the decade, but were nowhere very strong except in the South Yemen republic (formerly the British colony of Aden), where communist influence was strong in the mid-1970s; the strategic importance of this country for Soviet policy in the Horn of Africa was obvious. At the other end of this semicircle, the communist party of Indonesia, once an impressive force in a country of great riches and over a hundred million inhabitants, had been crushed in 1965; it showed few signs of recovery during the decade. The divided forces of communism in India declined through most of this period in their two main centers, Kerala and West Bengal, but the combination of mass poverty with a large supply of talented and restless intellectuals in West Bengal ensured that communism would remain a latent force. After the defeat of Indira Gandhi at the 1977 elections, the fortunes of the Bengali communists quickly revived. In the whole semicircle there was no state that could seriously be considered a great power. India had a vast population, but despite Indira Gandhi's easy victory over Pakistan in 1971, neither its military nor its economic organization was impressive. Much the same could be said of Indonesia. Another competitor for great-power status on the edge of the region was Iran. Undoubtedly its enterprising, talented, and ambitious monarch had presided over substantial economic progress, and had built large armed forces with the most modern hardware for use on land, sea, or in the air; but it seemed premature to attribute to Iran the relative importance in the world balance of power that it had known under Xerxes or Darius.

In the second semicircle almost the whole continental land mass consisted of states ruled by communists (the Soviet empire, North Korea, China, Vietnam, Laos, and Cambodia), the exceptions being South Korea, Thailand, and Malaysia.[1] Four island states (Indonesia, the Philippines, Singapore, and Japan) and one island colony (Hong Kong) had small communist parties in opposition, and only the northern islands belonging to the Soviet empire (Sakhalin and the Kuriles) were under communist rule. In the island of Taiwan no communist activity was visible. On the edge of the semicircle was Australia, a land of immense natural resources and small population, with a European society transposed into a non-European milieu. Powerfully present in the western Pacific was the United States, though its territory lay thousands of miles to the east.

For successive millennia the Mediterranean was the center not only of the main competing civilizations but of the main conflicts in world politics (Egypt against Mesopotamia, Iran against Hellas, Byzantium against Islam, Spain against the Turks). In the late twentieth century, when the speed of aircraft and missiles had caused distances to shrivel, it might be argued that the new Mediterranean was the Pacific, in which two super powers and two other states just below the super-power level could not avoid their leading roles. The ways in which America, Russia, China, and Japan might combine (two against two, three against one, or all four in individual isolation) seemed likely to affect mightily the fate of the whole human race.

The two semicircles were linked with each other in the blurred region where two great blocks of humanity, the Bengalis and the Turkic peoples, were exposed to domination or influence by Soviet Russian or by Chinese power. The Indians, aware of their numbers and of the age and brilliance of their culture, liked to think of themselves as potential equal partners of either of these giants, but the governments of India had vacillated uneasily since 1947 between dependence on the United States or on the Soviet Union. The rivalry between the Russian and Chinese giants seemed likely also to extend into the region of Iranian culture, which included the modern states of Iran, Afghanistan, and Pakistan, as well as the Tadjik and, to some extent, the Uzbek SSRs.

Any brief consideration of the role of communism in these regions in the 1960s and 1970s must touch both on the triumphs and disappointments of communists struggling for power and on the relations of the communist states with each other and with the United States.

Chinese Politics

This book is no place, nor is its author qualified, to analyze the political and social system of the Chinese People's Republic. It is necessary, however, briefly to summarize the main events of the period in Chinese internal politics that

---

1. This state includes not only the southern part of the Malay Peninsula but also portions of the island of Borneo.

clearly affected China's international status. It may be convenient to divide the whole period into three stages.

First were the years of the Great Proletarian Cultural Revolution, lasting roughly from the autumn of 1965 to the Ninth Congress of the Chinese Communist Party (CCP) in April 1969. The GPCR was officially launched at the Eleventh Plenum of the Central Committee of the CCP,[2] held from 1 to 12 August 1966. The general idea came from Mao Tse-tung himself. Its aim was to prevent the party and the state apparatus from congealing into the bureaucratic mold Mao considered to be the root cause of the degeneration of the Soviet system into "revisionism." Thousands of officials were removed from their posts and publicly humiliated, from such great figures as Liu Shao-ch'i and Teng Hsiao-p'ing at the top down to minor local potentates. The chosen instruments for carrying out this massive purge (in which it seems that fatalities were few), for disrupting government offices, industrial managements, universities, and schools, were at first the Red Guards, consisting largely of adolescents. From the beginning of 1967, however, the army began to take over the leadership, and the Red Guards lost ground. At the top the persons closest to Mao were his wife, Chiang Ch'ing, the ideologist Ch'en Po-ta, and the outstanding soldier Lin Piao. Lin Piao was officially described in 1966 as "Chairman Mao's close comrade-in-arms," and in 1967 he began to be referred to as Chairman Mao's successor.

The CCP was in effect deprived of power. In its place Mao intended to create a new structure of power, possessing the simplicity of the early Russian soviets, doing away with any sort of specialized bureaucracy, and providing transmission belts between the chairman and the grass-roots of Chinese society. In practice, the process was disorderly, producing chaos in administration in many parts of the country and leading to clashes between Red Guards and groups of workers or peasants or army units, and between competing Red Guard units. These incidents evoked periodic appeals from the center for moderation. The Cultural Revolution Group, a sort of headquarters of the movement led by Ch'en Po-ta and Chiang Ch'ing, came into conflict with the army when its "16 May Corps," an ultraradical group, began to attack alleged "capitalist roaders" in the armed forces, and was ordered by Mao to desist. There were major conflicts with the central leadership in Shanghai in January and February 1967, and in Wuhan in July. Eventually the new structure of government emerged in the form of a "revolutionary three-way alliance" composed, at each level, of locally based army units, revolutionary cadres, and the revolutionary masses. During 1968 revolutionary committees came into existence at the provincial level in twenty provinces, and in sixteen of these the chairman was an army officer. The ten-

---

2. That is, the eleventh plenary session of the current Central Committee, which had been elected by the Eighth Congress.

dency for the army to take over the GPCR was unmistakable. During the same period mass campaigns of reeducation in the Thought of Mao were conducted. Specialization of all kinds was repudiated; it was identified with the "capitalist road," and in any case it was unnecessary, since the Thought of Mao subsumed all wisdom. The principal slogans governing virtuous conduct were "Grasp revolution and stimulate production" and "Fight self-interest and repudiate revisionism."

By the end of the year it became possible to prepare the organization of the new purified party, and its Ninth Congress was held from 1 to 24 April 1969. In his political report to the congress Lin Piao stated that the GPCR had succeeded in finding the correct form to arouse the masses against the attempt by Liu's clique to restore the dictatorship of the bourgeoisie. The party was given a new constitution, which stated that the dictatorship of several revolutionary classes had now been replaced by the dictatorship of the proletariat. Marxism –Leninism–Mao's Thought was the party's foundation. Mao had in the last fifty years "inherited, defended and developed Marxism-Leninism" and "brought it to a higher and completely new style."

The Ninth Congress can be considered a landmark, though when it ended the structure of the new party was still flimsy. It was not until the end of 1970 that the organization of county and provincial committees of the party was effectively begun, and the process took another half year to complete. Two characteristics of the new party were the larger number of soldiers in key positions and the larger number of young people.

During the second stage, from the Ninth Congress until late 1975, something like a balance of power was established. Throughout all the convulsions Chou En-lai, the great administrator and the political genius of Chinese government, kept his position in the front rank, and was probably more successful in maintaining some continuity in government than it outwardly appeared. The media were in the hands of the radicals of the GPCR, but the picture they gave to the outside world was certainly distorted. The disastrous clashes with Soviet troops on the Ussuri river in March 1969 strengthened the arguments for a rapid restoration of order. At the Second Plenum of the Central Committee, in August-September 1970, Ch'en Po-ta was purged, and there was an open disagreement between Mao and Lin Piao. During 1971 Lin Piao and several of his closest colleagues were less and less mentioned in the media. At the end of September 1971 it became known that Lin Piao had been killed in an airplane crash in Mongolia. In the following summer official sources stated that he had planned a coup d'état and the assassination of Mao, and that when these failed, he had fled in the direction of the Soviet Union but crashed when his aircraft ran out of fuel.

The death and disgrace of Lin Piao left Chou the strongest personality in Chinese politics, though Chiang Ch'ing still remained in the party supreme leadership and had her influence on Mao. Other members of the former Cultural Revolution Group also remained powerful. Chou was responsible on the Chinese side for the conversations with U.S. Secretary of State Kissinger, and for the visit of President Nixon to China from 21 to 28 February 1972. In April 1973 Chou was able to bring Teng Hsiao-p'ing, one of the main victims of the GPCR, back into the leadership. Teng was made a vice-premier in April, was elected to the Central Committee at the Tenth Congress of the CCP in August, and became a member of the Politburo at the end of the year. On the eve of the congress the radicals made a counteroffensive with a campaign in the mass media against the teachings of Confucius, but Chou's followers responded with a campaign against Lin Piao. The balance of power in the leadership was symbolized by the ritual denunciations, in factory meetings and elsewhere, of an incongruous pair—Confucius and Lin Piao. In January 1975 Teng became first vice-premier and chief of staff of the army. An efficient administrator who put professional competence above ideological formulas, Teng showed that he intended substantially to reverse the policies of the GPCR, and was no respecter of persons. He thereby antagonized powerful people and incurred the wrath of Mao. Chou En-Lai appeared to be preparing Teng as his successor, but when Chou died on 8 January 1976 this was not what happened. The rather obscure Hua Kuo-feng became acting premier.

The third stage was an active struggle for power between the radicals and the moderates. On 5 April 1976 a demonstration of some 100,000 persons on Tien An Men Square in Peking, on the occasion of the annual festival of the dead, paid tribute to the memory of Chou with mass wreaths and inscriptions. This clearly was a protest against Chiang Ch'ing and the radicals. However, the radicals appeared to have control of the militia, because the wreaths and inscriptions were removed and arrests were made. On 7 April Teng was dismissed from all his posts, and Hua was confirmed in office as premier. The radicals' victory was short-lived, for Mao Tse-tung died on 9 September and the expected renewal of the struggle between moderates and radicals ended with the defeat of the radicals. Hua Kuo-feng inherited Mao's office of chairman, and Chiang Ch'ing and her three closest collaborators, who were denounced as the "Gang of Four," became the objects of a countrywide campaign of vilification. In the summer of 1977 Teng was restored to power, ranking in effect as second only to Chairman Hua.

China, the Soviet Union, and the United States

In the mid-1960s the breach between the Chinese and the Soviet leaderships was already complete, while hostility to the United States appeared to be as bitter as ever. The Chinese leaders represented themselves as the champions of

all true revolutionary movements and of all peoples fighting for their independence all over the world, in opposition to the hegemony of the two super powers.
China, they claimed, neither was nor wished to become a super power, and had
no pretensions to ''hegemony.'' This stance was not abandoned during the period, but in practice it became steadily more obvious, beginning with the major
armed clashes on the Ussuri river between Chinese and Soviet forces in March
and August 1969, that the Soviet Union was regarded as the more dangerous of
the two, and that China wished for limited cooperation with the United States.

Public polemics between Peking and Moscow were conducted on the ideological level, though specific issues of foreign and strategic policy were frequently mentioned. The Chinese accused the Soviet leaders of betraying socialism and of seeking to exercise, in cooperation with the United States, a joint
hegemony over the whole world. Later the accusation changed to that of preparing an attack on Western Europe, which could be avoided only if the West
Europeans and Americans remained militarily strong and united. At first the
Chinese denounced American imperialism in Vietnam, but when American withdrawal began, their fear changed: it was no longer that the United States was
an aggressive state threatening China, but that the American rulers had lost their
political will, and were retreating everywhere in the face of the resolute Soviet
aggressors. For their part the Soviet spokesmen accused Mao and his colleagues
of betraying socialism and of intriguing, by their calumnious attribution of aggressive intentions to the Soviet Union, to launch a world war from which they
would gain. Soviet polemists accused the Chinese of having abandoned the
''class analysis'' of the international situation in favor of a Greater Han imper-
ialistic attitude. The unstated assumption was, of course, that a true ''class analysis'' and a truly Marxist approach would inevitably lead to total acceptance of
the Soviet point of view. Whatever the Soviet leadership said at any moment
on any subject *was,* by definition, the truly Marxist view. On this massive foundation of impenetrable self-righteousness was built a mighty superstructure of
rhetoric, varying in style from bland condescension to shrill abuse. Two examples from the statements of each side may suffice to give the reader an impression of the political climate. A *People's Daily* leading article quoted in *Peking
Review* of 7 March 1969 headed ''Down with the New Tsars!'' asserted that
''the Soviet revisionist renegade clique . . . tries to whip up anti-China sentiment for the purpose of diverting the attention of the Soviet people whose resentment and resistance against its reactionary bourgeois fascist rule are growing
daily.'' In his report to the Tenth Congress of the party, published in *Peking
Review* on 7 September 1973, Chou En-lai warned that the object of Soviet
expansion was Europe. ''China is an attractive piece of meat coveted by all.
But, this piece of meat is very tough, and for years no one has been able to bite
into it. It is even more difficult now that Lin Piao the 'super-spy' has fallen. At
present, the Soviet revisionists are 'making a feint to the east while attacking

the west,' and stepping up their contention in Europe and their expansion in the Mediterranean, the Indian Ocean and every place their hands can reach.'' The Soviet leaders internally had "restored capitalism, enforced a fascist dictatorship and enslaved the people of all nationalities.'' The Soviet Union by its actions had "profoundly exposed its ugly features as the new Tsar and its reactionary nature, namely 'socialism in words, imperialism in deeds.' '' Chou rebutted the Soviet claims that China was trying to engineer a war, and that the Soviet government stood for détente:

> If you are so anxious to relax world tension, why don't you show your good faith by doing a thing or two—for instance, withdraw your armed forces from Czechoslovakia or the People's Republic of Mongolia and return the four northern islands to Japan? China has not occupied any foreign countries' territory. Must China give away all the territory north of the Great Wall to the Soviet revisionists in order to show that we favor relaxation of world tension and are willing to improve Sino-Soviet relations?

D. Vostokov in *International Affairs* (January 1972)[3] surveyed Chinese foreign policy since the Ninth Congress of the CCP in 1969. The whole article has an undertone of moralizing indignation, denouncing the Cultural Revolution and expressing horror at the efforts of the Chinese government to improve its relations with the United States and with various "capitalist" countries. The secrecy of Henry Kissinger's visits appeared especially to shock the Soviet writer, who was perhaps unaware in his innocence that secret dealings were not unknown in the diplomatic practice of governments, his own included. Chinese claims to stand for the interests of smaller states against the super powers infuriated him: "To-day the Peking regime is striving to win world-wide support for its hegemonistic aims by resorting to the slogan of uniting the 'medium and small' countries and by manipulating with anti-Soviet and anti-American catchwords." He was also shocked by signs of Chinese-Japanese reconciliation: "However, the Chinese leaders are developing contacts with Japan in practically all spheres and their relations with the Japanese ruling Liberal-Democratic Party have become very active."

An article of October 1975 in the same periodical entitled "Peking's Ideological Subversion," by I. Alexeyev and G. Apalin, declared that the "strategic direction" of Chinese foreign policy remained "Great-Han hegemonism." How different from the principles inspiring the Soviet leaders: "It is absolutely true that the Soviet Union is a great and mighty power; but in the first place it is a socialist state which pursues a class, socialist foreign policy. It has interests

---

3. The review of that name published in English in Moscow, not to be confused with the review of the same name published in London by the Royal Institute of International Affairs.

which it knows how to uphold, but these interests are not simply those of a state as such, but of a socialist state which combines national tasks with international ones, among which is support for the world socialist system, the international communist movement and the people's liberation struggle. Aspiration to hegemony in any sphere is completely alien to the nature of the Soviet system and communist ideology."[4] Among the crimes of the Chinese leaders was that in their telegram to Moscow "on the occasion of the 57th anniversary of the Great October Socialist Revolution they 'omitted' the words 'Great' and 'Socialist'; yet the Peking propaganda characterizes as 'great' the so-called cultural revolution which is designed to liquidate the socialist gains of the Chinese people."

The barrage of revolutionary rhetoric was, of course, intended by each side to win over all revolutionary communists struggling for power. In this competition there is no doubt that the Soviet leaders were more successful, during the whole period, than their Chinese rivals. The reason probably has very little to do with any superiority of Soviet ideological arguments; it is more simply that the Soviet Union was better able to supply money, arms, and training facilities than the Chinese.

The Maoist splinter parties that appeared in some Latin American countries, and the guerrilla movements that claimed Chinese inspiration, proved ineffective; despite his preference for unorthodox insurrectionary procedures, Castro eventually not only committed himself to the Soviet line but also publicly denounced the Chinese. In Africa, the construction of the "Tanzam" railway between Zambia and Tanzania doubtless won the Chinese some prestige and kind feelings, but these were soon forgotten; though many guerrilla fighters had received Chinese training, it was clear that the guerrilla leaders, once in power, would prefer Soviet big battalions to Chinese doctrinal attractions. This ingratitude was strikingly demonstrated by the victorious FRELIMO leader Machel in Mozambique in 1977.

More important was the allegiance of the communists in the Far East. The Japanese communist party maintained a comparatively independent posture in relation both to the Soviet Union and to China, and was viewed with mistrust by Peking. On the other hand, Chinese influence was strong in a section of the Japan Socialist party, and there were promising prospects that it would grow. The 24 June 1976 statement quoted in an earlier chapter[5] included agreement by Japanese socialists and Chinese officials that the Soviet government should return the southern Kurile Islands to Japan. Even the communists felt obliged

---

4. This statement, insofar as it is true, is tautological. The words mean essentially that the Soviet government supports the regimes it has imposed in other countries, supports those communist parties that obey its directives, and supports those nationalist revolutionary movements that owe allegiance to it.

5. See p. 46.

to make the same demand, in the long statement issued at their Central Committee Plenum of 2 June, though they also stated that negotiations to this effect should take place only after the abrogation of the U.S.-Japan security treaty.

The North Korean communists, like the Japanese, took a middle position between the Soviet Union and China. Kim Il-sung desired above all the reunification of Korea under his leadership. He was therefore bound not to antagonize either of his powerful communist neighbors, neither of which wished to risk the possible consequences of a renewal of war in Korea.

During the Vietnam war both the Soviet Union and China had given material assistance to the Hanoi forces, and both had denounced American policies as imperialist. However, the Chinese had impeded the transport of Soviet military equipment through Chinese territory, forcing the Soviet government to supply the Vietnamese communist government mainly by sea. The Vietnamese communists undoubtedly owed their victory much more to Soviet than to Chinese aid,[6] and it was to be expected that they would incline to the Soviet side. Yet they maintained relations with China, too, and appeared eager to preserve their position as an independent communist state, and an independent center for revolutionary activity in Southeast Asia.

The vast area of India and Pakistan was a principal theater of Sino-Soviet hostility. The Chinese declared their sympathy for Pakistan in the India-Pakistan war of December 1971, and denounced Bangladesh as another Manchukuo.[7] Conversely, the Bangladesh leader Mujib was praised by the Soviet leaders, and proclaimed his admiration for the Soviet Union. When Mujib was overthrown, as relations between Bangladesh and India deteriorated and the new Bangladesh rulers showed a more friendly attitude to Pakistan, the prospects of Chinese influence in that region greatly improved.

The conclusion of the war in Vietnam made it easier for the Chinese to cooperate with the United States; the limiting factors were the specific problems of Korea, Japan, and Taiwan, as well as the overall doubts as to whether the United States did not prefer cooperation with the Soviet Union (a joint imperialist hegemony over the whole world), or whether the United States leaders had the realism and strength of will necessary to uphold their own interests, and so make them a partner with whom serious business could be conducted. Of these two doubts, which were not entirely mutually exclusive, the first was felt more keenly by the "radicals," the second by the "moderates."

In the mid-1960s the Chinese leaders shared with the extreme left in Japan a passionate desire to abolish the U.S.-Japan security treaty; but ten years later

---

6. This is, of course, a relative comparison; the Vietnamese communists owed their victory above all to their own efforts, to their ruthless courage and inflexible fanaticism.

7. The name of the puppet state created by the Japanese in Manchuria in 1931.

it was quite clear to all concerned that it was to China's interest that the United States' presence in the western Pacific should be maintained, and this was dependent above all on the link with Japan. The ruling Liberal Democratic Party (LDP) in Japan was committed to maintaining the treaty, and this was also the view of the oppositional Democratic Socialist party. The main socialist group, the Japan Socialist party, was in effect divided on this basic issue: some supported the treaty, some bitterly opposed it, and some wavered. During the decade the LDP gradually lost some of its electoral support, and the Lockheed scandal, incriminating former premier Kakuei Tanaka in the receipt of large sums from that company, was readily exploited by the opposition in the campaign leading up to the election of 5 December 1976. The LDP lost its absolute majority, winning 249 out of 511 seats in the Lower House. Being still far the largest party, it was able to form a government, with Takeo Fukuda as premier. There was increased demand from within the party for a reform of its structure, and a certain mood of public disillusionment about the domination of Japanese politics by businessmen and bureaucrats. However, the traditional system of paternalism and welfare based on loyalty to the individual firm still worked; trade-union militancy was rather weak in industry, as opposed to public services; periodic bloody riots by rival extremist student groups made no dents of any importance in the structure of power; and the four opposition parties (JSP, JCP, DSP, and Komeito) were quite incapable of adopting a common program. Japan remained a relatively stable factor in an unstable world, and its links with the United States were not likely to be threatened unless U.S. policy showed a grotesque lack of realism and tact. Improvement of Japanese-Chinese relations was to the interest of both Japan and the United States.

In Korea there was a clear conflict between Chinese and American aims, which the two nations could not solve but could only tacitly agree not to exacerbate. The Chinese were committed to the union of Korea under communist rule, the Americans to the defense of the Republic of Korea. In practice, each power exercised restraint on its dependent, the Chinese on the northern leadership, the U.S. on the southern. The first priority for Kim Il-sung's government was union with the South on his terms; in order to achieve this, he must remain on good terms with both the Soviet and the Chinese leaders. The North Korean communist party therefore maintained, like the Japanese party, an independent stance toward both the great neighbors. The successes of the North Vietnamese communists encouraged Kim's hopes. In 1972 the two Korean governments began discussions about future reunification, but after a year these broke down. In November 1974 and March 1975 the South Korean authorities made the alarming discovery of tunnels under the Demilitarized Zone on the frontier— evident preparation by the North Koreans for a surprise attack on the South. The complete victory of the communists in Vietnam in 1975 increased Kim Il-sung's impatience, but to his annoyance neither of his potential great-power patrons would encourage him to take risks. Meanwhile the North Korean regime had acquired a special character within the communist world, owing to the extreme "cult of personality" of the leader and his promotion to high positions of members of his family, giving the impression that he was planning a hereditary dynasty.[8]

In the South, General Park Chung-hee remained an effective dictator, as he had been ever since 1961. He introduced a new constitution, approved by a referendum on 21 November 1972, which allowed only strictly limited opposition. His regime was bitterly criticized by left intellectuals and by exiles, but it was without doubt efficient. In the early 1970s the South Korean economy was extraordinarily successful; emulating the earlier "economic miracle" in Japan, South Korea became incomparably stronger, more united, and more prosperous than South Vietnam had been. It also had the great strategic advantage, in comparison with South Vietnam, that it had a very short and defensible border and could not be outflanked on land; where South Vietnam had had long borders with Laos and Cambodia that were used by its enemies to send troops and supplies to the south, Korea had the sea. It was also important that Korea represented a position of vital strategic importance to Japan. For more than a thousand years Korea had played much the same role between China and Japan that Flanders had between France and England—a base of invasion or an object of invasion. If the United States was committed to the defense of Japan, Americans could not in the last resort abandon South Korea, even if the American troops stationed on Korean soil were gradually removed in accordance with President Carter's declared policy.

Still more important as an object of conflict between China and the United States was Taiwan. The government in Peking would not for a moment consider the abandonment of its claims to the island, which (like its opponents in Taipeh) it considered an integral part of China. Taiwan, like South Korea, had achieved remarkable economic progress; its fifteen million people, like the four million of Hong Kong and the two million of Singapore, had shown what Chinese could achieve as private entrepreneurs in industry, agriculture, and commerce, given the chance. It was hardly conceivable that the United States could simply abandon Taiwan. It was even arguable that this would not be to the advantage of China, since so deadly a blow to the credibility of the United States as an ally could only promote a shift in the balance of power in the western Pacific to the advantage of the Soviet Union, the last thing that Peking could desire. In the long term it might be hoped that some arrangement could be found by which Taiwan would recognize Peking's sovereignty but continue to enjoy autonomy.

---

8. The nearest parallel in the communist world was Ceauşescu's elevation of his wife to membership in the Politburo of the Romanian communist party in 1977.

In the short term the United States and Chinese governments could do no more than try to play down the issue.

Vietnam and Southeast Asia

Without doubt the greatest success of communists in the whole world during this period was the conquest of South Vietnam, leading to the unification of Vietnam under communist rule. When the southern government surrendered on 30 April 1975, this action ended an armed struggle that had lasted for the best part of thirty years. The communist-led Vietminh started as a resistance group against the Japanese in 1944. After a period of unsuccessful negotiations with the French government, the communists reverted to armed revolt at the end of 1946. Nearly eight years later they had defeated the French and obtained complete control of the northern half of the country. After about three years of peace, guerrilla operations were started again in the South, at the end of 1957, and from then onward the war continued to final victory.

This is no place to discuss the rights and wrongs of the war in Vietnam, or the passions it aroused throughout the world; there is a vast literature on the subject. A few brief observations are, however, necessary.

It was a civil war of a peculiar kind. It took place in only one of two states inhabited by the same nation. Viewed on a nationwide scale, it was a simple civil war, in which the combatants were on the one hand the army and the state power of the South, and on the other the southern insurgents and the army of the North. Viewed within the framework of the southern state alone, it was in part a civil war and in part a war against foreign intervention—from the northern state. Foreign intervention in the fullest sense also played its part. In the first phase Chinese help was important in defeating the French imperial forces. In the second stage the southern state received enormous assistance from the United States, first in weapons and supplies and then in armed forces, which reached in 1968 over 500,000 men. The northern state in the second stage received enormous assistance in weapons and supplies from the Soviet Union, and some help from China. However, no Soviet or Chinese fighting units took part.

The southern state suffered from a basic geographical strategic disadvantage. Its very short frontier with the northern state would have been defensible if the fighting had been confined to it. In reality, however, it was bypassed to the west. Large parts of eastern Laos and eastern Cambodia were controlled by the North Vietnamese communists, and not only military supplies but many thousands of northern troops passed down the "Ho Chi Minh trail" to attack from the rear and to reinforce the southern guerrilla forces. These latter forces were controlled from the North, and it was the northern party secretary Le Duan who had prepared the insurrection in advance. It was not until 1970 that United States forces entered Cambodia, following the overthrow of Prince Sihanouk's government by General Lon Nol in March. They remained only from the end of April to the end of June, but South Vietnamese troops continued to operate on Cambodian soil. This American countermove did not succeed in liquidating the Ho Chi Minh trail. Whereas the northerners were able in this manner to invade the South, an invasion of the North by the southern and United States forces was never permitted. Even bombing of the North was on a very restricted scale and for limited periods. Systematic bombing of the cities of Hanoi and Haiphong was ruled out on the ground that it might lead to a danger of war with the Soviet Union. The result of this self-limitation by the United States Command was that whenever the communist forces suffered a serious military setback (such as the failure of the Tet Offensive of January 1968, the threat to their Cambodian bases in 1970, the failure of their Easter offensive in 1972), they were always able to retreat and recover, knowing that they need not fear pursuit into their own citadel.

Coverage of the war in the South by the mass media was of immense help to the communists. Hideous battle scenes in the South appeared on television screens, but nothing of the sort was seen in the North. Political life in the South was not monolithic; there were rival religious sects and rival cliques of politicians and generals, and none of these were accustomed to the rules of behavior considered respectable by Western democratic newspaper correspondents. Though stories of corruption and vice did not make as sharp an impact as visual images of the sheer horror of war, they had a cumulative effect on the American home public. The presence of hundreds of thousands of American soldiers with plenty of money to spend, of massive American army stores of goods unknown to Vietnamese, and of attractive young Vietnamese girls provided irresistible incentives to the pursuit of luxury, vice, and corruption. Cases of this kind provided "stories" to Western journalists. South Vietnam became known the whole world over as a sink of iniquity. A worldwide campaign rapidly grew up that placed the whole blame for the war on the Americans. They alone were aggressors and imperialists; the northerners were stern patriots, and the southerners at worst degenerate and vicious, at best silly little yellow men unable to appreciate Western liberties and likely to be much happier under the rule of their highminded northern compatriots. The element of racialist contempt in this last judgment was seldom explicit, but was unmistakably there, affecting the "left" at least as much as the "right."

This vast anti-American campaign on Vietnam was no doubt promoted by communists, and certainly it benefited them, but they had a comparatively small part in it. As usual, the most fanatical anti-Americans were Americans. There were several contributing trends of public opinion. The radical student movement of the second half of the 1960s started principally as a movement for civil rights for blacks. This courageous fight for justice, in which whites as well as blacks lost their lives at the hands of racist thugs, remains an imperishable glory of a generation of American young men and women. Having declared war on the authorities in this cause, it was understandable that the movement should pass on to attack all policies of the "establishment," and the most obvious of these was the war in Vietnam—though why commitment to justice for black Americans should cause one to urge that Vietnamese be handed over to the tender mercies of communist apparatchiks was not so obvious. There was a further special reason why students should oppose the war: the possibility that they might be conscripted into the army and sent to Vietnam. This, of course, also applied to persons who were not students, and whose parents saw on their televisions week after week the horrors into which their children might be plunged.

The war ate up more and more thousands of soldiers and more and more millions of dollars, and no end seemed in sight. The 1968 Tet Offensive, though defeated, enormously increased American war-weariness and was in effect responsible for Lyndon Johnson's decision in March 1968 not to stand for reelection. His rival and successor Richard Nixon was committed to ending the war, and so would have been any competitor for the presidency. The 1972 campaign was to some extent fought on the issue of which candidate was likely to be more efficient at getting America out of the war. This state of public opinion, rather than the growing but minority trend that positively espoused the northern cause (not with openly communist arguments, but with the argument that the North stood for national independence and democracy), made American surrender inevitable. The only question was how soon the North would concede peace, how much public humiliation its leaders would insist on imposing on the greatest power in the world before they graciously consented to stop the shooting. In the end it is possible that the Soviet leaders, desiring economic assistance from the West and therefore preparing the détente policy, put pressure on Hanoi, and it is possible that Nixon's decision to bomb the North in December 1972 was also persuasive. On 23 January 1973 the cease-fire was declared. The provisions in the settlement for guaranteeing the interests of the South Vietnamese state were, predictably, inadequate. When the northerners resumed their attack, the southern forces began to run out of supplies, the United States Congress refused to vote the sums required, and Soviet supplies to the North were maintained. The occupation of the South by the communist forces was followed by communist occupation of Laos and Cambodia. The victorious Khmers Rouges began their Cambodian reign by mass executions and by driving two million people from the capital, Phnom Penh, out into the countryside, healthy and sick and old and adult and infant alike. Neither these events nor the more restrained reprisals of the Vietnamese could appear on the television screen. Some stories got into the press, but the printed word could be more easily set aside in the mind than the visual image, and in any case, unconscious liberal white racism could offer the consolation that mere yellow men did not miss liberty as they had never learned to appreciate it.

The victorious Vietnamese communists owed more to Soviet than to Chinese help, but they took care to maintain correct relations with both communist states. It seemed possible that Vietnam would become a genuinely independent center for spreading revolution in Southeast Asia. The most promising direction was Thailand. Here centers of insurrection had long existed in the north, northeast, and extreme south, on the borders with Laos and Malaysia. Accumulated discontent with the military regime that had existed since 1958 overflowed in student demonstrations in October 1973 that led to the resignation and exile of the two dominant field marshals, Thanom and Praphat. The subsequent governments were weak coalitions of civilian parties, with cliques of soldiers in the background, until military rule was reintroduced in the autumn of 1976. None of these governments was markedly successful in resisting the guerrillas, though they derived some advantage from the fact that mutual hostility between the Vietnamese and Cambodian rulers, and Chinese suspicion of the Vietnamese, inhibited their opponents. They showed more resolution toward the United States, which by the end of June 1976 had been induced not only to withdraw all troops and military installations from Thai soil, but also to dismantle its radar monitoring station.

For the two hundred million inhabitants of the islands and the southern tip of the peninsula—Malaysia, Indonesia, Singapore, and the Philippines—Vietnamese-sponsored revolution was not very attractive. These lands of Muslim or Christian culture had long been separated from the Buddhist and Confucian cultural world of the mainland, and had little liking for its peoples. In 1977 communist activity was small, though it would be premature to assume that it would not revive. There was some increase in activity in the Malayan jungle, especially near the Thai border; and on 25 August 1975 the communists achieved a spectacular success by blowing up the National Monument in Kuala Lumpur, erected to celebrate the Malaysian government's victory in the Emergency—the long postwar struggle against the communist insurrection. In Singapore, Lee Kuan Yew's government seemed little inhibited by such latent communist sympathy as might exist among the Chinese population. In the Philippines some thousands of communist guerrillas of two rival dispensations kept up a struggle, while Muslim resistance on the island of Mindanao also kept the rulers busy. After twelve years of military rule in Indonesia, it was to be expected that there would be discontent, but there were few signs that the communist party (PKI), which had been mercilessly destroyed in 1965, was in a position to mobilize it. It was noteworthy that the exiled PKI leadership publicly accepted the Soviet line and denounced the Chinese, thus renouncing the pro-Chinese orientation of the PKI in its great days.

India and Its Neighbors

One of the causes of the conflict between China and the Soviet Union in the 1960s was the Soviet attitude to India. In the polemics between India and China about the frontier, Khrushchev had assumed an attitude of neutrality. This stance was repeated at the time of the frontier war between India and China in 1962. Soviet economic aid to India increased during the Khrushchev years, while Soviet aid to China seemed to the Chinese absurdly small. This refusal to give preference to a "socialist" state infuriated the Chinese, who also resented what seemed to them an assumption of airs of "great-power" conceit by the Indians. During the following years hostility to India, and support for Pakistan as its adversary, became a leading feature of Chinese foreign policy.

This conflict inevitably affected the communist movement within India. The official leadership of the Communist Party of India (CPI) followed the Soviet line; this forced it to moderate its opposition to the ruling Congress, and then to give it conditional support, justifying this posture by the argument that the party could best further its objectives by strengthening the "progressive" elements within the Congress (of which Indira Gandhi was the spokesman) against the forces of "reaction."

Discontent with this attitude brought the party to a split in 1964. A new Communist Party of India (Marxist) was formed that did not identify itself with the Chinese but refused to be drawn into the Soviet-Chinese quarrel, or uncritically to support the Soviet Union. In the next years the CPI(M) proved stronger than the CPI in the two states in which communists had enjoyed since independence the largest following—Kerala and West Bengal. However, in the latter state, which had not only the greatest volume of rural and urban poverty in India— and arguably the greatest concentration of misery in the world—but also an exceptionally high proportion of intelligentsia, the neutral stance of the CPI(M) was not enough. An extreme left wing emerged that favored armed rural revolt, looking to China as its model. In the summer of 1967 there was a local insurrection in the Naxalbari district, which was put down by the authorities. In 1969 a third party was formed, the Communist Party of India (Marxist-Leninist), whose members became known, because of the 1967 revolt, as Naxalites. At successive elections to the West Bengal assembly the CPI(M) gained at the expense of the CPI, in 1971 attaining 111 seats to its rival's 13, in an assembly of 280 seats. Congress lost its majority in the Bengal assembly in 1967, after which there was a succession of left governments alternating with intervention by the central government (left United Front in power in 1967, president's rule in 1969, United Front again from February 1969 to April 1970, president's rule until March 1971). In 1971 the CPI abandoned the United Front, and a coalition was formed to exclude the CPI(M).

This situation was drastically changed as a result of the India-Pakistan war at the end of 1971. India's sweeping military victory, and the formation of the new state of Bangladesh, enabled Indira Gandhi to win an overwhelming victory in the West Bengal assembly election of March 1972; Congress had 216 seats out of 280 and the CPI(M) only 14, while the CPI benefited from its association with Congress sufficiently to win 35.

Nevertheless, this was only a provisional success. In the following years disillusionment and discontent grew up again. In June 1975 Indira Gandhi proclaimed an emergency. The CPI, which supported her, continued to operate freely, but the CPI(M) and still more the Naxalites suffered police repression. When Indira Gandhi's Congress was defeated in the federal election of March 1977, the CPI shared its discomfiture, while in West Bengal the CPI(M) emerged as the strongest single party, far surpassing the Janata party, which had won at the federal level. In June 1977 it won 178 seats out of 294 in the West Bengal assembly.

Meanwhile there had been change in Bangladesh. The first leader of the new state, Mujibur Rahman, was devoted to India, which had brought him to power, and perhaps still more to the Soviet Union. However, he was unable to master the terrible situation of poverty, devastation, corruption, and internecine strife that confronted him. He was overthrown and murdered in August 1975, and a succession of military coups followed. The military rulers were much less friendly to India, and began to improve their relations with Pakistan. This trend was most welcome to the Chinese, who in 1971 had supported Pakistan and had regarded Bangladesh as a puppet of the Indian-Soviet alliance.

The prospects in the subcontinent were most uncertain in 1977. The appalling conditions in both West Bengal and Bangladesh seemed favorable to political extremists, and appeared to offer good opportunities for Chinese-type revolutionary communism. At the same time, the governments of Bangladesh and Pakistan, neither of which could be considered inclined to social revolution, were potentially useful to China as allies against India. Yet things were not as simple even as this. Indira Gandhi's government made what looked like a gesture of independence from the Soviet Union by restoring diplomatic relations with China in April 1976. It seemed probable that if the victorious Janata coalition were able to hold together, it too would seek better relations with both China and the United States, while maintaining the Indo-Soviet treaty of friendship, which did not commit its signatories very heavily. In any case the CPI appeared to have poor prospects. Indian communists in the future were likely to prefer an independent stance in relation to both the Soviet Union and China, such as was pursued by the Japanese, Vietnamese, and North Korean communists.

−7−

Communist Prospects in the Late 1970s

A Typology of Past Communist Successes and Failures

Twenty-five years ago, study of the struggles for power of communist parties between 1917 and 1952 appeared to show that the main victories (Russia, Yugoslavia, Albania, and China) had been won in countries with predominantly rural populations, in which industrial development was still in an early stage; and that in all cases it had only been possible to capture the state machine after it had been immensely weakened by defeat in war.[1] The state machines of advanced industrial societies had successfully resisted assault, even after defeat in war; Germany in 1918–1919 was the outstanding example. All other communist victories seemed at that time to fall into a different pattern; they were imposed as a direct or indirect consequence of the occupation of a territory by the invading Soviet army. Of this there had been different examples at different historical moments: Azerbaidjan in 1920 and Georgia in 1921; Mongolia, Tannu Tuva, Khiva, and Bokhara in the 1920s; Esthonia, Latvia, Lithuania, and eastern Moldavia ("Bessarabia") in 1940; and Poland, Czechoslovakia, Hungary, Romania, and Bulgaria between 1944 and 1948.[2]

An attempt some years later to look more thoroughly into the phenomenon of revolution led to some revision of this opinion.[3] Though the two main categories

---

1. These are the main conclusions drawn from a historical survey in my book *The Pattern of Communist Revolution* (London, 1953); later American edition entitled *From Lenin to Khrushchev* (New York, 1960), pp. 330ff.

2. This list does not include a number of minor territorial annexations by Soviet Russia, such as southern Sakhalin, Königsberg (renamed Kaliningrad), and northern Bukovina. A full list of these annexations does not seem necessary at this point. A recent survey of these cases by a large team of authors, some of whose contributions are outstandingly good, is Thomas T. Hammond, ed., *The Anatomy of Communist Takeovers* (New Haven: Yale University Press, 1975).

3. See my book *Neither War nor Peace* (London and New York, 1960), pp. 188–89, and especially 200–5.

mentioned above remained, it seemed that it was necessary to add a third. It seemed useful to distinguish between frontal assaults on the citadel of power and seizure of power from within the citadel with the complicity of part of the garrison. The communist victory in Czechoslovakia in 1948 seemed to be the only communist example of this type of revolution. It was true that though no Soviet forces were present in Czechoslovakia when the communists seized power, nevertheless during the second half of 1945 when they had been present they had enabled the communists to occupy numerous strategic positions in the. state administration that proved valuable in 1948. However, looking back from 1959 rather than 1952, it seemed that, on balance, it could be said that the Czechoslovak communists had made their own revolution, assisted by the complicity, complacency, or passivity of other political groups. In this respect their seizure of power closely resembled that of the Italian fascists in 1922 and of the German National Socialists in 1933 (which, of course, is *not* an assertion that Czechoslovak communism was *the same thing* as Fascism or National Socialism).[4] Further evidence that has come to light as a result of the events of 1968 reinforces this view; observers from outside in 1948, including myself, had overrated the element of Soviet pressure and underrated the element of ingenious manipulation, suborning, deception, and intimidation by the Czech communists of influential members of other political parties and of noncommunists in positions of authority.[5]

Twenty-five years ago it also seemed possible to form some general conclusions about the social forces that supported or opposed communist movements. In advanced industrial societies communist support came from a section of the industrial working class—in a few, from a majority of that class[6]—and from a section of the professional classes. Arrayed against them were businessmen, government officials, farmers, a majority of professional people, and many or most workers. In the rural, agricultural, partly industrialized, or "developing" societies, communists had good chances of winning a following among the "intelligentsia"—the modern-educated intellectual elite that was equally alienated from the culture of its own people and from the prevalent political system—as well as among the small industrial working class and the much larger unorganized, exploited, and uprooted urban poor; they had opportunities to mo-

---

4. It does, however, involve the assertion that *none* of these three actions (by Gottwald, Mussolini, and Hitler) were mere coups d'état and that all three *were* revolutions. For the argument in support of this judgment see the reference in the preceding note.

5. For some details, see the chapter by Pavel Tigrid entitled "The Prague Coup of 1948: The Elegant Takeover," in Hammond, *Anatomy,* pp. 399–432.

6. A clear majority in France, and at that time about half the class in Italy.

bilize peasant discontents and instinctive xenophobia in conditions of crisis.[7] Against them stood not only the few rich landowners and capitalists but also the bureaucracy, either indigenous or—in the case of the vast areas still belonging to colonial empires—foreign. The state machine weighed heavily on the people, and its methods of repression were more brutal than those of governments in advanced industrial societies, but it was more vulnerable than the latter, for it had fewer horizontal links with the various layers of society, or shallower roots in the soil of society—it was brittle, though heavy, like cast iron. It seemed at the end of the 1950s that the prospects for communism were much more favorable in the "developing societies" than in the industrialized societies of Europe, North America, or the South Atlantic and South Pacific.

Let us consider how this type of analysis stands up to the realities of the late 1970s.

Changes in the Political Environment

There seem to me to have been four main changes in the general world situation, apparent already in 1960 but much intensified since then, that have radically modified the political environment in which both communists and their opponents operate.

First is the disappearance of the West European colonial empires and the proliferation of new states, most of which have had very small and diverse populations. This process has usually been peaceful, but in three important cases— Vietnam, Algeria, and the Portuguese colonies—it was extremely bloody. Hostility to the West in the lands that have become new states has not diminished but has notably increased, though there are exceptions; there is no clear correlation between the degree of consent or resistance by the former colonial rulers to nationalist claims and the degree of friendliness or hostility in the new states.[8]

---

7. There is a large literature on the "cultural gap" between intelligentsia and masses, and on the forces pushing the intelligentsia toward revolution. As I have been writing about this for longer than most, I may perhaps recommend my own essays of 1951 and 1954, republished in *Nationalism and Communism*, (London, 1964), pp. 36–67, as well as two sections in my book *The Russian Empire 1801–1917* (Oxford, 1967), pp. 225–26 and 478–80. Of those who have developed these concepts in their own way in recent years, I must especially express my admiration for Richard Lowenthal and John Kautsky.

8. To take a few random examples: Kenya, in which the British tried to repress nationalism, has pursued a rather friendly policy toward Britain and its Western allies, while India, which obtained independence after tremendous manifestations of goodwill on the British side, seemed until the defeat of Indira Gandhi in 1977 to be well on the way to becoming a semi-vassal of the Soviet Union. The hostility of Somalia does not seem explicable by British policy in the 1950s. It is perhaps arguable that the French have maintained better relations with their former colonies than any other European nation—Guinea and Congo (Brazzaville) are obvious exceptions, but Algeria is a surprising reinforcement to the argument.

Hostility has been promoted and exploited by Soviet policy, and has given communists growing opportunities.

Second is the growth of expectations, stimulated by the growth of the mass media not only in advanced societies but also in at least the urban enclaves of the developing societies. It has been reinforced by the less and less inhibited demagogy of politicians (most of whom would sincerely claim to be "democrats") and the contemptuous repudiation by the intelligentsia of all concepts of hierarchy and of any service ethos. Everyone is entitled, according to the new conventional wisdom, to every luxury, and it is his right to grab it. Obviously, this is a more convincing argument in rich Western societies than amid Asian or African poverty, but it has its devotees there too.

In advanced industrial societies may be observed the systematic propagation by commercial interests, through the mass media, of short-term hedonism as the only desirable social value. These interest groups find powerful, if unconscious, allies in that section of the intelligentsia that considers itself the enemy of plutocracy and of capitalist advertising. It is especially noticeable in the attitude of these people to religion. Not only do they cast off religious dogmas in which they cannot themselves believe, but they treat with militant derision those who keep their faith; believers must be idiots or barbarians. A still further paradox is that they receive strong indirect aid and comfort from a growing number of priests of all Christian denominations who almost reduce the sphere of church activity to material welfare and preach a bizarre combination of material equalitarianism and spiritual elitism. This strange half-unconscious alliance between capitalist salesmen, atheist intellectuals, and progressive churchmen is most visible in the northwestern corner of the world (from Vancouver to Hamburg). It is as yet only latent in the developing societies, where the possessing oligarchs with their flamboyant luxuries are genuinely hated by the radical ideologues. However, a religious phenomenon that is somewhat analogous is the attempt to assimilate the great universal religion of Islam to Arab nationalism; atheist intellectuals will argue that Islam is a splendid thing, not for its divine revelation to the Prophet or for its ethical teaching, but simply because it was invented by an Arab.

Only in communist-ruled states and a few Muslim dictatorships is short-term hedonism rejected in favor of a service ethos. It is true that the ultimate goal held up to communists is satisfaction of material wants several generations hence (long-term hedonism); meanwhile, however, devoted service to the communist cause and self-sacrifice for it when necessary have first place. In communist-ruled states this means uncritical obedience to the party. Within communist parties *in partibus infidelium* the same ethos is obligatory, though the surrounding climate of Western short-term hedonism makes inroads into the ranks.

Third is the continued nuclear stalemate, reinforced by the Cuban missile crisis of 1962. Fear of nuclear war gives an advantage to those states that are well equipped with conventional forces. Conventional war involving millions, in the center of Europe, continued to seem improbable through the 1970s-to-date, since the Soviet rulers could not be *sure* that if they were to use their superiority in conventional weapons to attack Western Europe, the United States government would *not* resort to nuclear retaliation. The possibility that the Soviet Union might develop so great a superiority over the United States in nuclear weapons and in antinuclear defense that it would possess a first-strike capability is something that the present author is unqualified to judge, and which lies outside the scope of this work. Meanwhile, however, it seemed clear that conventional-force superiority in regions outside the main European and Far Eastern theaters might make war an attractive proposition to those who had it. In the Middle East this superiority lay with Israel, whose leaders had strong reasons for not taking the initiative. Elsewhere the situation was less clear. The Cuban invasion of Angola in 1975 appeared to be a brilliant success for the communist cause. The temptation to repeat it further south was strong, but the risks were also large. The Indian invasion of Pakistan in 1971, undertaken in quite different circumstances, was also a success for the invader. Massive interventions of Soviet-equipped communist forces in civil wars in South America, tropical Africa, southern Asia, or even southern Europe, possibly with Vietnamese, Iraqi, Bulgarian, or other "volunteers," were not absurd hypotheses. An unknown factor was the total number, and the fighting quality, of the Africans, Asians, Latin Americans, and Arabs who had received various forms of training in communist-ruled states since the early 1960s.

Fourth was the unquantifiable phenomenon often described as the "failure of nerve" of Western rulers and Western public opinion. At the level of ideas, this was a strange combination of material greed and moral scruple. Short-term hedonism, discussed above, was more widespread among the larger community of the influential (professionals, businessmen, medium-rank officials, trade-union hierarchs, and mass-media manipulators), who may be described by Gaetano Mosca's phrase "political class," than among the small number who made decisions of policy (top politicians, bureaucrats, soldiers, and captains of industry), for whom C. Wright Mills' phrase "power elite" perhaps still remains more appropriate. The members of the power elite probably still retained more self-confidence and more will to keep power than appeared. Yet the values spread by the media among the political class had a feedback (which defied quantification, even with the use of the political scientists' most esoteric jargon) upon the power elite. These values were a combination of short-term hedonism with a collective guilt complex. This latter sentiment took various forms. In Britain it was breast-beating about the British Empire, a kind of inverted imperialism that saw the map of the world painted not in the cheerful red of the prewar Blimps who were proud of the empire on which the sun never set, but in deepest black, indicating that no great political horror could occur anywhere in the world without its having been due to the sins of the defunct empire. In France in 1977 this phenomenon was less obvious, but an equivalent had been much in evidence during the Indochina war and the Algerian troubles of the 1950s. In the United States it began with the sense of guilt toward the blacks in the civil-rights marches, swelled mightily during the Vietnam war, was re-fuelled by the overthrow of Allende, and was kept going by knowledge of the contrast between American wealth and Third World poverty in general, and the misbehavior of American tycoons in banana republics in particular. Guilt com-plexes require ritual scapegoats—hence the "witch hunt" against the CIA in the United States.[9] Disinterested desire to deal with unemployment, poverty, and race prejudice; greed to grab for oneself every luxury flaunted on the tele-vision screen; honest shame at the crimes or blunders that had been committed by one's own rulers, and from which other peoples had suffered; unwillingness to spend money on armed forces that could be spent either on the relief of poverty or on the increase of one's own comfort; indifference to the preparation of war in distant lands or the inhumanity of man to man in "faraway countries of which we have never heard"; and the plain wish to run away from unpleasant facts and live a quiet life—all contributed to a climate of opinion in which more and more members of the power elite became convinced that they could get nowhere by talking of the public interest, and that they could only keep in power, and do at least a little good, by cynically adopting for the public record the values in which they did not inwardly believe, whose ultimate consequences they viewed with dismay.

Communist Prospects in the Third World

An examination of the communist record in the power stakes since 1960 can perhaps usefully begin with the following oversimplified statements:

Communists have obtained power, or placed their nominees in power, in five states: Cuba, South Vietnam, Laos, Cambodia, and Angola.

Communists came close to power, but were overthrown, in Chile.

Communists maintained themselves in power in all those countries in which they had obtained it before 1960, but were faced with the danger of a drastic modification of the nature of communist party rule in Czechoslovakia. This dan-ger was averted by Soviet military intervention.

---

9. It is almost impious to use this word, long reserved for the misdeeds of Senator McCarthy against the left in the early 1950s, to denote the antics of the trendy antipatriots of the 1970s. Yet the analogy seems obvious, and its use compatible with equal dislike of both phenomena. The CIA did discreditable things; so did American supporters of Stalin in the 1940s. McCarthyism wrecked the careers of innocent and honorable men and women; so did the campaign against the CIA (though it is true that most of those whose lives it ended were not Americans but foreigners who had risked death to serve the cause of freedom as they saw it).

Communist rule diverged greatly from the Soviet model in China and Yugoslavia, and rather less so in North Korea; the future development of communist rule in Vietnam remained uncertain. Elsewhere institutional forms remained essentially similar, though differences in cultural content were substantial.

Prospects of communist access to a share in power, or even to predominance, in several states of southern Europe appeared rather good: in Italy, France, and to a lesser extent, Portugal, Greece, and Spain.

Prospects of communist access to power in Third World states were obscure. Complete political control by a modern disciplined communist party did not look likely, but rule by nationalist parties with a stiffening of genuine communists, and with "advisers" from communist-ruled states, seemed a likely hypothesis. Mozambique, Congo (Brazzaville), and that part of Ethiopia effectively ruled by the revolutionary *dergue* under Colonel Mengistu provided examples. The experience of Egypt showed that Soviet influence, and indigenous communist infiltration into the ruling party, could be suddenly reversed. A similar process took place in Somalia in the autumn of 1977.

To what extent do these successes and failures fit the pattern summarized above, as it was seen in the 1950s?

The victories were a combination of the first two types (assault on the citadel and conquest by a foreign army). The case of Cuba is quite peculiar. Castro's victory was the result partly of his guerrilla warfare against the Batista regime and partly of the collapse of that regime itself through the defection of most of the political class and the failure of nerve of the dictator. However, two years passed before Castro declared himself a communist, subordinated the existing communist party to his own leadership, and was recognized by the leaders in Moscow as the head of Cuban communism. The unification of Vietnam under communist rule was largely due to invasion of the South by the North Vietnamese army, but this was also facilitated by the efforts of the Vietcong guerrilla forces. Guerrilla warfare certainly weakened the defenses of the citadel of power, but the final assault was conducted by the regular army of the North rather than by the revolutionary forces of the South. Victory in Laos and Cambodia was a direct result of victory in Vietnam; the Pathet Lao and the Khmers Rouges were the beneficiaries of others' victories rather than the makers of their own. Victory in Angola was the result of a civil war that arose only after the abdication of power by the Portuguese; this in turn was the result of a noncommunist revolution in metropolitan Portugal, which was an example not of assault on the citadel of power but of seizure of power from within the citadel. However, the victory of the MPLA in the civil war was made possible only by the invasion of a Cuban communist army.

All these victories took place in predominantly rural, predominantly nonindustrial societies. The cadres of the communist parties and communist-supported guerrilla movements came mainly from the intelligentsia, but the masses who were mobilized into them, by persuasion or by threats, consisted mainly of peasants. The pattern generally resembles those of the Chinese and Yugoslav revolutions; industrial workers were scarcer, and played a smaller role, than in the Russian.

The Enigma of Eurocommunism

It was in relation to the opportunities for communists in advanced industrial societies that prospects appeared to have changed significantly since the early 1960s. A seizure of power from within the citadel, through communist entry into left coalition governments and the gradual removal of rivals, seemed possible in the years ahead. Admittedly, the attempts in Chile and Portugal had failed. In both countries an ultraleft, of persons who (whether labelling themselves Trotskyists or Maoists or neither) considered themselves better communists than the communist party, had undermined communist policies. In both countries also a large part of the middle classes had been frightened not only by the antics of the ultraleft but also by the more soberly menacing attitudes of the communists. In other European countries the communist parties had to steer between the same Scylla and Charybdis: they had to talk revolutionary language if they were not to be outflanked by the ultraleft, yet they had to moderate their rhetoric if they were not to send liberal-minded professional people scuttling into the conservative camp.

In France, Italy, and Spain communist leaders had to take account of the changes in the social structure resulting from the economic development of the last two decades. They could no longer hope to achieve their aims by relying on a solid block of class-conscious manual workers forming half or more of the population. The old working class had lost ground in relation to the growing white-collar labor force and the lower-level bureaucracies of both government service and private business. Most members of these increasing social groups tended to adopt middle-class attitudes, but a significant minority were attracted by ultraleft slogans. In France the ultraleft was quite powerful both within and outside the socialist party. In Italy the strength of the extraparliamentary left was hard to judge, but it could not be ignored. In Spain numerous groups of extremists, whether separatist or anarchist or both or neither, lurked below the turbulent surface. In Greece the communist party was divided, the maximalist demagogy of Andreas Papandreou was an unknown factor, and the steaming floods of anti-Turkish, or more generally xenophobic Panhellenic fanaticism could be channelled in almost any direction or indeed overrun all regular channels.

If the forces that communists would have to mobilize for their purposes were unpredictable, the same was true of the forces of their enemy. Was it still true in 1977 that the state machine of the democratic state in an advanced industrial society was stronger than that of the despotic state in a developing society, that its links with the population were firmer, that it was based more on consent than on coercion?

A second and connected question of some importance could also be raised. In the 1930s the great depression—a "crisis of capitalism" if ever there was one, and thus a process from which Marxists expected that the triumph of socialism would arise—had in reality led to loss of power by the left. The businessmen had proved stronger than the workers. In Britain the conservatives had won a huge majority in 1931, had maintained democratic government, but had imposed harsh social policies. In the United States, Franklin Roosevelt had introduced social reforms, but he had also saved American capitalists from any form of socialism. In Germany the National Socialists, financially supported by a large section of big business and aided by Prussian landowners and army officers, had harvested the votes of urban lower-middle-class persons, of peasants, and of a substantial minority even of the workers, and had used their victory to destroy the socialist and communist parties as well as to suppress democracy. The question that arose in 1977 was whether the economic troubles of the industrial West, the new "crisis of capitalism," would once more strengthen the business and bureaucratic elite, or whether it would this time bring communists and socialists to power.

In Italy the communist party favorably impressed thousands of middle-class Italians by its efficient administration of several large cities and provinces. It continued to woo the Catholic church and to court individual politicians of the Christian Democratic party. To outside observers such as the present writer the details of this process were not known, but the example of the suborning of noncommunist politicians in Czechoslovakia under the second presidency of Dr. Eduard Beneš provided a warning. In any coalition government it was to be expected that the communists would at first ask for no "sensitive" ministries, but confine themselves to those in which they could establish a reputation for constructive work. They would outwardly behave in a most respectable manner —as the communists of Gottwald had behaved between 1945 and 1948—while burrowing away beneath the surface, installing their own men in the apparatus of government, and doing all they could to split the parties of the right. In this last action they could have recourse to the same procedure adopted by Mátyás Rákosi in Hungary in the 1940s—to denounce as "fascists" those persons on the right who tried to resist their actions. The word "fascism" still had in 1977 the power to rouse fear and hatred among men of liberal outlook in Italy, especially in the professional middle classes, many of whom had suffered, or had seen their parents suffer, from Mussolini's tyranny. There were also enough real neofascists on the political scene to make the "fascist peril" more than a nightmare. If one group after another could be discredited by the fascist label and sliced off from the Christian Democratic party (Rákosi's famous "salami tactics"), the communists might in time become the dominant partner in the coalition.

In France the communists were still too much a society apart, and had had too little experience of local government, to inspire middle-class confidence. In a left coalition government in France it even seemed possible that the socialists would have more power than the communists—that they would not only control more prestigious ministries but also prove more than the equals of the communists in sophisticated understanding of how real power works, and in the human talents available to assert their primacy. In Britain the communist party was negligible as a parliamentary force but not as an influence in the trade unions or in the Labour party apparatus, though it was sometimes difficult to distinguish between CPGB stalwarts and Trotskyists. The question about the effects of economic crisis was especially relevant to the case of Britain. In the 1930s large-scale unemployment weakened trade unions throughout the industrial world; indeed it seemed a law of economic theory that this should be so. But in Britain in 1977 growing unemployment did not seem to diminish either trade-union militancy or the fear, amounting almost to defeatism, with which conservative politicians and businessmen regarded the unions. It might therefore be considered possible that if economic conditions so deteriorated as to produce a crisis in the British political system, the victors would not be, as in 1931, the business class and the bureaucracy, but the new radical leadership in the trade unions, inclining in sympathy toward the communists.

It was clear that there were serious disagreements between the leaders of these three parties and the Soviet rulers; that accession to power by the French or Italian communists in a democratic framework would have a feedback on Eastern Europe that could encourage a repetition of Dubček-type policies; and that the Italian or French Eurocommunists might conceivably welcome NATO as a defense against Soviet attack. It was, after all, true that the Chinese and Yugoslav governments had long reckoned with the possibility of armed resistance to Soviet forces; why should not West European communists do likewise?

Against this it must be said that the one point in foreign policy on which the communists of Portugal, Spain, France, Italy, and Britain were united was hostility to the United States. "American imperialism" was the source of all international tension and danger. If the speeches of their leaders to date were serious evidence, all these parties would do their best to minimize expenditures on defense and to loosen, and if possible break, their countries' links with the United States. This would mean that whatever their leaders' feelings about Soviet policies, they would be placing their countries at the mercy of Soviet military power. The same applied in general to the Trotskyists and to most of the ultraleft in Europe—of their loathing for the Soviet regime there was no doubt, but they too would place their countries at the mercy of the Soviet army. Thus, though the Soviet leaders might distrust and despise Western communists and Western Trotskyists, acceptance of the policies of either would be "objectively" beneficial to Soviet interests. This was not, however, true of Maoists, or at least of those who fully supported Chinese policies: these were bound, on the contrary, to recommend energetic defense policies and Atlantic unity.

Similar considerations applied to the attitudes of communists, ultraleftists, and Maoists in Japan.

Summing up, the events of the last decade showed less progress for the communist cause in developing societies, and more progress in advanced industrial societies, than was to be expected in the early 1960s.

Prospects for the Soviet Empire

Finally we must consider the prospects of the Soviet Union, the most powerful state ruled by communists, which was still, despite the defections of some communist parties or the lack of enthusiasm of others, by far the most important communist center in the world.

The public posture of the rulers of the second super power was arrogant, boastful, and self-righteous. They had indeed plenty to congratulate themselves about. Russia had come a long way since 1917: its giant factories were turning out huge quantities and varieties of industrial goods, its schools and universities were training and indoctrinating millions of boys and girls, and its barracks were full of soldiers and hardware. But behind the braggart rhetoric and the unctuous professions of virtue lay both anxiety and hope.

Some of the anxiety was economic. Soviet agriculture remained backward, output per head little if at all higher than in 1913. The magnificent arable and pasture lands of Russia, Siberia, and the southern mountain valleys should have been able to produce crops in sufficient quantity for massive exports, and dairy products to meet the growing demand of a population whose standard of living steadily grew. Achievement in both these tasks fell far behind, and for this the decades of neglect and of doctrinaire contempt for rural second-class citizens were to blame. In their agricultural failure the Soviet leaders had harmed not only their own subjects but also the hungry nations of the Third World. Russia and Siberia were capable of producing agricultural surpluses equal to those of the United States and Canada, but bad husbandry prevented it. Soviet propaganda made much of the starvation that threatened Indians or Africans, but neither they nor "world opinion" noticed that their own incompetence was a major cause of the threat.

Industrial growth had been impressive; but it was uneven, inhibited by rigid controls, and lacked the network of auxiliary services essential to a modern economy. The gap between the technological progress of Soviet and of Western industry appeared to be widening. It was mainly in order to reduce this gap, to enlist the assistance of advanced Western industrial organization, that Brezhnev sought a policy of détente.

There were also political anxieties. It seemed in 1977 that the groups of dissenters, ranging from critical Marxists through radical reformers of a scientific and nonideological outlook to neo-Slavophil Christians of varying persuasions, were but a small minority. They displayed not only heroic courage but a penetrating insight into real problems; six decades of censorship and of ritual exhortations had not blunted the fine-precision instrument of the Russian-intelligentsia mind. There was little evidence that they had a large following, and some evidence that the "know-nothing" prejudices of the Soviet urban herd were being successfully mobilized against them. Yet it was also obvious that the rulers feared them; and perhaps in this they were not wrong, for the Russian critical thinkers of the nineteenth century too had had no large following, yet they had sown dragon's teeth.

It often seems strange to Western observers that the Soviet rulers will not take the risk of giving their subjects the liberties that are listed in their written but unpracticed constitution. Cannot such a powerful government afford some criticism? Cannot it expect, in view of its great achievements, to receive the support of the many millions of patriotic subjects? Part of the answer to this question is that as soon as political liberties became effective, there would be demands for national liberties, for free independent development of national cultures, and before long for sovereign independence: Ukrainians and Tadjiks would claim the rights that are enjoyed by Mauritanians and Zambians. To half the population of the Soviet Union, "socialism with a human face" would mean "socialism without Russians." This is why the Soviet government would not take chances with liberty inside the Soviet Union. It is also why it would not permit chances to be taken in Eastern Europe, and why influential Soviet leaders looked with horror on the postures of Italian or Spanish communist leaders, why Brezhnev at the Twenty-fifth Congress of the CPSU administered a sharp rebuke to Berlinguer, no less wounding because no names were mentioned.

The Soviet rulers were faced with alternative policies, each of which had its dangers. Should they encourage the liberalization of the Western communist parties in the belief that once they had obtained substantial influence in their countries, they would be able gradually to reduce their defenses and to loosen ties with the United States, to the point at which Europe would be handed over militarily naked to Soviet political dictation, with or without invasion? Or should they recommend undiluted dogmatism, at the cost of abandoning hope of communist political influence, in order to avoid exposing the communist parties of Eastern Europe to infection with the liberal virus? Should they continue their efforts to attract Western know-how and industrial aid in order to improve their economy, at the cost of accepting the status quo at least in the northern half of the world? Or should they take courage from the signs of failure of nerve among the leaders of the West, and go all out to dominate Europe, even at the risk of war?

There were clear signs of genuine disagreement within the Soviet leadership on these issues, especially on the merits or faults of Italian-type constitutional communism and on whether the capitalist system was or was not on the verge of collapse. Some Western observers tended to play down the disagreements between the Western communists and the Soviet leaders, and even to suggest that they formed part of a conscious maneuver, secretly approved by the Soviet leaders, that was designed to make the Western communist parties attractive to the electors. This view did not appear to be supported by the facts. The attack by the prominent Soviet journalist Zarodov in *Pravda* (6 August 1975) on the policies advocated by the Italian communists, and the insults hurled at Carrillo by the Soviet journal *New Times* (June 1977), to take two outstanding examples, seemed unmistakably genuine. Moreover, the repeated appeals by Polish, Czech, and Soviet dissidents for support by Western communists, and the frequent rather positive responses they evoked, must have not only infuriated but alarmed the Soviet leaders.

A more likely explanation of the fluctuating Soviet attitude to "Eurocommunism" was that this was one of the issues on which the aspirants to the succession to Brezhnev in Moscow were taking opposite sides. All past periods of succession rivalry in Soviet history (1922–1925, 1953–1955, and 1963–1964) had been marked by polarization at the top about the main issues that faced policymakers. Rivals competed to seek popularity, offering better material conditions or appealing to Russian or other national feelings, or to pride in the military power of the Soviet Union. At a time when Brezhnev's days as quasi autocrat were numbered, similar polarization was to be expected, and "Eurocommunism" was bound to be one of the main issues on which opinions would differ at the top.

Conclusions

It seemed unlikely in 1977 that the United States would abandon Western Europe or Japan; but the weakness of European governments in the face of demagogic pressures, and their persistent refusal to provide for defense from their own resources, might in time create a massive revulsion of American opinion against them.

In other parts of the world it was far from clear what would be the consequences of American withdrawal from the postwar policy of worldwide commitments—how and where the Vietnam trauma would make itself felt. Communists were few, and Soviet influence was in decline, in the Muslim lands; but if one or two rulers on either side of the Persian Gulf were to fall before an assassin's bullet or bomb, things might change very quickly. The ability of the United States to compete with the Soviet Union in support of Arab nationalism was limited by its inability to leave Israel to the mercy of her enemies. It was difficult to see how the United States could outbid the Soviet Union in support to black nationalism in Africa. It was difficult for the American public to see simultaneously the two levels of the South African problem—both the struggle of the blacks against white racism and the struggle of the Soviet Union to deny the minerals of central and southern Africa to Western Europe and to control the southern Atlantic. Even words of conditional support for any South African government were believed to be unthinkable for any American administration dependent on black votes; yet the spectacle on American TV screens of white corpses slaughtered by blacks (should things ever come to that) would not be likely to improve race relations in American cities.

Persons of goodwill and rational mind were bound to feel that the leaders of the two super powers should abandon their sterile mutual hostility and refuse to let themselves become involved on opposite sides in every conflict between classes or nations in western Asia, Africa, or Latin America, but rather work together to produce acceptable compromise solutions, and face together the worldwide problems of population, poverty, and pollution. The foremost exponent of this view was a Soviet citizen, Academician Sakharov. But Brezhnev and his colleagues ignored Sakharov, and tirelessly proclaimed that détente was compatible with intensified "ideological competition," a bland phrase that covered not only leading articles in *Pravda* but also butchery in the bush.

Perhaps the most important of all the unanswered questions affecting the future of communism and the future of the human race was the place of China in world affairs. Would the leaders of the United States succeed in creating solid relations with China, as well as with Japan? Or would the new Chinese leaders decide that there was nothing to be gained from the Americans, and seek a new compromise, on the best terms they could get, with the Soviet empire?

The word "communism" could denote an abstraction, a movement, or a power. The abstraction could be a terrifying bogey or a glorious dream, neither of which had much relation to reality—though it remained an undeniable reality that millions of persons around the globe believed in the one or the other. Of the movement, consisting of parties of varying strength pursuing power around the globe with varying degrees of success, something has been said in the preceding pages. As to the power, this meant essentially either China or the Soviet empire, and of these two the latter was incomparably the stronger.

Talk of the "menace" or the "promise" of "communism" was usually no more than empty rhetoric, but the menace or promise of Soviet power remained very real. The Soviet empire possessed a large population, great natural resources, a vast but technologically rather backward industry, a vast and cumbrous bureaucracy, and an enormous military apparatus. Judged by the efficiency of its economy, the skill of its operatives, and the sophistication of its educated class, the Soviet Union lagged far behind the United States. In other respects, however, it appeared as strong or stronger. Its armed forces were equipped to fight any sort of war at short notice: in nuclear weapons and missiles it might still be inferior to the United States, but for all other types of war it was much better prepared. The rulers who commanded these forces had an unshaken will to power, and an impenetrable carapace of self-righteousness reinforced by the simplified residual Marxist-Leninist ''science'' whose tenets they ritually intoned. They were able to command the obedience of their subjects, who were mobilized by a compound of loyalty and fear that defied analysis of its constituent parts. How different was this from the United States, where Congress, press and media prevented any certain commitment of American power for the future, and citizens vied with each other in publishing state secrets to the world, knowing well that no action would be taken against them.

The rulers of the Soviet Union were getting old, and soon younger men would take their place. A generation would come to power that had not known the horrors of war (in all communist wars since 1945 the Soviet rulers had made other people do the fighting for them). These men, like their predecessors, would face the sullen hostility, sporadically breaking out in violence, of their East European subjects. To remedy this condition by treating Poles or Hungarians with generosity, by respecting their culture and letting them live in their own way, was inconceivable. The example would cause ferment among their non-Russian subjects, and in any case generosity toward other nations was something unknown in five hundred years of Muscovite bureaucracy. To admit that the hostility was due to their own policies was almost equally inconceivable. The correct explanation could only be that it was artificially maintained by the intrigues of the capitalist governments of Western Europe. At the same time these governments were demonstrably weak, incompetent, and cowardly, unable to manage their economies or their peoples. The Soviet Union had this magnificent armed might. The time must come to use it.

There are historical parallels. Bismarck's wars faded from German memories and Tirpitz and Ludendorff had their hour. One begins with small risks; if the enemy does not respond, one takes bigger risks; then a point of escalation is reached where either the enemy surrenders or the big war starts.

Surrender of the civilized, technologically brilliant, hedonistic, and indifferent West to the semibarbarous, industrially inferior, but militarily superior and politically ruthless Soviet empire was not inevitable, but it was possible. Escalation into a nuclear war between the giants was also not inevitable, but it too was possible.

Both disasters can be avoided. Avoidance depends on the choice and execution of intelligent policies—that is, of hundreds of particular decisions on particular problems that present themselves to officials and politicians over long expanses of time. Those outside the process of government cannot know all these details, and so are in no position to tell the politicians what to do. However, this much can be said, and needs to be said, by the layman: unless current attitudes of mind can be changed, even the best of policies will fail. When citizens reject the ethos, so prevalent today, that they should just seize what they can today, forget the future, and deny all solidarity with anyone outside their trade, their class or their nation; when the intelligentsia apply their much-vaunted critical powers—so liberally lavished on miscellaneous scapegoats (establishments, foreigners, red agitators, and so on)—to their own utopias and their own ambitions; and when the rulers find in themselves the civil courage that ruling requires; then the ghosts that haunt Western man will lose their terrors, and may even begin to fade away.

Notes on Sources

The most useful single source in the preparation of this book was the series of volumes of the *Yearbook on International Communist Affairs* from 1966 to 1975 published by the Hoover Institution Press. These volumes also contain short bibliographies of works appearing in each year that will be most helpful for readers of this book who wish to pursue the study of its subject.

Second to this source is the periodical press, both general and specialized, whether communist, neutral, or hostile to communism. This includes both periodicals that I have been reading more or less regularly throughout the period covered, and cuttings prepared for me by Myron Hedlin, to whom I acknowledged my debt in the preface. First I must mention *The Times* and *The Economist* (both of London), which are my regular fare, and *Le Monde* (Paris), which I read less regularly, yet often. Among the specialized periodicals from which I derived much information are *World Marxist Review, Peking Review, International Affairs* (Moscow), *Kommunist* (Moscow), and *Africa Communist* (exiled South African). The most useful communist weekly has been the Italian *Rinascita*, and the most useful dailies, the Italian *Unità* and the French *L'Humanité*. In the category of periodicals I should also mention the *Annual of Power and Conflict*, which has been appearing since 1971, and *Conflict Studies*, both published by the Institute for the Study of Conflict (London).

It would be pointless to try here to produce a bibliography of books I have read during these years. Some of those I have found useful within the past year, however, are listed below.

On France, Annie Kriegel, *Les communistes français* (Paris, 1968) and A. Laurens and T. Pfister, *Les noveaux communistes* (Paris, 1973). Madame Kriegel's new work, *Un autre communisme* (Paris, 1977) did not reach me until my book was in the proof stage.

On Italy, Paolo Sylos Labini, *Saggio sulle classi sociali* (Bari, 1974) and Giorgio Napolitano, *Intervista sul PCI* (Bari, 1976). Though the memoirs of a leading communist, Giorgio Amendola, *Una scelta di vita* (Rome, 1976) relate to an earlier period, they were very revealing on the background to the growth of communism among Italian intellectuals.

On Spain, Santiago Carrillo, *Hacia la libertad* (Paris, 1972) is an authoritative exposition of PCE policies while Franco was still in power. The long interviews with Carrillo that were published in book form by R. Debray and M. Gallo, *Demain l'Espagne* (Paris, 1974) were also informative. Carrillo's book *L'Eurocomunismo y el estado,* which aroused the controversy mentioned in chapter 2, was not available to me when I was writing this book and I had to rely on press summaries. A valuable analysis of the changing Spanish social structure was Amando de Miguel, *Recursos humanos, clases 7 regiones en España* (Madrid, 1977).

On Japan, Robert A. Scalapino, *The Japanese Communist Movement 1920–1966* (Berkeley, Ca., 1967); Paul F. Langer, *Communism in Japan: A Case of Political Naturalization* (Stanford, Ca., 1972); and Antonio Lombardo, *Il sistema politico del Giappone* (Milan, 1976).

On Africa, Robert Legoold, *Soviet Policy in West Africa* (Cambridge, Mass., 1970); Bruce Larkin, *China and Africa 1949–1970* (Berkeley, Ca., 1971); Basil Davidson, *In the Eye of the Storm: Angola's People* (London, 1973); Aristide R. Zolberg, *One-Party Government in the Ivory Coast* (Princeton, 1969); and Jean-Suret-Canale, *La république de Guinée* (Paris, 1970). All these are incomplete sources, and none is wholly satisfactory, but there is useful material in them, as well as in many other books there is no room to list.

On Latin American communism, the most useful work that is up-to-date is William Ratliff, *Castroism and Communism in Latin America, 1959–1976* (Stanford, Ca., 1977). On Chile, Robert Moss, *Chile's Marxist Experiment* (London, 1973) is clear and cogently argued, though it has been bitterly attacked by those who sympathized with Allende. I have done my best to compensate by reading some of the vast volume of pro-Allende journalist literature.

There is also a vast literature on Soviet "nationality policy," though the quality is seldom high. Useful basic facts are available in Zev Katz, ed., *Handbook of the Main Soviet Nationalities* (Cambridge, Mass., 1976). A competent exposition of current Soviet doctrine is M. I. Kulichenko, *Natsionalnye otnosheniya v SSSR i tendentsiya ikh razvitiya* (Moscow, 1972). Sources on the communist-ruled countries of Eastern Europe consist overwhelmingly of periodical articles or of collective works with chapters by different writers. Two single-author works that are on a notably higher level are Gordon Skilling, *Czechoslovakia's Interrupted Revolution* (Princeton, 1977) and Dennison Rusinow, *The Yugoslav Experiment, 1948–1974* (London, 1977). *The White Paper on Czechoslovakia,* published in Paris by the International Committee for the Support of Charter 77 in Czechoslovakia, is a well-edited collection of documents.

Index of Names